An American Epic

The Guns Cease Killing and the Saving

of Life from Famine Begins

1939–1963

VOLUME IV

**THE HOOVER INSTITUTION ON
WAR, REVOLUTION, AND PEACE**

HERBERT HOOVER

An American Epic

The Guns Cease Killing and the Saving

of Life from Famine Begins

1939–1963

VOLUME IV

**THE HOOVER INSTITUTION ON
WAR, REVOLUTION, AND PEACE**

HENRY REGNERY COMPANY

CHICAGO: 1964

I dedicate these volumes to those able and intrepid American men and women whose compassion and conscience saved hundreds of millions of lives from the two greatest famines of all history. They gave America's answer to that imperishable question: "Are we our brother's keeper?"

IN ACKNOWLEDGMENT

In the preparation of this volume, as in the three previous ones in this series, I have received helpful assistance and comments from old associates and friends: W. Hallam Tuck, Lewis L. Strauss, Maurice Pate, Perrin C. Galpin, Neil MacNeil, Frank E. Mason, Tracy S. Voorhees, Dennis A. FitzGerald, Louis P. Lochner, and Hugo Meier.

My appreciation goes to those of my staff and of the Herbert Hoover Archives, Stanford, California, who assisted in research, in checking various documents, and in the mechanical preparation of the text for publication: Loretta Camp, Bernice Miller, Joan Dydo, Maureen D'Honau, Dr. Rita Campbell, Crone Kernke, and Eileen Shaw.

My grateful thanks go to Herbert Hoover Hyde, who has edited all four volumes of this series, and to Mrs. Arney R. Childs, who has been responsible for the indexing of the series.

They have been devoted helpers.

CONTENTS

SECTION VII

Famine Continues in Germany, Austria,
and Japan

SECTION VIII

More American Relief Activities

SECTION IX

Some Last Remarks

THE SECOND WORLD WAR

My colleagues and I, who had organized and conducted famine relief and reconstruction of more than a billion people in forty-five nations during the First World War and its aftermath, had a notion that we had performed our share of such labors. But, not so. When twenty years later we received appeals to use our experience again to fight raging hunger on an even greater scale, we could not, in good conscience, refuse. And so for six years more we struggled with the greatest famine and war destruction of all history.

It seemed to me that I was the only living person who could tell the whole story of a great epic in American compassion, and I prepared three volumes on the relief activities of the First World War, concluding with famine relief to Communist Russia in 1923. Now comes this fourth volume of *An American Epic*, dealing with America's aid and action in the Second World War, which by the necessary margins of food and medicine accounted for the saving of more than 800,000,000 people overseas.

* * *

During these famines of both world wars, the American people furnished the margins of food and medicine which saved the lives of more than 1,800,000,000 human beings, largely women and children, most of whom otherwise would have perished.

Starvation is a vague term covering many stages from hunger to death. Very few people die from insufficient food; because of lowered resistance, they die from disease. Contagious diseases at once join in the attack. The aged, the infirm, and the children are the first victims. When children no longer play in the streets, starvation is near.

The term "mass starvation" is used in these volumes to mean wholesale death in villages, communities, or areas.

There is no arbitrary yardstick by which starvation can be measured. However, in the First World War, from long experience in dealing with the many aspects of food consumption and from specifications set forth by nutrition specialists, it was accepted that about 1,500 calories, with appropriate components of carbohydrates, proteins, and fats, became a kind of medial line between starvation and its companion, chaos, and a sufficiency for public health and maintenance of civil order. Hard workers needed more than this, and children posed some special food requirements.

As a basis for calculation of required overseas food, we computed the average number of people in each nation who were below the 1,500-calorie line and required food from abroad to hold to that level. From the very nature of things, no such computation was accurate in detail. However, the fact that there was no mass starvation in war-torn areas after both world wars gives a warranty for this basis of estimates.

*   *   *

When the two greatest dictators on earth joined in an alliance on August 23, 1939, not only did they launch the Second World War, but another world-wide famine became inevitable. As the war moved along, Stalin and Hitler divided Poland and Lithuania between them. Stalin occupied Estonia and Latvia, Bukovina and Bessarabia, and attacked Finland. Hitler, already in possession of Czechoslovakia and Austria, drove his Panzers over Holland, Belgium, Luxemburg, and France almost unimpeded. Denmark submitted to his treacherous invasion in one day. Norway, after her initial recovery from the German blow, fought back hard and held out longer than Belgium, Holland, Luxemburg, and France, but finally surrendered to Hitler's armies. Italy, having formed a partnership with Germany, avoided invasions for a time. Most of the conquered nations had been dependent upon food supplies from overseas.

Although her armies were driven from the Continent, Great Britain possessed the most powerful navy in the world. With it, she imposed a rigid blockade on all of German-occupied Europe, even though ample food supplies and shipping were available.

With the background of our experience and reputation from the First World War, it was natural for the small invaded democracies to appeal to my colleagues and me again, in 1939, to build up supplies for them, with the necessary protective agreements. We initiated some relief to Poland and Finland, but after a few months the blockade was put into action against it and our efforts were brought to an end. Our continued attempts to have the blockade removed met with failure. For the following four years after the war began, we were prevented from taking effective action.

The United Nations Relief and Rehabilitation Administration (UNRRA) began to ship food in the last months of the war, but only to about 20 per cent of the famine-stricken areas—primarily Communist dominated.

Under President Truman, the blockade was lifted, and the liberated countries were supplied by America. At this time, in May, 1945, Mr. Truman enlisted my services. One of my major activities was to co-ordinate the food resources of all nations in the battle against this world-wide famine in 1946. In 1947, my activities were expanded by the President to cover the economic policies of the Allies in Germany and Austria.

Volume IV concludes with a brief review of several other postwar American relief activities in which my colleagues and I participated.

FOUR YEARS OF FRUSTRATION
1939

CHAPTER 1

APPEALS FOR HELP
TO THE OLD HANDS

With the outbreak of World War II in 1939, the small democracies —Poland, Finland, Belgium, Luxemburg, Holland, Norway, and Greece—were dependent upon the import of overseas food in exchange for their industrial exports. Now the war ground them between the millstones of invading armies and the British blockade. They all remembered the service my colleagues and I had rendered them during the famine after the First World War, so it was natural for them to appeal to us again for help.

The first appeal came from the Polish Government on September 16, 1939.

The second came from Finland on December 3, 1939.

The third was from Belgium on May 14, 1940.

The fourth was from the Duchy of Luxemburg on May 17, 1940.

The fifth country to seek aid was the Netherlands, on July 24, 1940.

The sixth call for help, from the people of Norway, arrived on September 3, 1940.

The seventh was an appeal from Greece in July, 1941, which was made to President Roosevelt.

When I received the Polish appeal, I suggested that this was properly a task for the American Red Cross. I had long held the view that, to avoid such waste and confusion as that caused by more than two hundred different competing relief organizations in the First World War, the sole managers of our compassion in foreign countries this time should be the American Red Cross. I therefore proposed to Chairman Norman Davis that in this Second World War all relief should be undertaken by his organization, and I offered to join his administrative staff as an adviser. However, he decided that the Red Cross would confine its efforts to medical aid. This was only 10 per cent of the problems.

With the refusal of the American Red Cross to undertake the major burden of relief—food and clothing—my old colleagues in the American Relief Administration and I concluded that it was our duty to do our utmost. We had maintained the continuing interest of these men during the years since the First World War through the administration of charitable agencies which we had created after that war. In consequence, we had offices, organized leadership, and experienced staff at hand.

No other group of men in the world had comparable experience in the administration of relief, or an understanding of the terrors and suffering from starvation. These men were now about twenty years older than they were in the First World War. In the meantime, they had risen in national service and in their professions: among them were Cabinet members, judges, governors, generals, admirals, and high officials in our Foreign Service.

There appeared to be no insoluble problems in responding to these appeals, except possible opposition from the combatant governments. In fact, the problems were less complicated than those we had resolved in the First World War.

During the first two years of World War II, there was an ample surplus of food to be had from the United States, and during the entire war there was enough food from the neutral nations to fill requirements for the countries making these appeals. Unlike the shortage of shipping in the First World War, ships were available from Sweden without diminishment of the transportation facilities of the Allies. That country, to preserve its neutrality, withheld charters to the belligerents. However, the Swedish shipping companies offered ships for charter to neutrals for relief purposes.

The exiled governments of Poland, Norway, Luxemburg, Holland, and Belgium, with headquarters in London, could purchase the food and pay for transportation. The Dutch and Norwegians had brought their gold reserves with them. Each government, with the exception of Luxemburg, still had control of its shipping, and Belgium and Holland retained their colonial possessions.

We had proved for four years in the First World War that by means of suitable agreements with the combatant countries we could assure that no benefits from imports of food for relief would obtain to either side. In fact, the only unsolved problem was again to secure the co-operation of the British and the Germans for immunity of these supplies through some neutral organization.

In order to engage the co-operation of the exiled governments in securing such an agreement, we sent our old hands Hugh Gibson to London and Frederic C. Walcott and John Hartigan to Berlin. Gibson, a retired ambassador, was familiar with the agreements made in the First World War, Walcott had been an administrator on our relief staff, and Hartigan had served in the trusteeship of the Saar after that war.

During the first months of the war, we were able to secure co-operation from both belligerents through their ambassadors in Washington, and we organized relief to Poland and Finland.

CHAPTER 2

POLAND

In response to the appeal of the Polish Government in Exile—including the Prime Minister, General Władysław Sikorski, and the Ambassador in Washington, Count Jerzy Potocki—we organized the Commission for Polish Relief, Inc., on September 25, 1939.

The officers of the new organization were: Chauncey McCormick, Chairman; Maurice Pate, President. The Directors were Hugh Gibson, W. Hallam Tuck, Edgar Rickard, Perrin C. Galpin, Lewis L. Strauss, Theodore Abel, Frederic C. Walcott, and Mrs. Vernon Kellogg. They sacrificed important positions to answer this call of suffering. I was made Honorary Chairman of the Commission. It was my responsibility to conduct negotiations with the various governments concerned, to secure financial support, and to enlist public support by making speeches and by issuing public statements. My colleagues attended to the major problems of purchase of supplies and transportation.

For the Polish operation, a staff was quickly recruited in Europe by cable. Mr. William C. McDonald, a former associate of Mr. Pate in Poland who had remained in Warsaw and had courageously helped in the evacuation of American citizens during the bombardment and German occupation of the city, was located in Switzerland. Mr. McDonald enjoyed high confidence in Poland. He went to Berlin immediately to conduct negotiations with the Germans and then proceeded to Warsaw, where he set up arrangements for the distribution of food and medical-relief supplies.

Mr. Gilbert Redfern, who knew Poland very well and who had been one of my foreign attachés in the Department of Commerce, was recruited in London and sent promptly to Vilna, where he performed an outstanding task in caring for Polish refugees in the Baltic States. Mr. F. Dorsey Stephens, one of my former colleagues in Belgian Relief, aided by his wife, Zora, did equally devoted and useful work among the fifty thousand Polish refugees in France.

In the New York headquarters of the Commission for Polish Relief, McCormick and Pate had the invaluable devotion and experienced work of Columba P. Murray, Jr., Colonel Joseph Krueger, and Bernard Fraser, all veterans of the American Relief Administration. Hugh Gibson and Frederic Walcott voluntarily gave generously of their time on the negotiating and diplomatic side. Mrs. Vernon Kellogg was a zealous raiser of private contributions in the United States.

In one of my addresses in support of Poland, I endeavored to give encouragement to the despairing Poles. In New York on October 11, 1939, I said:

The spirit of a great race does not die from oppression. Poland is not dead. Poland will rise again. There is more to nations than their soil, their cities, their wealth, and even their governments. There is a soul in a great people. That soul is forged in the instincts of their race, their traditions, their heroic struggles, their heroic men, and their genius in art, music, and literature. It is steeled in their sufferings. They may be occupied by armies; they may be oppressed; they may be enslaved; they may be impoverished. But the soul of a great people cannot be crushed. From that their national life and their independence will rise again and again from the ashes of their homes.[1]

In the initiation of relief to Poland, we concentrated upon two programs: the supply of food and clothing to the underfed children in the congested districts and ghettos in Poland, and the care of Polish refugees, now scattered over Europe. Mr. Pate set up canteens, under the care of Polish women, which provided special meals to 200,000

[1] Herbert Hoover, *Further Addresses Upon the American Road, 1938–1940* (New York, Charles Scribner's Sons, 1940), p. 227. The full text of all documents quoted in Volume IV of *An American Epic* may be found in the Hoover Institution on War, Revolution, and Peace or in the places indicated in the footnotes.

undernourished children and aged persons daily in Poland. The Polish Government in Exile had set up refugee relief, and our organization supplied it with food and clothing. Our route for shipments was from the United States to Sweden and thence to Hamburg or Danzig. When it was cut off because of the German invasion of Norway on April 9, 1940, the Commission was able to ship through Genoa or Lisbon and thence by rail to Poland.

FINANCING THE POLISH RELIEF

To finance the relief, the Commission supported the appeals of the Polish-American organizations in the United States, from whom we received about $400,000. The Polish Government in Exile made an initial donation of $186,225.

It was certain that if the Commission were to be successful in carrying out a substantial program, it would cost more than the combined resources of both charity appeals and the exiled Polish Government. Therefore, on February 29, 1940, I obtained a hearing before the House Foreign Affairs Committee and advocated a fifty-million-dollar appropriation to the Red Cross for relief for Poland.[2] I urged Norman Davis, Chairman of the American Red Cross, to undertake this relief. When the Congressional appropriation subsequently became law, the Red Cross undertook medical aid, but our organization received no part of it for the major need: food.

To stimulate charitable contributions, the Commission organized a mass meeting at New York City's Madison Square Garden on March 12 at which I spoke. It organized a mass meeting in Chicago at which I also spoke, and another in New York on April 28, where both General Joseph Haller, Minister of State of the Republic of Poland, and I spoke.

In the meantime, August Zaleski, Minister of Foreign Affairs of the Polish Government in Exile in London, took a hand in the finances of the Relief Commission. As a result, on May 11, I received the following cablegram from him:

[2] For full details, see H. Doc. 835, 76th Cong., 3rd sess.

[The Polish] Government have given most earnest and urgent consideration to your communications in light both of developments in their discussions in London and Paris and of recent information from Poland. Polish Cabinet in special session adopted following resolution last night:

"Government invite President Hoover to accept responsibility for relief of populations in Poland and request him to start operations immediately. In view of hardships of situation within Poland and of limited resources in disposal of Polish Government we beg President Hoover to agree to following proposal:

"Government will negotiate with British and French Governments terms of blockade clearance for food supplies for famished urban and rural populations in Poland on principle of continuity of relief action. Relief will cover in first place milk, fats, and clothing, and in second place only wheat and flour.

"*First,* immediately thereupon Polish Government will place at President Hoover's disposal in U.S.A. sum of one million dollars for dollar purchases.

"*Second,* Bank of Poland have placed at President Hoover's disposal their gold deposited with Bank of Rumania at Bucharest, hoping that Mr. Hoover will exert all his influence to obtain delivery of this gold or else to utilize it for purchases of relief supplies in Rumania or elsewhere. Should it prove impossible to utilize this gold in aforesaid manner, Polish Government will place at President Hoover's disposal requisite means of payment for relief purchases on markets designated by Allies and in consultation with Allies' purchasing organizations up to amount of Rumanian gold deposit not otherwise utilised.

"*Third,* furthermore Government place at President Hoover's disposal equivalent of one million dollars in sterling and French francs for relief purchases in pound and franc monetary area. . . ."

Our total resources with these additions amounted to about $6,000,-000, including $3,060,704 in Polish gold deposited in the National Bank of Rumania. We sent Dorsey Stephens to Bucharest to bring out the gold. The Bank of Rumania refused to hand it over. After all patience had been exhausted in negotiating with it, we attached its balances in New York and won our case on July 15, 1941, in the lower courts.[3]

---

[3] Later, at the time of America's entry into the war in December, 1941, such litigation was suspended. After the war was over, the new Polish Government claimed

OUR RELATIONS WITH THE BRITISH
BLOCKADE OF POLAND

Although the British blockade was in action against delivery of food to German-occupied territory, we had no difficulty in obtaining permits for relief shipments during the Chamberlain ministry. However, when Churchill succeeded Chamberlain as Prime Minister in May, 1940, he soon stopped all permits of food relief to Poland.

I will discuss Mr. Churchill's blockade policies later.

OUR RELATIONS WITH THE GERMANS

At the outset of our Polish relief operations, I conducted negotiations with the Germans through their Embassy officials in Washington. They were most co-operative, and issued certificates of immunity from submarine attack, provided neutral vessels were used.

WE KEEP UP A TRICKLE OF FOOD TO POLAND

After we were prevented by Mr. Churchill from sending overseas supplies to Poland, the Relief Commission deployed its American staff over Europe to seek food outside British control. They were able to make some purchases in the Baltic nations and in Russia, but in the end, the blockade closed in upon us, and this effort to aid Poland was ended.

It was only by the incredible tenacity of Maurice Pate and our men in Europe that a meager stream of food and medical relief continued to trickle to Poland for nearly two more years. Beyond doubt, this saved thousands of lives.

---

this gold in favor of Poland, and the Commission released the Bank of Rumania. By way of appreciation, a donation of $100,000 for subsequent relief operations was made by the Polish Government out of these funds.

The further relief of Poland was now dependent on whether or not the British blockade could be relaxed for relief shipments. We did not abandon our effort to secure relaxation of the blockade, but merged this problem with those of the other small democracies which I describe in later chapters.

That the Polish people were appreciative of our efforts is indicated by the following:

September 15, 1940—A message from the Committee of Poles in Poland, which had been set up to co-operate with our efforts, read:

American gifts sent into Poland are a blessing, an alleviation to the hardship and misery of our country. . . . We therefore beg that help from America should be continued, and if possible continued on a larger scale.

November 1, 1940—Another cablegram to me from the President of this committee said:

I take this occasion to express deepest gratitude as President of Polish Central Relief Committee for assistance which Commission for Polish Relief has given. . . .

March 15, 1941—A letter from August Cardinal Hlond, Primate of the Catholic Church in Poland, read:

As the head of the Church in Poland, I express to you my gratitude and recognition for the help given already to my compatriots both in the persecuted country and on this sorrowful emigration. Especially I send the expression of my gratitude to Mr. Hoover, the former President of the United States, who, after the other war, had rendered us great services, saving many of our children from starvation.

I beg you to continue your efficient help for the Polish people, which since September 1939 has suffered the hardest catastrophe in its history. We, Poles, hold now the primacy of suffering, which encourages me in this request.

CHAPTER 3

WE SECURE RELIEF FOR FINLAND

In the Stalin-Hitler alliance of August 23, 1939, Stalin had exacted as part of his share in conquest the annexation of the helpless Baltic States. Estonia and Latvia complied with Stalin's demand for "protective garrisons." Lithuania was divided between Stalin and Hitler. Finland alone refused.

When Stalin attacked Finland on November 30, 1939, I made the following statement:

Civilization struck a new low with the Communists' attack on peaceful Finland. It is a sad day to every decent and righteous man and woman in the world. We are back to the morals and butchery of Ghengis Khan. . . .

They [the Finns] will make a brave fight. They may be overwhelmed by the hordes whose morals are the morals of Communism; whose methods are cowardly. They are to be brought into subjection by the killing of defenseless women and children. Brave men do not do that. Even if Finland falls, the day will come when it will rise again—for the forces of righteousness are not dead in the world.

On December 3, the Finnish Minister to the United States, Hjalmar J. Procopé, through my old associate, Lewis L. Strauss, asked if our group would undertake to organize relief for Finland as we were already doing for Poland. Before replying, I again, as in the case of Poland, urged Norman Davis, Chairman of the American Red Cross, that this relief be undertaken by that organization. I proposed that

10

our group would serve under him if he wished. He decided the Red Cross would limit its services to medical aid and would collect garments through its chapters. However, Finland's most critical need was food.

Our old colleagues incorporated the Finnish Relief Fund, Inc., under the laws of Delaware on December 6, 1939. Except for part of the clerical help, this American organization consisted entirely of volunteers. The following officers were elected:

HERBERT HOOVER, *Chairman*
EDGAR RICKARD, *President*
LEWIS L. STRAUSS, *Vice-President*
JOHN JAY HOPKINS, *Vice-Chairman and Director of Organization*
Additional Directors

PERRIN C. GALPIN	JOHN L. SIMPSON
FRANK C. PAGE	H. ALEXANDER SMITH
RAYMOND SAWTELLE	CLARE M. TORREY
EDWIN P. SHATTUCK	

After its formation, I received the following cablegram from the Premier of Finland, Risto Ryti:

People of Finland rejoice very much that you, Mister President, known by people of Finland as their cordial friend since twenty years, are again heading a movement for our distressed people. In the uneven struggle against the outrageous attackers for their existence and the holiest and the best human values, the people of Finland need every material and moral assistance that possibly can be given. The sympathies and the support extended to us by the great people of America have a highly encouraging effect on ourselves, and strengthen our confidence in the final victory of justice and the good forces over injustice and violence.

On December 7, I made the following address on Finnish relief:

America has a duty to do its part in the relief of the hideous suffering of the Finnish people. Our people should have an outlet in which to express their individual and practical sympathy. I have consented to organize a nation-wide Finnish Relief Fund for this purpose.

I appeal to the American people for its support. Finland is not a rich country. The people have little reserve for emergency. They are making a heroic defense. Air attacks have compelled the evacuation of civilians from their towns and cities. Hundreds of thousands of women and children have been driven from their homes in the middle of northern winter. Many are already, and more will be, refugees outside of their own country. Many are destitute. Others are without adequate shelter, clothing, and food. This Fund is for the purpose of serving these broad needs.

The American Red Cross has appealed for funds to furnish medicines, hospital supplies, and many garments will be provided through their chapters. They should be supported. The two funds will cooperate fully. . . .[1]

We believed that we could secure public support from a nation-wide appeal which would give emergency aid. But we realized that nothing short of American Government assistance could support the Finns. We hoped that our drive for funds would aid in inspiring action by the Congress.

To avoid overhead expenses, I addressed a telegram to the publishers of America's leading newspapers, asking whether they would receive contributions, report the donors in their columns, and remit the money to us. The press responded in extraordinary fashion— some 1,400 newspapers established such funds.

We organized the usual radio programs and theatrical benefits, issued press statements, and arranged public meetings. I spoke at Madison Square Garden in New York (December 20, 1939), at Minneapolis (December 29, 1939), Duluth (December 30, 1939), Detroit (January 21, 1940), New York (January 29, February 2 and 4, 1940), Scarsdale, New York (February 18, 1940), Elizabeth, New Jersey (February 23, 1940), Brooklyn (February 26, 1940), Pittsburgh (March 8, 1940), and Peoria, Illinois (March 14, 1940).

Our organization sent our old hands of the First World War, F. Dorsey Stephens and later W. Hallam Tuck and Robert Van Wyck Maverick, to Helsinki to aid in organizing the purchase of supplies abroad as well as their distribution. In the spring of 1940, Congress appropriated $30,000,000 to aid the Finns. The total response from our public appeal was $3,546,526.11.

[1] Further Addresses Upon the American Road, 1938–1940, p. 236.

The Finns called every able-bodied man to the front—about 300,000 men. Such a call in the United States would mean roughly 11,800,000 men. With great losses after a valiant defense against overwhelming Communist armies, the Finns agreed to terms of peace on March 12.[2] Stalin forced them to surrender a large part of their fertile lands, from which 400,000 Finns were expelled almost overnight.

On March 13, I made this statement:

The terms imposed on Finland mark another sad day for civilization. The Finns have made a heroic defense that will live for all time. But the odds were insuperable.

The Finnish Relief Fund must continue. . . .

On the same day, we received the following cable from Kyosti Kallio, President of Finland:

We are deeply grateful to the Finnish Relief Fund for the humanitarian aid which we have received during the Finnish War for the relief of the distressed. I hope with all my heart that you will continue to alleviate the lot of those suffering on account of the war for the population of the ceded areas will be moving into the territory of the republic.

We have signed a compulsory peace yet we hope that our struggle for the right has gained us the sympathy of the civilized world and trust that we shall not be left to our own resources in the work of reconstruction.[3]

On March 14, we received a telegram from former Premier Aimo K. Cajander, who was head of the Finnish Government's relief organization (Suomen Huolto):

Having defended our independence Finland after persistent fight as an outpost of western civilization and ideals and justice has been compelled to conclude a hard peace. The activity of the Finnish Relief Fund becomes even more acute as the number of evacuated has increased and the misery great among the families of men killed by battle and air raids. The mortality is dreadful among the evacuated children. Until this situation is

---

[2] The Russians subsequently admitted that their loss in dead and wounded exceeded 200,000.

[3] *Further Addresses Upon the American Road, 1938–1940*, p. 239.

settled assistance is imperative more so than ever before. I address to you a pressing appeal for continued help.[4]

Although we could expect little public response to a further appeal in view of the Congressional appropriation and the Finnish surrender, on March 14, I issued the following statement, which tells at least part of the story of Finland.

. . . The scene in Finland today is one of smoky ruins. Thousands of destroyed homes and villages. Thousands of destitute men, women and children. Thousands of sick and wounded. Now come thousands forced from their land and homes, which they have held for a thousand years. . . .

I commented that Finland's example to the free world was

. . . not alone of human suffering. There are questions which affect the whole defense of freedom and liberty in the world.

The Finns have been subjected to an unspeakable aggression by Communists. With the knowledge that they faced probable doom they fought not alone for themselves but for all free men. . . . Not in centuries have we seen such a heroic stand of free men against such odds.

. . . A star has risen which lights the No-Man's Land of civilization. Its glow will light the minds of men and women and give hope to liberty for a thousand years to come.[5]

[4] *Ibid.*
[5] *Ibid.*, pp. 239–40.

FOUR YEARS OF FRUSTRATION
1940–1941

CHAPTER 4

ENTER MR. CHURCHILL

When Winston Churchill succeeded Neville Chamberlain as Prime Minister of Great Britain, the future of our relief to women and children in the occupied democracies became doubtful. He came to office when practically all of Western Europe had fallen before Hitler's onslaughts. Great Britain was in the greatest danger of her entire history. In the preservation of his country, Mr. Churchill was serving the cause of freedom for the whole world. I admired him for his constancy to that purpose, his courage, and his abilities.

I was familiar with Mr. Churchill's public life from its beginnings. He was a militarist of the extreme school who held that the incidental starvation of women and children was justified if it contributed to the earlier ending of the war by victory. He was the only member of the British Cabinet at the outbreak of the First World War who opposed the relief of Belgium. He was overruled. The relief of Belgium —with guarantees of noninterference from the Germans—proved to be of no military advantage to them. This was acknowledged by Prime Ministers Asquith and Lloyd George.

In 1939, I had reason to believe I could secure the same guarantees from the Germans again. During the First World War, German experience with our men proved that we had devoted ourselves solely to our relief jobs and never engaged in espionage. But far more important was the recollection by the German people and their leaders of the service of our group in saving their people from starvation in 1919 and our rehabilitation of their children, which continued for four years after the end of the war.

During my visit to Germany in 1938, I had obtained ample evidence that the Germans, by every device, were increasing their food production and storing large shipments from abroad. I believed we could get a contribution of cereals from them for relief purposes.

On July 26, 1940, Mr. Gibson, then in London, with Jan Ciechanowski of the Polish Foreign Office, Viscount de Lantsheere, Counselor of the Belgian Embassy, and Dr. E. N. Van Kleffens, Minister of the Netherlands, called on British Foreign Minister Lord Halifax. In this meeting they jointly urged that the British permit relief through the blockade, subject to satisfactory arrangements with the Germans for protection of ships and supplies from which no military advantage would accrue to them. Lord Halifax was not encouraging. I also took up the matter personally with Lord Lothian, the British Ambassador in Washington, who seemed sympathetic.

In the meantime, we were receiving poignant appeals for supplies from the local relief committees in these countries, which had organized soup kitchens for the children and the destitute. On August 11, I issued the following statement to the press:

Somebody must raise a voice for food supply during the coming winter to the 27,000,000 innocent civilians, mostly women and children, in Norway, Holland, Belgium and Poland. Possibly France also will be in difficulties. This subject needs clarification. It is impossible to understand what the Administration in Washington means by statements that they do not have any facts, or why they recall an Ambassador because he states a fact. The obvious truth is that there will be wholesale starvation, disease and death in these little countries unless something is done about it.

The situation is obvious, because the Belgians are always dependent upon imports for from 60 to 70 per cent of their food, the Dutch 30 to 40 per cent, the Norwegians 20 to 30 per cent, and Central Poland, as now set up, about 30 per cent. France imports about 15 per cent. Their food must come over their borders, either from other parts of the Continent or from overseas. The situation will be even more acute than these figures imply, because the farmers and villagers consume most of the domestic production and the cities mostly live on the imports. The native production degenerates during war by inability to import feed for animals.

These little nations are being ground between the millstones of the food blockade—Great Britain and Germany against each other. They are blockaded by Germany from Continental supplies and by Great Britain from overseas supplies. The Germans blame the British blockade. The British say the fault is the German invasion.

If these little nations are allowed to keep their accumulated stocks of food and their present harvest, the situation will not begin to be acute until some time in the Fall and will become fatal in the winter or spring next year—as domestic supplies are exhausted.

Something must intervene if these people are to be saved. There is no reason why it should not be done again by a neutral non-governmental organization as was the case in the first World War. That case as applied now would require:

1. That Germany agree: (a) To take none of the domestic produce of these people. (b) To furnish an equivalent of any food already taken. (c) To permit imports from Russia and the Balkan States. (d) To allow free passage of ships without attack. (e) To permit adequate control of distribution by the organization, so as to enable it to assure that those guarantees are carried out.

2. The British to agree that ships carrying cargoes solely of food for these people should be allowed to pass their blockade so long as the guarantees are fulfilled.

The de facto or fugitive governments of Holland, Belgium, Norway and Poland should finance such an organization with their resources in the United States and elsewhere, which are considerable. It would probably cost $20,000,000 a month at the start, and $40,000,000 a month before the winter is over. This sort of method applied to the then circumstances worked for four years from 1914–19. It can be done if there is the goodwill to do it.[1]

The portion of my press statement which referred to the conditions to be secured from the Germans was censored out of the British press.

Nine days after my press statement, on August 20, Mr. Churchill

---

[1] Herbert Hoover, *Addresses Upon the American Road, 1940–41* (New York, Charles Scribner's Sons, 1941), pp. 117–18.

attacked our proposals in a speech to the House of Commons. He ignored the guarantees we proposed to secure in advance from Germany and also ignored our record in the care of Belgium in the First World War. He said:

> . . . It is our intention to maintain and enforce a strict blockade not only of Germany but of Italy, France and all the other countries that have fallen into the German power. . . . What, indeed, would be a matter of general complaint would be if we were to prolong the agony of all Europe by allowing food to come in to nourish the Nazis and aid their war effort, or to allow food to go in to the subjugated peoples, which would certainly be pillaged off them by their Nazi conquerors. . . .
>
> Many of the most valuable foods are essential to the manufacture of vital war material. Fats are used to make explosives. Potatoes make the alcohol for motor spirit. The plastic materials now so largely used in the construction of aircraft are made of milk. . . . Let Hitler bear his responsibilities to the full and let the peoples of Europe who groan beneath his yoke aid in every way the coming of the day when that yoke will be broken. . . .[2]

There were at least four errors in Mr. Churchill's statement. It ignored the basis of our proposal—that we would secure adequate guarantees from the Germans, as well as a contribution of cereal supplies from them; it also ignored the fact that if the Germans failed to keep their agreements, relief would be stopped instantly. Furthermore, the notion that the special type of food we needed for children (milk, chocolate, fats, and meat) would be used for munitions was sheer nonsense. Even if the Germans seized and used them, as Churchill claimed they would, our stocks in their territory at any one time would not supply the German Army for one single day— relief would have ended. As to the assertion about ending the war more quickly, the amount of food we proposed to have in stock in German-controlled areas at any one time would not, if seized by the Germans, feed their own people for six hours.

I asked both General John J. Pershing and Admiral William V.

---

[2] British Parliament, House of Commons, Parliamentary Debates, Official Reports, 5th ser., v. 364, August 20, 1940, pp. 1159–62.

Pratt, who had commanded the American forces in the First World War, what they thought of these arguments of Mr. Churchill against our proposals. They both characterized them as "nonsense." I include in a later chapter the text of their statements.

It has been rightly said that truth is the first fatality of war.

CHAPTER 5

ENTER THE BRITISH PROPAGANDA ORGANIZATION IN NEW YORK

The United States was now heading into the Presidential campaign of 1940. My colleagues and I believed that it would be most unfortunate if relief matters should get into that debate. Therefore, we decided to postpone any further action until after the election. Also, if the Republicans won, I would be in a position to get action. We therefore made no public reply to Prime Minister Churchill.

The British Information Service in New York at once organized an attack upon me and my colleagues under the direction of a well-known American journalist, Herbert Bayard Swope. A meeting of Americans active in British interests was convened in New York, and as a result of this meeting, a manifesto denouncing our proposals was released to the press on October 6, 1940. It was a long and repetitive argument, the essential parts of which were:

The American people are deeply sympathetic with the civilian populations of Europe in their sufferings and threatened sufferings. And especially with those who, already enduring subjugation by a pitiless conqueror, now face the further ordeal of food privation. Were it possible to alleviate this distress, without strengthening the conqueror and so prolonging his conquest, every impulse would prompt the American people to seek to do so.

However, by the declared intention of the totalitarian powers, this is a total war, imperiling the life of every citizen in the nations within its orbit. No one can hope to evade a share in the common suffering.

Further, the issue of the war lies between two strategies, each of which threatens intense suffering for civilians. The totalitarian powers aim by studied and relentless assault upon civil populations to drive them into subjugation. The toll of that strategy is being taken daily and nightly in the lives of women and children. For the democratic nations, overwhelmingly outnumbered in military strength, the only instrument of defenses available to them is the imposition of a naval blockade by which their adversaries shall be barred from the raw materials, including food essential for their aggression. This blockade cannot fail to occasion privation among peoples already suffering virtual enslavement at the hands of their conquerors.

The American people have given overwhelming evidence of their sympathy with Great Britain and her Allies. . . . It is the keystone of American policy that we will lend ourselves to no plan which might directly or indirectly strengthen the enemies of democracy. . . .

Any proposal to feed civil populations in conquered countries would naturally have to rest upon the consent of both belligerents. . . .

The manifesto stated that the Germans had already removed great quantities of food from the small democracies, which was not true at this time because they had no need for it. The manifesto continued:

. . . The Allied forces would be expected to permit food ships to pass their blockade.

. . . It is our strong conviction that any effort by private American citizens to bring pressure to bear upon other governments or to arouse American sentiment for that purpose would be improper and unfair as well as directly contrary to America's essential interests, and should be firmly resisted by every clear-sighted leader of public opinion.

We do not raise questions as to the practicability of the undertakings which it is proposed to demand from the totalitarian governments. But, in view of the habitual violation by those governments of every solemn undertaking entered into, it is obvious that no confidence could be placed in any pledges which they might give. . . .

Unless the British Government gives its free consent, uncoerced by any external pressure, it is our reluctant but considered judgment that the American people should have no part in the scheme. It may well be that the issue is between restraining the natural impulse to relieve privation, and giving a measure of immediate relief, the effect of which will be to make the status of slavery more tolerable. Between the agony of empty stomachs for a time in one part of the world and the agony of stricken souls in every part of the world there can be but one choice.[1]

Among the fifteen prominent signers of this document were men and women in the legal profession, education, labor relations, farming, and the clergy.

The whole argument was based on the assumption that the margin of food needed by these small democracies and the stocks of imports on hand at any one time would determine victory or defeat in the war. This was wholly fallacious.

At the meeting, one of the clergymen refused to go along with the attack on the relief program and furnished me with an advance release of the manifesto. Therefore, prior to its distribution to the press, I telegraphed each signatory on October 4. I stated that they could not have been fully informed with regard to our proposals and concluded:

. . . As an instance of this, all proposals are conditioned upon such safeguards as would be no injury to the British cause. These are not fully stated in your release. Second, your statement does not present the fact that these little nations are not asking for government aid or charity but are prepared to pay for their own food, to furnish their own ships, and even to obtain their food elsewhere than in the United States if necessary. All they ask is that someone raise a voice for them in negotiation of an agreement between the contending powers to prevent their starvation and create an organization to protect their supplies. There are other important considerations not disclosed in your statement which involve too much discussion for this telegram.

By the newspaper controversy which must ultimately ensue if your statement is to go to publication, three dangers are incurred. The first is an injury to the British cause which necessarily arises from such a public controversy, and the second is that the full facts have obviously not been presented to the public by your statement, and third it may jeopardize millions of lives that otherwise may be saved.

Out of consideration for these people I sincerely feel you should with-

[1] *The New York Times,* October 6, 1940.

hold your name from this statement which, as I have said, is based upon a lack of full information and faulty conclusions.

I regret that I have not had an opportunity to personally discuss this matter with you . . . and I am at your disposal at your convenience.

Under these circumstances I am wondering whether you would not think you should delay your signature to such a statement until the full facts could be known to you. If after full and free discussion of the situation you still feel that your statement should be published I could have no right to object.

Carrie Chapman Catt, a leading suffragette, replied to my telegram:

Unaware of signature mentioned. I authorize you to withdraw it.

However, she signed later.

My press reply to the manifesto, made on October 6, was:

. . . The problem is not one of America feeding Europe, as some headlines would imply. The problem arises from the appeals of the Belgians, the Dutch, the Norwegians and the Poles of Central Poland that some agreement be brought about by which, with their own money, they be allowed to import food . . . with an international organization supervising the operation and protecting their supplies from the occupying armies. Such an agreement would of necessity have to be made by some third party, with the British on one hand and the Germans on the other.

These 30,000,000 people, of whom 10,000,000 are children, have always been dependent upon imports from over their borders from somewhere, and without such imports they see a catastrophe during the present winter. . . . They are not asking for American government appropriations or for charity or ships, or for even the right to purchase food in the United States. . . . They are hoping some outside group will aid them in working out an agreement by which they can be saved. They know that such solutions were found in the last war which proved successful and they plead for solution now.

This is no doubt a side issue in the gigantic problems with which the world is confronted. But with the rising tide of famine in these countries, the problem will constantly grow more vivid. The American people are interested, by their deep sense of humanity, by the fact that these democratic peoples have fought, sacrificed and suffered for the very things we stand for, and the fact that fifteen or twenty millions of our citizens are relatives or descendants of Poles, Norwegians, Dutch and Belgians.

. . . It is a problem for co-operation and not controversy.[2]

The staff in Swope's office was quickly expanded to include two other writers adept in personal attack, and a violent campaign was begun. It had the backing of responsible but misled clergymen.

On October 19, a broadcast by J. B. Priestley was transmitted from London via the British Broadcasting Corporation (a British Government agency) and aired over an American network. He dismissed our prerequisite of proper German conduct with the argument that the Germans never kept agreements. He engaged in much painful ridicule and showed a complete disregard for the human lives at stake. I asked for similar time on BBC to present our case to the British people, but my request was denied.

To my utter surprise, a few days after the issuance of the manifesto by Swope's committee, the British Ambassador, Lord Lothian, made an appointment to call on me in New York on October 8. Since this seemed strange in view of their propaganda activities, I asked William R. Castle, former Undersecretary of State, to attend the interview. The meeting took an astonishing turn in that Lord Lothian, a naturally humane man, assured me that he favored our relief program. He said he expected to go to London shortly and that one of his principal objectives would be to convince Churchill of our "rightness" and of the necessity for the relief. I had little confidence that he could succeed in this, but I was also sure that he represented the real spirit of the British people, whom I had known for more than twoscore years. He asked me to supply him with information about our plans. I told him frankly that we intended to put on a campaign for public support after the American election and inquired whether it would possibly embarrass his efforts. He thought, on the contrary, that it would help him. Apparently he was totally at variance with the official propaganda line.

Lord Lothian returned to Washington from England early in December. Without a word to me, on December 10 the British Embassy

<hr>

[2] *New York Herald Tribune*, October 7, 1940. The reply also appears in *Addresses Upon the American Road, 1940–41*, pp. 119–20.

issued a statement to the press flatly saying that no relief would be permitted through the blockade. The Ambassador was evidently carrying out Churchill's policy.

The press release was supposed to squelch us. On December 11, our committee issued a reply, pointing out its misrepresentations.

Lord Lothian died a few days after the Embassy statement was issued. Since he and I had been friends during the First World War and for long years thereafter, I concluded that a record of his visit of October 8, 1940, which really represented his true character, should be preserved for history. Therefore, I addressed the following note to Mr. Castle, who was present at my interview with Lord Lothian. I now make this note public, together with Castle's reply:

December 13, 1940

DEAR BILL:

While I think of it, it seems to me desirable that we make a memorandum of the conversation which we had with Lord Lothian on October 8th, a few days before he started for England, when he visited me at the Waldorf and you were present.

We had a general discussion as to the unquestioned disaster that was facing these little democracies before the next harvest, with which facts he fully agreed. We discussed at length the methods successfully used in Belgium during the last war, which prevented relief having any military disadvantage to the British. This he also confirmed, as he was in the British Government at the time. In closing he stated that he personally favored our proposals, and that he would make it one of the purposes of his visit to London to urge the Government's approval. In reply to a question of mine as to whether he wanted us to keep on agitating the question, he said: "You must not stop."

It may become important some time to establish Lothian's humane outlook and the knowledge of an experienced British official that . . . [relief] was practicable and necessary.

Kindly let me have any corrections if my memory is faulty.

HERBERT HOOVER

December 18, 1940

MY DEAR MR. HOOVER:

I made a few notes after leaving you in October on our conversation with Lothian. What you said and what I remembered coincide.

With what you had to say about the Belgian relief work during the last war, Lothian wholly agreed and, in fact, spoke of it with enthusiasm.

When the interview was about to end, the Ambassador said that he was glad to say to you that he personally favored your proposal and he did so because he believed that it would be of great benefit to Britain. He said that his plans were a little uncertain, but that he expected to go home shortly and that he would urge the government to give its approval. He said that he was sure that during the German blitzkrieg, the government had not really faced the situation with all its implications.

BILL

CHAPTER 6

THE CREATION OF THE NATIONAL COMMITTEE ON FOOD FOR THE SMALL DEMOCRACIES

The Presidential election over, we determined that the only way relief could be brought to the women, children, and destitute in the small democracies was to awaken public opinion in the neutral countries to the inconsequential dangers from our proposals. Both the British and Germans were sensitive to neutral opinions. They needed actual support from the neutrals, or at least the continued neutrality of these nations.

On November 18, 1940, we launched an organization called "The National Committee on Food for the Small Democracies." In addition to myself as Honorary Chairman the original membership comprised those who had taken part in the famine relief of forty-five countries after World War I. However, we were quickly joined by leading Americans, including: former Vice-President Charles G. Dawes; former Secretary of the Navy Charles Francis Adams; former Secretary of Agriculture Arthur M. Hyde; former Undersecretaries of State William R. Castle, J. Reuben Clark, and James G. Rogers; former Assistant Secretaries of the Treasury James H. Douglas and Walter E. Hope; former Undersecretary of the Treasury Dr. Roswell Magill; Speaker of the Lower House of the Massachusetts Legislature Christian Herter; former Assistant Secretary of War Hanford MacNider; former Ambassadors F. Lammot Belin, Henry P. Fletcher,

John W. Garrett, and Dave Hennen Morris; former Foreign Ministers Laurits S. Swenson and Richard M. Tobin; former Governors Lewis O. Barrows, Ralph L. Carr, W. Cameron Forbes, Theodore Roosevelt, Jr., and Leverett Saltonstall; and General John J. Pershing and Admiral William V. Pratt.

The Committee included such clergymen as William Cardinal O'Connell, Daniel A. Poling, John R. Mott, Oscar E. Maurer, Archbishop Edward Mooney, Archbishop John T. McNicholas, Rabbi Edward N. Calisch, Bishop Ralph S. Cushman, Bishop James E. Freeman, Bishop William A. Griffin, George E. Barnes, Robert I. Gannon, Dr. Rufus M. Jones, Preston Bradley, and more than two hundred other well-known churchmen representing fourteen denominations.

Also among the members of the Executive Committee were Perrin C. Galpin, M. Preston Goodfellow, Richard W. Lawrence, Chauncey McCormick, Maurice Pate, Raymond S. Richmond, Edgar Rickard, Lewis L. Strauss, W. Hallam Tuck, and Allen Wardwell.

There were 204 university and college presidents and prominent educators, as well as many hundreds of professional, business, and farm leaders. About 60 prominent publishers, editors, and writers joined; among the latter were Temple Bailey, Faith Baldwin, Mary Hastings Bradley, William Henry Chamberlin, Irvin S. Cobb, Margaret Deland, Dorothy Canfield Fisher, Will and Inez Hayes Irwin, Rose Wilder Lane, Charles G. Norris, Kathleen Norris, George Sokolsky, Ida Tarbell, and Hendrik Willem Van Loon.

Many men and women joined our office staff as volunteers, including Mrs. Courtland Barnes, E. E. Fogelson, Mrs. Eve Garrette, Mrs. Helen Walker Homan, Robert MacAlarney, and Tracy Voorhees.

Out of gratitude for their loyal support, I should like to mention the names of all of the one thousand persons who joined with us, but space forbids their inclusion.

In addition to our National Committee, we set up more than twenty-five hundred local committees in forty-eight states, embracing representatives of the Church, business, labor, and agriculture. The organization included members of every creed, race, and color.

It was probably the most complete representation of true American spirit ever assembled by a civilian organization.

The Committee stated its purpose, which was

to raise a voice on behalf of the peoples of Finland, Norway, Holland, Belgium and Central Poland so that agreements may be made by the German and British Governments with a neutral organization—

(a) by which their domestic food supplies can be protected from the occupying armies;

(b) by which supplemental supplies can be imported through the German and British blockades and protected;

(c) to secure the efficient operation of such a neutral organization.

To the end that the lives of millions of children, women and men can be saved from the inevitable famine and pestilence which confront them, and that renewed hope may be given to them in the ideals of mankind.

I presented our case in detail in a nation-wide broadcast from a meeting at Vassar College on November 15, 1940. Some paragraphs of that address were:

I . . . present to the American people the plight of some millions of children, women, and men in the little nations of Finland, Norway, Holland, Belgium and Central Poland. . . .

I am asking for no gifts, no government appropriations, no use of American ships. . . . I simply wish to present the case of these people to America. I will suggest that their lives and infinite suffering can be saved. And I will suggest that we have a moral responsibility.

I have postponed discussing this question at length for the past two months because I did not wish so tender and difficult a subject to be stained with any color of [political] partisanship. That election is behind us and my obligation to participate further in partisan questions is ended. It is a problem that calls for cooperation and not for controversy. . . .

These little nations—all of them—sacrificed and fought against overwhelming odds to maintain freedom. . . .

They normally obtain a large part of their food supplies from outside of their borders in exchange for their products. Most of their food imports have come [from] overseas. . . .

They will reach the acute . . . [hunger stage of millions] some time this winter or next spring. . . .

. . . The only hope lies in restoration and protection of their domestic food by the Occupying [German] Army and in the import of food from overseas through the British and the German blockades under full safeguards. . . .

I then discussed the plans and safeguards we proposed and gave the answer to the arguments of our opponents. I continued:

I am perhaps one of the few living Americans who had full opportunity to see intimately the moving tragedy of the last great war from its beginnings down through the long aftermath of famine, pestilence and depression. I witnessed its misery and its backwash upon civilians in its most hideous forms. I saw the nightmares of roads filled for long miles with old men, women and children dropping of fatigue and hunger as they fled in terror from the oncoming armies. I saw even then the terrors of a score of air raids. . . . I saw the dreadful effect of the blockade in starvation. I have seen the women and children of whole cities practically at the exhaustion point of food. I have seen the raging of pestilence that is the implacable companion of famine. I witnessed their sufferings in over 20 nations.

When one speaks of war to me, I do not see the glorious parade of troops marching to tunes of gay music. . . .

I cannot forget the faces of the hungry, despaired, and terrorized women and little children, who are the real victims of modern war. . . .

There are things in this world that are not silenced by ideological argument or armchair strategists or declamation as to who is responsible. They are not to be settled that way because of the teachings of Christ which have resounded down these two thousand years. That teaching gave to mankind a new vision and part of that vision was mercy and compassion. . . .[1]

On November 23, *Collier's* published an article of mine in which I reviewed the food situation in Europe. The final paragraphs were:

. . . compassion is part of the woof and warp of democracy. . . . Today the Christian world is confronted with preserving the lives of . . . million[s].

[1] *Addresses Upon the American Road*, 1940–41, pp. 121–31.

We cannot as a Christian nation dismiss our concern. . . . And the parable of the Samaritan has pungent implications other than the compassion of the Samaritan alone. Perhaps some will remember the condemnation, which has echoed over centuries, of the priest and the Levite who passed by on the other side. And perhaps some will remember that the Greatest Teacher of all time did not allow His immortal vision to be clouded by a debate on the previous sins or the ideology of those who "stripped him of his raiment and wounded him . . . leaving him half dead. . . . He had compassion on him." [2]

I had hoped this reference might be of some influence on the minds of those people who had signed the manifesto attacking the relief program a month before.

[2] The article is reprinted in *ibid.*, pp. 132–46.

WE CHANGE TACTICS

In the face of Mr. Churchill's adamant opposition to the urgings of the exiled governments, it was clear that any plan for relief on the basis of the necessary food for the whole population in the occupied democracies, as administered in Belgium during the First World War, was hopeless at this time. So, on January 4, 1941, we determined to propose an experiment that not even the most violent British or German militarist could honestly challenge. We suggested it be applied initially to Belgium. If it proved successful and obviously without military damage, then it might be accepted for the other occupied democracies.

Our new proposal was based upon the fact that in each of the German-occupied democracies, devoted citizens had built up a system of soup kitchens where such food as they could obtain was being provided for the children, the aged, and the destitute. These kitchens were functioning in every needed place, but the food supplied was wholly inadequate.

In Belgium at this time there were two million underfed children and about one million destitute adults. To make the soup-kitchen ration more adequate, they needed additional bread, which would require 25,000 tons of cereals monthly. They also needed 20,000 tons monthly of meat and fat products, condensed milk, and other special foods for children.

Our proposal was that each month the Germans should supply from their large stocks on hand the 25,000 tons of cereals and that the 20,000 tons of special foods for soup kitchens should be permitted through the British blockade. Since no one could get the soup-kitchen ration without a ticket from the Belgian authorities, it was certain that the food would reach only the needy. We proposed that our stocks of imported soup materials on hand in Belgium should not at any one time exceed 10,000 tons, with a reserve in Holland, which would be less than one day's supply for Germany, even if it were seized. Moreover, the supply could be stopped instantly with any German violation, so from the arrangements there could be no military danger to the British cause.

On January 4, 1941, we telegraphed the details of our experimental plan to Hugh Gibson in London and to John Hartigan in Berlin and asked them to present it to those governments. In the meantime, we had sent three of our old hands, then in Poland, into Belgium to report on the situation. They were F. Dorsey Stephens, Columba P. Murray, Jr., and William C. McDonald.

Upon receiving their report, Mr. Gibson informed M. Paul Henri Spaak, the Minister of Foreign Affairs of the Belgian Government in Exile in London, of our new plan and our reports from Belgium. On January 30, Minister Spaak presented the matter to British Minister of Foreign Affairs Anthony Eden. The essential paragraphs of Spaak's memorandum to Eden were as follows:

At the beginning of this month Mr. Hoover commissioned three experts to make an inquiry into the food situation in Belgium. I have just been given their conclusions. You will find them enclosed (Annex I). They reveal a situation of extreme gravity. . . . Mr. Hoover considers that no population could subsist with the ration that is foreseen at present. . . .

You know our point of view. Like the British Government we desire above all the victory which will bring the liberation of our country. The whole question is to know whether, without compromising this victory, it is possible to lessen the effects of the famine that threatens our people.

A project of food relief conceived on a limited basis of public soup kitchens has been presented to me. . . .

The organization proposed permits an easy control and it is not susceptible of furnishing any substantial aid to the enemy. . . . Putting it in operation would . . . permit us to demand that the Germans put a complete stop to the levies on individual stores.

In the present circumstances I think that it is impossible to reject it purely and simply. A trial of it ought to be made, even if only on a limited scale as an experiment.

If the trial fails due to the Germans' fault, we will have demonstrated before the whole world that they, after having stripped the occupied territories of part of their resources, have besides prevented us from helping their victims. . . . no one will be in doubt about the responsibility for it; the case will be clear, all the responsibility will be on one side. In this war it is not only material force that counts, moral force also must contribute to the victory.

We wish, as you know, to formulate our policy in close agreement with the British Government. . . . That is why [we] . . . insist . . . that the question be thoroughly examined and discussed between our two Governments.

Spaak did not succeed.

On February 4, together with Hallam Tuck, I accepted an invitation, inspired by a mutual friend—a former member of Parliament, Captain Victor Cazalet—to lunch in Washington with British Ambassador Lord Halifax, who had succeeded Lord Lothian. After this meeting Mr. Tuck and I prepared a memorandum of our conversation with the Ambassador. We again presented to him our plan and the gist of the report from our three American representatives on the situation. We pointed out that if the Germans refused our proposal, the responsibility for starvation would rest on them before the world. If the Germans agreed and did not carry out their end of the program in good faith, the relief would stop instantly and again the responsibility would be theirs. We bluntly stated that British propaganda in the United States was being offset by their adamant attitude on this proposal for relief. We also pointed out that there were twelve to fifteen million descendants of the races of the small democracies in the United States. We suggested this was poor public relations for the British, who were spending large sums of money for favorable propaganda in America.

Lord Halifax dismissed our arguments with the opinion that the Germans would never enter into the agreement we proposed. He reiterated Britain's determination not to relax the blockade.

To explain our new proposal to the public, on February 16, I addressed a mass meeting in Chicago organized by Chauncey McCormick. There I reviewed our previous proposals of relief and pointed out that the same relief measures applied in the First World War had been supported and approved by the British Government. I related our failure to secure their approval of a similar program again. I explained our proposal and continued:

. . . [As to the] opposition on military grounds I am able to give you the highest military authorities in the world. Your Chairman, Mr. Chauncey McCormick, has received tonight the following telegram from General John Pershing. He says:

"I wish to send my greetings to those who are endeavoring to find a method by which food supplies can be furnished to the democracies in Europe occupied by the German armies. There is no doubt millions are in jeopardy unless they are given aid from somewhere. From my own war experience and some knowledge of the problems involved, I have every confidence that the salvation of these people can be worked out along the lines proposed by Mr. Hoover without military loss or benefit to either side. The interest of this committee in maintaining American ideals and the friendship to America of these nations by saving these millions is worthy of every support."

Your chairman has also received greetings from Admiral William V. Pratt, who dealt with the blockade in the last war and long commanded the United States fleet. Admiral Pratt said:

"I wish you would extend my greetings to your meeting in furtherance of aid to prevent wholesale starvation among the people of the occupied democracies in Europe. I have no hesitation in saying that this aid can be given under Mr. Hoover's proposals without any damage to Great Britain. Taking the long view of the future of constructive forces in the world and America's relation to it, it is of vital importance to America that Mr. Hoover's plans be carried through. Not only is the need pressing now, but what is of equal or more importance, an organization must be perfected now to start a more extensive campaign when the war is over. Only America will be able to meet this emergency."

I continued:

I am opposed to the whole philosophy of dictatorship. I want to see a world of free men and women. Here are six or seven nations whose whole philosophy of life and government has been and is yet opposed to totalitarianism. If the spirit of free men in the long years to come is to survive on the continent of Europe, it will be among these people devoted to freedom by their every instinct. Over centuries they have maintained their systems of free men from subjugation, time and time again. They have done it not by military action but by sheer moral and intellectual resistance. If the democracies of the west are to say to them now—as some of our citizens have said to them—"We will make no effort to save your millions of women and children, that they must die or grow up with stunted minds and bodies," then there is little encouragement to them to hold fast to our ideals of life. If confidence in the ideals of democracy is to be held, now is the time to hold it. . . .

We are asked for aid to Britain of stupendous dimensions. I believe we should give to them that aid generously and including ample food. But if that aid is to be given to preserve free nations, have we not a right to suggest that these other free peoples—friends of America all our national life—be allowed also to live? . . .

And overriding all this there is the question of humanity. There are things in this world that are not silenced by ideological argument or declamation as to who is responsible. They are not to be settled in these ways because of the teachings of Christ which have resounded down these two thousand years. . . .

Can you believe that American public opinion or the spiritual leadership of America has so lost its bearings as to be opposed even to an effort to aid those who lie in the ditch of war? . . .

I have seen the agonies of famine. I have listened to the pleadings of children, the fierce demands of mothers for the right of their children to live. I have seen relief stations and hospitals filled with its consequence in distorted minds and bodies. I have witnessed it in twenty nations. . . . I have seen starvation's unending blight upon the world. I know starvation in the last war had a large part in the causes of the world's agony today. I had hoped it would never again come to the world. But it has come, and I would be untrue to myself and to my country if I did not fight it to the end.[1]

[1] *Addresses Upon the American Road, 1940–41*, pp. 147–55.

At this meeting a new form of British Government opposition to relief appeared. Before the Chicago meeting, pressure was brought to bear upon the local representatives of the small democracies to disavow our efforts. The Polish, Belgian, Norwegian, Finnish, and Dutch Consuls had agreed to be present at this meeting, but the British Consul visited each of them and persuaded all but the Finn not to come. The Consul also tried to dissuade a leading Chicago pastor, the Reverend Preston Bradley, who had agreed to preside at the meeting, from doing so. This courageous clergyman not only resisted the Consul's attempt, but indignantly disclosed the whole story at the meeting.

CHAPTER 8

THE GERMANS AGREE TO THE GUARANTEES—SECRETARY HULL'S ATTITUDES

On February 26, 1941, the Germans agreed in full to our proposals. The following is a summary of the cable from John Hartigan in Berlin:

Conference held with FO [Foreign Office] officials resulted in following statement principles accepted by German Government proposed activity in Belgium Hoover Relief.

One Permanent Commission . . . will be permitted operate Belgium with headquarters Brussels. Only one American [Relief] Commission envisaged. . . .

Two No exportation or requisitioning any supplies furnished by Hoover Commission or of equivalent domestic supplies.

Three German Government continuing efforts to extent ability supplement supplies Belgium from own reserves—notably bread, grains and potatoes. . . . This contribution independent of our contemplated operations. . . .

The German Foreign Office gave Hartigan a memorandum confirming their agreement:

German Government have with interest taken account of Mr. Hoover's plan for relief Belgium and fully appreciate humanitarian motives. Competent German authorities prepared assist Mr. Hoover in execution his plan.

Gathering from proposals submitted beginning January its intention place relief program on soup kitchen basis giving necessitous Belgian civil population one meal daily with one meal extra for children and infants. Competent German authorities agree with this form distribution. As Hoover Delegation could ascertain on visit Belgian Winterhelp co-ordinating all Belgian organizations of social welfare and working in close cooperation with and aided by German military administration and German Red Cross. Competent German authorities gather that relief plan intends to grant additional foodstuffs to population of occupied Belgium. They will take necessary measures that foodstuffs imported from overseas within frame relief work shall fully be turned over to Belgian civil population and that neither these foodstuffs nor foodstuffs of the same kind shall be withdrawn from Belgium or be requisitioned for purposes of occupying forces. . . .

. . . If notwithstanding Germany in times of war is prepared to assist Belgium with German or other European grain supplies this means considerable concession. Concerning question of control raised by Mr. Hoover may be pointed out that Belgian organizations united in Belgian Winterhelp offer fullest guarantees for just distribution of relief foodstuffs all over Belgium. If in addition relief plan calls for small neutral control commission competent German authorities . . . prepared to admit such commission composed of 3 or 4 persons acceptable to German Government with headquarters in Brussels. . . .

The same day, we cabled the text of the German agreement to Hugh Gibson, stating that the agreement covered every honest objection that anyone could raise. We directed him to present it to the Belgian Government in Exile, they in turn to give it to the British Foreign Office. We added the following general observations:

The rescue of democracies in Europe to find them only empty husks does not appeal to thinking Americans. If the ideals of democracy are to be upheld in the minds of these suffering people it can only be done if we show them sympathy and support now. The friendly attitude of the peoples in these countries to the higher purposes of peace when this war is over are of no little importance.

I gave a copy of the German agreement to the Belgian Ambassador in Washington, and he presented it to Undersecretary of State Sumner Welles.

On February 28, because of an unfriendly statement of Undersecretary Welles to the Belgian Ambassador in Washington, I called on Secretary Hull and complained. Mr. Hull said Welles's statement was made when he was away, ill, and that he had not authorized it. I reviewed our latest proposals and the German agreement with the Secretary, recounting the opinions of General Pershing and Admiral Pratt. The Secretary appeared sympathetic to our proposals and expressed astonishment at the British lack of propaganda sense.

An incident occurred at this meeting which had no immediate bearing upon our activities, but it was of momentous importance for the future of our work. Mr. Hull informed me in detail of the positive evidence in his hands that Hitler was preparing to attack Russia. I called his attention to some other evidence which appeared to me to confirm that such an attack was pending and that it would at once assure the safety of Great Britain.

Mr. Hull asked me for a memorandum on our proposals and our activities. I sent it to him on March 5, and included my Chicago speech, the German agreement, and a covering letter, the important paragraphs of which were:

March 5, 1941

MY DEAR MR. SECRETARY:

Apropos of our conversation Friday I have increasing reports that the Administration is opposed to relief for the occupied democracies. Whether this is true or not, certainly the representative of some of these small democracies and of Britain understand that this is the Administration view.

I feel deeply concerned that America should ever be thought of as opposing the saving of these millions of people.

I know that the statements being made are not your views. They probably originate from an entire misunderstanding of the actual situation in these countries, of ignorance of our proposals. . . .

As you know, I have said on several occasions that for our Government to undertake active negotiations between Germany and Britain to cover such arrangements could only lead to embarrassments; and to avoid these embarrassments they should be left to informal bodies. But when the representatives of some of the governments in Washington, who are concerned, are given an impression that our Government does not approve this implies influence by our Government, and of course it puts obstructions in the way to the relief of these starving people.

As I have said, I am sure this does not represent your own view. I am wondering if under the circumstances you could informally let all of these representatives [of the small democracies] know that our Government does not in the least disapprove, and is not opposed. I of course believe it would be greatly in American interest aside from the lives that will be saved for our Government to go further and say that it hopes that this solution may be carried out. . . .

Please accept my great respects.

HERBERT HOOVER

I also sent to Mr. Hull the names of the men in Belgium directing the soup-kitchen organization, known as the "Winter Help Committee," whose head was Paul Heymans, former Minister of Economic Affairs. He was known to Hull.

THE BRITISH OPEN NEW ATTACKS UPON US FROM WASHINGTON— AND WE REPLY

On March 10, 1941, ten days after my discussion with Secretary Hull, the British Embassy let loose a blast at our proposals in the press. I give this verbose statement in full:

The attitude of His Majesty's Government in the United Kingdom toward the problem of the relief of the civilian populations in the German-occupied territories was first stated in detail by the Prime Minister in his speech to the House of Commons on August 20, 1940. It was amplified in the statement made public by the late Lord Lothian just before his death. Nothing has since occurred to alter the view of His Majesty's Government that it is the responsibility of the German government to see to the material welfare of the countries they have overrun, nor to weaken their conviction that no form of relief can be devised which would not directly or indirectly assist the enemy's war effort.

Nevertheless, His Majesty's Government would not think it right to pass over in silence the various proposals put forward by certain organizations and by Mr. Hoover. They recognize that there is a body of opinion in the United States and elsewhere which, with motives which cannot be impugned, would like to be able to play an effective part in the prevention or relief of distress. Although convinced that the vast majority of the American people are determined to do nothing which would impair the war effort of the British people and their allies, His Majesty's Government nevertheless recognize that this great body of opinion feels itself unable entirely to dismiss the possibility of giving relief unless it can be satisfied that such action is, in fact, incompatible with its desire for a speedy British victory and the release of Europe from enemy domination.

For these reasons, His Majesty's Government have considered afresh the whole problem of relief, including the proposal for the institution of soup kitchens in Belgium. They consider it desirable to restate certain basic facts and principles on which their policy rests.

The blockade is not a food blockade nor an oil blockade, but a blockade directed against the whole economic war machine of the enemy. It is intended to deprive him of imported goods, to drive him into using in uneconomic ways goods which he possesses or produces, to aggravate his transport difficulties and to render as costly and burdensome as possible distribution of supplies within the areas which he controls and utilizes for his military operations and war potential. Every import of foodstuffs into an occupied territory conflicts directly with one or other of these objectives.

Just as the blockade extends over the whole range of supplies and transport, so it must extend over the whole range of countries overrun by the enemy. The Germans are attempting to organize these territories to form an integral part of their war machine. Their factories and their agriculture are forced to work for the enemy; their laborers are attracted into Germany by promises of more food and better wages. Their surplus products are taken by the enemy and this helps to create the disparity which exists today between rations in Germany and those allowed to the civilian populations in the occupied territories. All these territories are used by the enemy as bases for his attacks on Britain by sea and air. Railways and roads which should be used to carry food from one part of the occupied area to another are devoted instead to the transport of troops and of fuel and bombs for the campaign against Britain. The rolling stock of the occupied countries has been looted, and as far afield as the Balkans, Belgian and French wagons are even at this moment carrying German troops and munitions.

As a result, surplus products of one district are prevented from moving freely to others where they are urgently required. The surplus production of Norwegian fisheries and of the farms of Denmark and the Netherlands is not equitably divided among the Norwegians, the Danes and the Dutch; it is the Germans who claim the right to profit by all local surpluses in each separate area under their control. They disclaim the obligation to make good any local deficiencies except those in Germany itself. Every arrival of foodstuffs into any one part of the occupied area thus constitutes a direct encouragement to the German technique of exploitation. Unfortunately, therefore, there can be no doubt that the admission of relief supplies would benefit the enemy. It is not simply a question of ensuring that any supplies admitted are consumed only by the subject peoples for whom they are intended, but a question of whether the German economy is thereby relieved in another direction.

The British government have already promised full support for the relief of distress in these territories the moment they are freed of German occupation. Speaking in the House of Commons on Aug. 20, the Prime Minister stated:

"Meanwhile we can and will arrange in advance for the speedy entry of food into any part of the enslaved area when this part has been wholly cleared of German forces and has genuinely regained its freedom. We shall do our best to encourage the building up of reserves of food all over the world so that there will always be held up before the eyes of the people of Europe, including—I say it deliberately—the German and Austrian peoples, the certainty that the shattering of the Nazi power would bring to them all immediate food, freedom and peace."

It may be urged that even although it is not possible to devise acceptable conditions, the duty of feeding the hungry overrules all other considerations. This is an argument which the British government must respect, although they cannot accept it. It presupposes firstly that there is and will be hunger on a serious scale; and secondly, that hunger is a greater evil and one more urgent to be remedied than the prolongation of the war, the continued subjection of many nations to German oppression and tyranny, and the wounding and killing by the most barbarous means of countless thousands of people. But there need be no scarcity amounting to famine and starvation if the enemy would distribute his supplies equitably, and devote to the welfare of his conquered peoples a tithe of the ingenuity which he devotes to his attack on the civilian population of Britain or of the solicitude shown to his own armies of occupation. Germany has, in fact, proclaimed on many occasions that the so-called new order can assure all food supplies in the countries under her domination. The existence of local shortages in certain districts of the occupied territories is not an admissible argument; for it was not to be expected that the enemy would make good his depredations or restore the supplies he has looted, while he is still hopeful that supplementary supplies from overseas may be forthcoming. Provided that we do not play into his hands by admitting

such assistance, it can hardly be supposed that he will allow hunger to impair the efficiency or to increase the discontent of the vast subject population which is essential to the functioning of the German war machine.

The British government do not deny that the oppressed peoples are likely to suffer some degree of hardship and privation, and they are deeply moved by the sufferings of their allies. The civilian population of Great Britain itself is suffering and has suffered many thousands of casualties from the brutal attacks which the German air force has directed against it.

The British people are, moreover, now deliberately subjecting themselves to privations; they are lowering their own standard of living to a minimum so that more and more shipping space can be allotted to the implements of war. They are doing all this in the common cause and they are confident that their allies in the enslaved countries will scorn to shirk their share of the distresses which must be borne by each and every one if the common victory is to be assured.

Even if it were admitted that immediate shortages of food were likely, *the British government would regard it as false humanitarianism to agree to the admission of foodstuffs to the areas concerned, knowing as they do that the result of this action would be to prolong the war and to add in the long run to the sum of human misery.* They believe that the conquered peoples have now had sufficient experience of German domination to realize the justice of this view.

For these reasons the British government are satisfied that relief of countries in enemy occupation would, whatever the conditions might be, postpone the day of victory. They regard it as their primary duty to rid Europe of Nazi tyranny and to restore the conquered peoples to physical and spiritual freedom. They cannot allow themselves to be deflected from this goal and, in full realization of their responsibility, they therefore feel obliged to reaffirm their determination not to permit the blockade to be weakened or undermined by the admission of supplies from overseas into any territory under enemy control.[1]

The same day (March 10), the Committee on Food for the Small Democracies issued its reply:

The British Ambassador has courteously furnished me with an advance copy of the British statement. The American people have a right to know

[1] *New York Herald Tribune,* March 10, 1941; italics mine.

the views upon it of myself and the executive committee on food for the small democracies. Before giving those views, we wish no misunderstanding of our sympathy with the British cause, or that we have any doubt that the original plight of the people in the small democracies is due to the German invasion.

We believe that the British statement was prepared before they were fully informed upon the undertakings we have now secured. And, in this light, our full proposals in no way impair the British war effort. At the same time they uphold the ideals of democracy to the world and these little nations. They would save the lives of multitudes of children and others. . . .

We do not agree that there are enough supplies on the Continent to care for these people. . . . British reports state that the fat supply of the Continent as a whole has been reduced 40 per cent. Our reports show over 50 per cent. And, as the Germans are not likely to reduce their fat supplies below fighting levels, the shortage falls even more violently upon the occupied democracies. And the Belgians are the first to be exhausted.

In order to check our own information again, we requested a committee of experts, comprising Mr. John Lee Coulter, former member of the Tariff Commission; Professor J. I. Falconer, of Ohio State University; Professor Asher Hobson, of the University of Wisconsin; and Dr. E. V. Mc-Collum, of Johns Hopkins University, to review objectively all of the data; not only our own investigations on the ground in Europe, but also the data of the Department of Agriculture, the Department of Commerce, British reports, and actual rations on the Continent. They fully confirm our conclusions.

We repeated our proposals in detail, the required German guarantees, and the opinions of General Pershing and Admiral Pratt, then continued:

This Committee wishes to make it clear that none of its members seeks to administer any relief. The American Red Cross has been given permission by Britain to import supplies through the blockade for French children, and this committee would favor the extension of their fine service, or those of the Friends Service Committee, to the Belgians.

. . . It is no false humanity which saves the lives of countless children, and the committee has every evidence that millions of Americans wish it to continue its efforts toward finding a solution by which the lives of these helpless people may be saved.[2]

SECRETARY HULL REPLIES TO MY LETTER OF MARCH 5

On March 14, 1941, I received a long letter from Secretary Hull. He wrote that the Government of the United States had great sympathy for human suffering, was constantly considering possible measures of relief, did not endorse any particular plan, was securing the views of various persons, and welcomed any information from us.

Since our Committee felt that in view of the long British statement of March 10 some of our members might think that Churchill was right and that we should cease our efforts, we communicated with each member to ask whether he wished us to continue. Out of a total of 1,000 members, only one withdrew. The other 999 urged us to more action.

But the propaganda against us continued. In the following editorial, *The Tulsa Tribune* answers a particularly unfair attack:

Henry Wise Hobson is the Episcopal bishop of the diocese of southern Ohio. For some time past he has been, and perhaps still is, chairman of a war propaganda organization known as "The Fight For Freedom, Inc." . . .

Its issue No. 20, dated October 10, 1941, referred to the ex-President of the United States, Mr. Herbert Hoover, as "The Father of America's Hoovervilles, the man who bayoneted the bonus marchers and who refused to lift a finger for the hungry millions who pleaded for relief during the early days of the depression."

That is an unmitigated and diabolical lie. Mr. Hoover never bayoneted a human body, and if the Reverend gentleman from Cincinnati knows enough recent history to fill a thimble he knows that Herbert Hoover has fed more hungry human mouths than any man who ever lived.

All this infamy of falsehood has been pointed out to the allegedly reverend gentleman from Cincinnati, and he has refused to repudiate the falsehood, or to in any way correct it. . . .

[2] *Ibid.*

Such an un-Christian attitude as Henry W. Hobson has assumed, with the responsibilities of chairman of an enterprise that deliberately maligns one of the noblest Americans who ever lived, is infamous. The reverend gentleman should read the Ten Commandments. . . .[3]

To me, the Bishop's reasons for opposing food for hungry children seemed a little *non sequitur*.

[3] *The Tulsa Tribune*, February 16, 1942.

CHAPTER 10

WE HAD NEED TO FIND SOME
OTHER NEUTRAL SPONSOR

By the passage of the Lend-Lease Act in March, 1941, we were confronted with the fact that the United States was in reality no longer neutral. The Germans would not be likely to admit American citizens into countries occupied by her armies to supervise relief. Therefore, through a former American ambassador on our committee, we secured assurances that the Swiss and Swedish governments would undertake the work of inspection if the combatant governments were brought into agreement.

Although the Washington Administration was against us, we expanded the activities of our committee. We hoped that we might persuade the Washington authorities with evidence of deep American feeling, and beyond that we wanted to demonstrate to the world that a great majority of Americans held to their Christian obligations.

Among other things, we started the publication of a weekly bulletin entitled *Facing the Facts* and gave it wide circulation to the press and our many local committees. In one week alone we received editorial support from newspapers and periodicals with a circulation of over twenty-five million. At the same time, the religious leaders on our committee undertook to secure the opinions of their colleagues. A group of Protestant leaders issued a statement on March 17, 1941, supporting our proposals. It contained these significant paragraphs:

"If we produce another generation of shriveled bodies and distorted minds there will again (as after the last war) be an unbalanced future.

51

Europe cannot be built on starved, diseased people with minds and emotions charged with hate.

"We believe it our Christian duty to feed the starving peoples in the small democracies of Europe with their 37,000,000 needy people. While we debate the issue thousands continue to die. Great Britain cannot do it. Her hands are tied. The United States government cannot do it without many involvements. The only relief, as was the case in the last war, must come through some informal neutral body such as Mr. Hoover proposes. There is no Christian reason for continuing among these friendly people the tragedies of famine and epidemic."

It was the belief of those who signed the statement that the Hoover plan, if accepted, would safeguard the interests of Great Britain and contribute nothing to Germany.[1]

It was signed by eighty-four Protestant clergymen.

A few days later, on March 25, a statement by leading Roman Catholic clergymen in support of us was issued by William Cardinal O'Connell, Archbishop of Boston. The other signers were two Archbishops—the Most Reverend John T. McNicholas of Cincinnati and the Most Reverend John A. Floersch of Louisville—and seventeen Bishops of Catholic dioceses throughout the United States. They asserted:

As individual American citizens—in cooperation with religious leaders of every denomination, who have publicly expressed their support and approval of Herbert Hoover's plan to relieve starvation within the occupied countries of Europe—we join in giving expression to our strong belief that the exigencies of even a just war do not require that millions of innocent children, women and non-combatants be made to endure famine.

A victory built on the dead bodies of starving women and children, innocent victims of the war over which they have no control, will destroy human sentiments that must necessarily enter into any form of enduring peace.

We hope and pray that those who guide the destinies of nations will be conscious of their obligation to protect the innocent, and not lay obstacles in the path of a movement whose sole object is to alleviate dire

[1] *The New York Times*, March 17, 1941.

distress without affording aid to those who have invaded the lands of these many millions of starving and helpless fellow humans.

With the Holy Father, Pope Pius XII, we believe that "we can desire nothing more in such a convulsion of things than to help the bodies and raise the spirits" of the innocent victims of war.[2]

Later, a statement of approval was issued by sixty-two leading American rabbis. It said in part:

The state of unlimited emergency which the President has proclaimed cannot blind us to human needs and should not stifle our humanitarian impulses. . . .

We, as religious leaders, cannot be indifferent to the suffering that, in increasing measure, is the lot of the innocent civilian population of western Europe. . . . We recognize the practical problems involved in any effort to bring food to Belgium and other stricken areas, and we also recognize that segment of American opinion which fears that help to starving civilians may mean aid to the Nazis. . . .

. . . The Biblical command to feed even our enemy when he is hungry is reiterated by our sages. How much the more then are we obliged to seek to save the lives of these starving innocents who are not our enemies but vanquished friends of democracy, the unfortunate victims of events beyond our control.

We record our approval of the quiet courageous way in which the National Committee on Food for the Small Democracies has striven to carry out the mission entrusted to it, working to win support for its proposals without entering the realm of political controversy or using these methods of intense campaigning which might evoke debate and stir up unwanted prejudices.

We regret that, despite this fact, the committee has been the target for unjustified attacks. . . .

In the name of the God and Father of all men and of our common humanity we commend the work of the National Committee on Food for the Small Democracies in the blessed effort it is making.[3]

In the meantime, poignant appeals poured in from local relief committees inside Belgium, Holland, Poland, and Norway. These

[2] *The New York Times,* March 25, 1941.

[3] *Congressional Record,* Senate, 77th Congr., 1st sess., September 4, 1941, v. 87, pt. 7, pp. 7278–79.

we duly published. For instance, a Belgian appeal, written by Paul Heymans, former Belgian Minister of Economic Affairs, and signed by Belgium's leading citizens, read in part:

In the name of the Belgian General Relief [Winter Help] Committee which has been formed to bring relief to the Belgian people in the hour of their gravest need we express our gratitude to you and your colleagues on our behalf. . . . we have laid great hopes in the materialization of your plan *to at least rescue our children.*[4] As time is passing and as we are unfortunately the powerless witness of a situation which is already extremely grave we must make a pressing appeal to give assistance to these innocent victims. . . . we beg for help. . . .

On May 6, we received a long report on the situation in Belgium from John Cudahy, who had been Mr. Roosevelt's Ambassador to Belgium. Mr. Cudahy had retired from the diplomatic service but had now revisited Belgium. The report contained more than five thousand words. It was published, in substance, in *Life* on June 2, 1941. A few paragraphs are sufficient indication of Belgium's plight:

They ask for bread. Belgium is hungry. Of 8,400,000 Belgians more than 8,300,000 are subsisting on rations which means rapid depletion of physical forces and gradual starvation. In nearly every Belgian home there is cruel suffering and the future is cast in shadow which grows blacker each day. . . . Young Belgians to number of 2,000,000 will be cursed for the rest of their lives by stunted and impoverished physique, weakened and degenerate brain and discolored, embittered character unless relief comes soon. There are tens of thousands of aged and invalided whose tenuous days will be brought to a close. . . .
 . . . I met people everywhere who told me fearful harrowing stories of famine in Belgium and because I have lived in the country and have a genuine affection for the people I felt sympathy but I cannot say my heart was really affected until I met my friend René Colin. He was ten-years-old when I went away from Brussels last July, a robust juvenile specimen with cheeks the same pigment as that apple from Washington State [with] . . . sturdy legs like bulging old-fashioned supports of pianos. . . . We were such good friends that one of my first calls on my return to Brussels was to . . . [René]. But I shall not soon recover from the shock

[4] Italics mine.

of my reunion with René. It was not that high color in his sunken cheeks
. . . had turned to pasty gray, and that he had grown so thin that his neck
resembled a pipestem, nor was it heavy smudged shadows under his eyes,
not his limbs like those of a tree withered by blight. No it was complete
metamorphosis of the pink, hearty, happy Belgian boy I had left ten months
. . . before into a dejected tired little old man that stood before me, now
spiritless as the wounded bird, all bloom gone from him as the light fades
from the ending day. He had given up school, his mother . . . told me.
. . . There was very little milk and very little bread and potatoes, she said,
and the boy could not keep awake. Two weeks ago he had fainted in the
classroom and so she had decided to wait for better days before resuming
his studies. . . .

Ambassador Cudahy had many articles published stressing the suffering in Belgium.

In view of United States co-operation with Great Britain through
the Lend-Lease program and an agreement by the Washington Administration to supply food to Vichy France, I again addressed Secretary Hull on March 27. The essential paragraphs were:

Since my letter of March 5th and your reply two events entirely change
the situation as to food relief to the German-occupied democracies.

The passage of the Lend-Lease Act obviously involves us deeply in
the consequences of the war. But it also gives our government a measure
of responsibility to see that the policies pursued by the British are in the
interest of both winning the war and winning a peace, and [thus] in the
interests of the United States.

The British have opened the blockade on food to Southern [Vichy]
France and with that event 95 per cent of all the so-called principles they
have advanced for the absolute wall of food blockade to the democracies
is negatived. . . .

I reviewed the food situation in Europe and pointed out that

. . . *Germany and Italy cannot be starved by the food blockade.*
. . . *The effect of the food blockade is to starve the women and children*
of the democratic peoples who have been lifelong friends of the United
States.

I then restated the reasons why the United States should take in hand the problem of food for these small German-occupied democracies and concluded:

I know that millions of Americans would be gratified. And I know it would bring to the British cause support that is now lukewarm or doubtful. And it brings to Americans the feeling that the standards of Christianity have not been abandoned by our country. It can have no military advantage to the Germans; it has immense values to our future.

On April 7, Camille Gutt, the Minister of Finance and War in the Belgian Government in Exile in London, gave an interview to the New York press in support of our efforts. *The New York Times* reported the interview, saying:

Belgium is on the verge of starvation. . . .
"People are actually hungry. . . . Boys and girls are seen fainting in the schools from want of food, babies are dying and the number of destitute increases everyday." . . .
"We are cooperating to the fullest extent with the British in our common end, which is to win the war," he continued. "Certainly we are not going to break or impair a weapon in their hands. On the other hand, we do fight to liberate Belgium, and not to liberate a generation of crippled and disabled men and women. . . ."[5]

OUR OPPONENTS ARE STILL IN ACTION

On March 26, 1941, Sir Gerald Campbell of the British Legation called on me in New York. I dictated a summary of the conversation immediately after he left. Some of the paragraphs indicate the forces in motion against us:

. . . He stated that they felt particularly bad at the way things had developed, that the British Blockade Minister had received very bad treatment in the House of Commons. . . . He said he could not help but feel that our campaign was against the British. . . . I told him British

[5] *The New York Times*, April 8, 1941.

suffering was a daily shock to all our people, but that we could see no reason why the death of British children required also the death of Belgian and Dutch children—their own Allies.

. . . He said they felt that the propaganda we were carrying on was distinctly anti-British. I replied that I could find nothing of this in any of our statements and asked him to be specific. On the contrary, I felt the British people were being misled because they would not allow the conditions demanded of the Germans to appear in the British press. . . .

I reminded him that there had been a broadcast to the United States from Great Britain attacking me but not one indication of the conditions we had imposed on the Germans. I stated that I had asked for broadcasting time over the British Broadcasting Company because I had wanted to tell the British people exactly what we were proposing and also express our sympathies with their cause. But I was told I would be given no opportunity.

He said that the Germans would not make any such agreement as I proposed. I told him that, to the contrary, I had secured an agreement from the Germans, of which the British . . . had a copy, stating they would furnish 25,000 tons a month of breadstuffs if 20,000 tons of soup kitchen supplies were brought in from overseas. . . .

He said that even if the Germans agreed, they would not keep their word. I replied that then the operation would cease and the responsibility would be upon the Germans. . . .

He again reiterated that we were anti-British. I said that to disagree with British government policies was a right even of Englishmen and certainly I had not surrendered that by being an American. . . .

He expressed regret that we could not find some kind of basis of common action. I said it could be found if the British government would stop misrepresentation in their propaganda and try to find humane policies. He closed the conversation with a remark, "we will need take measures."

Campbell's statements did not unduly alarm us.

CHAPTER 11

THE ROOSEVELT ADMINISTRATION JOINS WITH CHURCHILL IN OPPOSING RELIEF

On April 11, 1941, Secretary Hull answered my letter of March 27, in effect informing me that despite the opening of the blockade for food to France, our government would not interest itself to secure similar action to provide relief to the small democracies. He said:

MY DEAR MR. HOOVER:

I have received your letter of March twenty-seventh, and am glad to have your further observations regarding food relief within certain countries in Europe. I am not aware, however, that there has been any change in the situation since my letter to you of March fourteenth, which would warrant a modification of this Government's attitude. I think I have heretofore indicated that conditions are not such at this stage as to make practicable the application of the general policy of the Government, which has been rather fully defined, to the individual or group undertaking, of which you are the official head.

CORDELL HULL

On April 24, I replied to his letter and more vigorously reviewed the obligation of our government to give the small democracies the same consideration being extended to France. As the full text appeared in the *Congressional Record,* I give only the two concluding paragraphs:

10. I do not believe the American Government, in the long corridor of history, can escape the moral responsibility of making an effort on behalf of these millions of human beings who have sacrificed their all on the altar of democracy.

11. We wish it clearly understood that neither this Committee nor its members wish to administer any such actual relief, and have before suggested that it should be done by agencies already established for such purposes and not in any way affiliated with this Committee.[1]

On May 10, Secretary Hull replied to the above letter. The important paragraph was an admission that Mr. Churchill was dictating the policies of the American Government:

. . . to insist upon the fulfillment of a program which is at variance with the aims and objectives of the British Government and its endeavors to bring about a victorious conclusion of the war and thereby release the peoples of Europe from military domination and the menace of possible food shortage, would not appear to be in harmony with the declared policy of this Government to give all aid to Great Britain and other countries which are resisting aggression.

All this did not explain why German-occupied France could have food, while it was denied to adjacent German-occupied Belgium and Holland.

On June 2, Senator Elmer Thomas of Oklahoma introduced a resolution in the Senate in which he strongly urged relief. He said in his introductory remarks:

Mr. President, several days ago I said that a resolution would be submitted in the Senate urging the Secretary of State to work out with the British Government and the accredited representatives of stricken and hungry countries of Europe some formula whereby the lives of millions of defenseless and destitute people might be saved.

. . . The resolution I am about to submit actually has 37 signatures of Senators. Other distinguished Senators who are not in Washington at the moment have signified their intention of supporting it. Thus, it is seen that

[1] *Congressional Record,* Senate, 77th Congr., 1st sess., October 16, 1941, v. 87, pt. 7, p. 7929.

there is in this body substantial support for this humanitarian resolution. That support cuts across party lines.

If, by raising our voice, we can save the defenseless, hungry, unarmed millions—save them from starvation or from the pestilences that unfailingly follow mass malnutrition—we shall have done something Christian, compassionate, and merciful in a war-torn world. No other nation is able to help; hence, unless we raise our voice in their behalf, they surely will perish. . . .[2]

The resolution called upon the Administration to

. . . endeavor as quickly as possible to work out, in cooperation with the British Government . . . the setting up of systematic and definite relief for all stricken . . . countries . . . based on agreements by the belligerents for the protection of the native and imported food. . . .[3]

Many Senators signed the resolution. Among them were sixteen Democrats, twenty Republicans and one Progressive. Our Committee on Food for the Small Democracies at once furnished the Senator with more than six thousand resolutions which had been passed by public bodies, plus a mass of evidence of support from every segment of American life.

The resolution was later formally presented to the Senate, and a number of Senators spoke effectively for it. However, it was referred to the Senate Committee on Foreign Relations, where it received an administrative burial.

On June 3, I again addressed Secretary Hull. This time I "spoke my mind" fully on the Administration's policies in relation to this matter. The full text appears in the *Congressional Record;* I give but a few paragraphs here to indicate its tenor:

What you have said in effect is that the American Government accepts the views of Britain in this matter; that you will not even attempt to moderate those policies so as to save the lives of literally millions of women and children in these small democracies. Yet these countries have sacrificed their all for Britain and in the cause against aggression which you properly state is also an American cause. . . .

[2] *Ibid.*, June 2, 1941, v. 87, pt. 4, p. 4586.
[3] *Ibid.*, p. 4586.

. . . You say, "The moral responsibility and the clear duty to supply relief rest with the occupying authorities." That certainly is true. The hard answer is that the Germans will not do it in so far as the British blockade prevents them from doing it. . . . The British themselves admit that a 40 per cent fat deficiency exists in German-occupied Europe. And that hits Belgium today to the extent of 90 per cent.

. . . You say, "To insist upon the fulfillment of a program which is at variance with the aims and objectives of the British Government, etc." In other words, our Government adopts the policy of starvation and death to these democratic peoples because it is British policy. Therefore the American Government—no matter what the cost is to our own standards of humanity, to our own interests, to the destruction of these peoples—is blindly following the policies of another government with no voice of its own. . . . This refusal to aid the Belgians contrasts with the vigorous and effective action of our Government in 1914 by which we saved 10,000,000 lives in Belgium and Northern France. . . .

The peoples within these democracies have from the day of their invasions looked to America for leadership. . . . We now apparently abandon these peoples to their fate, and that without consideration of the sacrifice they have made against aggression. . . .[4]

On June 28, Secretary Hull replied to my letter of June 3. He simply repeated all of the British arguments and assertions.

Early in September our Senate friends pressed for hearings on the resolution directing aid to the small democracies. In an attempt to block the hearings, Hull addressed to the Foreign Relations Committee a letter which was issued to the press. It did not seem fair that one side alone should be published; therefore, through Senator Arthur Capper, two of my letters to Secretary Hull were introduced into the *Congressional Record* on October 16, 1941, and were widely published in the press. The result was to increase our support.

STILL MORE ATTACKS UPON OUR PROPOSALS

A violent attack upon me appeared in London in *The Times* on April 10. Hugh Gibson cabled it to me. *The Times's* Washington cor-

[4] *Ibid.*, October 16, 1941, v. 87, pt. 7, p. 7930.

respondent, in a dispatch to his paper voicing strong opposition to our plan, had quoted from an article written by a minister of the Gospel in the United States, Dr. Henry P. Van Dusen:

What of "politics" in the United States, particularly as they affect Mr. Hoover and his interest in the "little democracies"? Professor van Dusen, of the Union Theological Seminary, writing in a new periodical, "Christianity and the Crisis," points out that while Mr. Hoover insisted that he would contemplate no move to weaken the British defence, he was "meeting rather secretively in Washington with the most extreme isolationists" to plan the defeat of the Lease and Lend Bill, a measure which every intelligent citizen of his "little democracies" hailed as the brightest hope for their future liberation. And what of Mr. Hoover's demand that the Governments of these democracies have certainly not echoed? Mr. van Dusen says:—"The little democracies can hardly be expected to trust one who is employing the full weight of his immense political influence to defeat the succour upon which their very existence depends; nor can their friends in this country. The Biblical figure is altered: 'Men cry for freedom and are proffered bread.' "

The American Government has no alternative but to consider as "political" the attempts to secure their influence for lifting the British blockade.

I thought this might provide a good opportunity to get our case before the British public, and I therefore sent a cablegram to *The Times*. To my astonishment, it was published on April 16.

THE EDITOR   April 12, 1941
THE *Times*
LONDON.

SIR:

I have been informed of the content of a dispatch which appears in the *Times* of April tenth. As it is a wholly inaccurate presentation of my views and purposes, I should like my old British friends who do not read the American press and are therefore not aware of the facts to have a word on the subject. They should know that these quotations are from a small but zealous group whose distortion of fact does the British cause daily harm.

I have differed from part of one policy among many British policies and it is one that particularly affects many Americans. That difference is in the question of food for the starving women, children and unemployed men in the occupied democracies. An Englishman is not a traitor when he constructively criticizes a policy of his Government, nor is it enmity to England for an American to express such a differing opinion.

I start with two assumptions: first, that no Englishman wishes, any more than I wish, to let their former Allies starve; and second, that there must be no military advantage to either side or no project could be accepted. Therefore every proposal of mine has been founded upon the requirement of a prior agreement with the Germans covering

(a) Cessation of all requisition of native food supplies;

(b) Contribution of foodstuffs from German controlled breadstuffs in amounts equivalent to the food already taken;

(c) Imports through the blockade of soup kitchen supplies and special food for children;

(d) Efficient neutral control.

That such an agreement is not impossible is indicated by the fact that the Germans on February 26th last accepted these terms in respect to my proposal of an experiment in Belgium. They agreed to supply 25,000 tons of breadstuffs per month from their own sources. Such an arrangement decreases rather than increases their supplies. It does not support men working for Germany. Other parts of this proposal assured that neither food, ships, nor money now available to Britain were to be called upon. It is said in Britain that the Germans will not keep such an agreement. If that should prove so, the relief would stop instantly. The maximum violation would be the seizure of all the imported stock of food in Belgium. Those stocks at any one time would not feed Germany for one day. Therefore it has no military importance in prolonging the war or violating any real purpose of blockade.

I have no wish to enter here the many reasons which impel an extremely large and growing number of Americans to favor these proposals, except one. Such an action would advance the British cause in America.

I have no need, either, to discuss my personal attitude towards the British people, so incorrectly stated in the dispatch referred to; but my friends in England should know that quite to the contrary of those implications, I last year advocated aid to Britain with "tools of war" in six nationwide broadcasts and on innumerable other occasions, and that also included advocacy of the Lend-Lease Bill so far as it was "short of war" (to use the President's assurance) and so far as it was not a vehicle for abandonment of constitutional responsibilities of the Congress. Those reservations were not based on unfriendliness, but on the conviction that if the expressed purposes of this war are to be sustained, then those purposes must be maintained in our American domestic life.

In America usually we do not take the trouble to reply to what we know as "smear" material. I would not do it now if I did not have so deep a feeling for the agonies of the British people, a feeling the roots of which lie deep in many years of personal contact and the memories of a joint association in winning the last war.

HERBERT HOOVER

In a brief but emotional address before the Senate on April 18, 1941, Senator Robert A. Taft reviewed our difficulties and the need of food for the invaded democracies. He added that there had been much misrepresentation regarding our committee's work in the press, some even in the British press. He stated that my letter of April 12 to *The Times* effectively met those misrepresentations but that only parts of the letter had been cabled back to the United States. He therefore requested that my entire letter be placed before the Senate and inserted in the *Congressional Record.* This was done immediately following his remarks.[5]

On May 6, *The Times* published a cabled letter from Dr. Van Dusen—this time I was pro-German and anti-British. Gibson answered it effectively, and it, too, was published in that newspaper, on May 12. I reproduce his letter here as an indication of the stuff Van Dusen's committee engaged in.

8th May 1941

TO THE EDITOR OF THE TIMES

On May 6th THE TIMES published a letter received by cable from Dr. Henry P. Van Dusen devoted chiefly to portraying Mr. Hoover as an enemy of aid to Britain. This personal attack on a former President of the United States seems to me to require a reply because of the complete inaccuracy of practically all of the statements it contains.

[5] *Ibid.,* April 18, 1941, v. 87, pt. 3, pp. 3175–76.

Mr. Van Dusen, who is a professor of systematic theology, is obviously not familiar with the subject he discusses.

For instance he lifts from its context an extract from a speech made by Mr. Hoover six months ago to appeal for more scientific economic research in preparation for the future. Mr. Van Dusen represents this speech as a proposal for American collaboration with a victorious Axis economy. Anyone who reads the address can see that this is a complete misrepresentation of Mr. Hoover's clear and obvious meaning. The speech was an exposition of the measures of economic defence and offence which should be developed *against* totalitarian economics, parallel with the development of military defence. In other words its meaning was exactly contrary to that attributed to it by Mr. Van Dusen. The speech received highly favourable commendation from the American press supporting Britain, including the New York Times, Washington Star, San Francisco Chronicle, and scores of other papers.

Mr. Van Dusen also describes an alleged "secret" meeting of Mr. Hoover with republican leaders in an effort to defeat the Lease and Lend Bill. This meeting was scarcely "secret" as it was fully reported in the American press. Far from laying plans for the defeat of the Lease and Lend Bill it represented an effort by Mr. Hoover to shorten delay in consideration of the Bill by securing its acceptance in principle by the republican leaders and persuading them to confine opposition to those features which involved American constitutional questions. In fact in order that delay in consideration of the Bill might not be prejudicial he went a step further and proposed simplification and effective aid by the voting of an outright gift of five billions of dollars to Britain to get on with.

These are samples of the fundamental inaccuracy of Mr. Van Dusen's statements.

I might add that if Mr. Hoover's purpose was to prevent aid to Britain as alleged by Mr. Van Dusen, it is curious that he should have begun last year by making six nationwide broadcasts to advocate aid to this country, and that he should have supplemented them with innumerable speeches along the same lines including advocacy of the Lease and Lend Bill. This clear record is difficult to reconcile with Mr. Van Dusen's statement that Mr. Hoover is an obstacle to effective aid to Britain.

These facts are generally known in the United States. However, in times like these when all our efforts should be devoted to common purposes, it is deplorable that there should be such an effort to create the impression here that influential and friendly elements in America are opposed to aid for Britain. On the contrary, if the people are given the facts I hope they will find comfort in the knowledge that actively friendly forces are more widespread than they had realized.

HUGH GIBSON

One of the charges made by our opponents was that my colleagues and I had never received appeals from the small democracies urging that we organize their aid. Therefore, our committee issued a complete statement to the press, giving verbatim the text of every such appeal. It is too long for reproduction here, but I list the titles of those government leaders and officials of the small democracies who signed the appeals:

BELGIUM

The King
The Minister of Foreign Affairs
The Minister of Agriculture
The Minister of Finance and War
The Minister of Public Health
The President of the Internal Relief Committee
The President of the Belgian Red Cross
The Belgian Ambassador in Washington
The Belgian Ambassador-at-Large

POLAND

The Prime Minister
The Minister of Foreign Affairs
The Polish Ambassador in Washington
The Chairman, Central Polish Relief Committee

NORWAY

The Norwegian Minister in Washington
The Minister of Supply
The Minister of Public Health
The President of the Norwegian Parliament
The President of the Norwegian Red Cross
The President of the Norwegian State Bank
Former Cabinet members
A committee of eighteen leading Norwegian citizens

HOLLAND

The Cabinet
The Minister of Foreign Affairs
The High Commissioner for Relief
(The Queen urged support of an American-Dutch Relief Committee)

FINLAND

The President
The Prime Minister
A former Prime Minister

LUXEMBURG

The Grand Duchess
The Prime Minister

CHAPTER 12

THE AMERICANS AND BRITISH PRESSURE THE EXILED GOVERNMENTS TO REPUDIATE US

On April 9, 1941, former American Ambassador Dave Hennen Morris, a member of our committee, informed me that Undersecretary of State Sumner Welles had notified him that the two Belgian Ambassadors, Georges Theunis and Robert van der Straten-Ponthoz, had stated that there was no immediate need in Belgium. I concluded that the hostility of the British and American officials was just about enough of a load and that if the Belgians were turning against us, it was time for a change. The next day we cabled Hugh Gibson:

We have done our best for sane handling of this problem. . . . We do not propose to longer receive here or in London private urgings and public obstruction. Under the circumstances we have the impression you should come home. . . .

On April 12, Gibson cabled us that the exiled Belgian Government in London wanted him to remain and that they disavowed the action of their Embassy in Washington. I informed our friends inside Belgium of the situation through our "grapevine" [1] and suggested they

---

[1] The grapevine was simple enough. The United States had not yet formally declared war. There was no American prohibition or censorship of communications abroad. The Belgians were engaged in vast mining operations in the Congo, whence they shipped large quantities of metals to the United States and Britain. They had offices in New York and Lisbon, and some of their officials had been members of our

set officials in the United States straight about the needs of their people, which they had so repeatedly pressed upon us.

On April 14, the Belgian Minister of Finance and War, Camille Gutt, called on me in New York. He reported that the British authorities were pressing him very hard for a statement that the people in Belgium did not need food and to proclaim that our committee was not acting at Belgium's request. He stated that the Belgians were wholly dependent upon the British.

Two weeks later, on April 28, Mr. Gutt again called on me, accompanied by Ambassador Theunis, who was a special representative to the United States. Gutt was obviously embarrassed, but revealed they had concluded that my presence in the movement for food was the stumbling block to their relief. He said they had been told by top State Department officials that there was no chance of the Belgians' obtaining food as long as I was in the picture. They thought it might be a good idea if I resigned as head of the Committee on Food for the Small Democracies and someone more agreeable to the Roosevelt Administration were selected to take my place.

I reminded them that I had taken up their cause only at the urgent and repeated requests of their government and their people at home, and did so at great sacrifice of my own resources and sleep. I said we did not like spending our time and money while enduring constant vilification. I suggested they return to Washington and ascertain from Sumner Welles and the British Ambassador whether food would be allowed to go to Belgium if I removed myself from the scene. I added that I would be only too happy to withdraw if it would assure food and relief for Belgian women and children.

On July 24, Belgian Ambassador van der Straten-Ponthoz wrote and reprimanded us for continuing our crusade.

Meanwhile, in response to my communication sent through the grapevine to Belgium, a delegation of prominent Belgians under the leadership of a former Minister, Paul Heymans, was en route to Lon-

---

relief organization in the First World War and were members of local relief committees in Belgium. They subscribed funds to our organization. Those stationed in New York sent messages to the Congo in their own codes by radio and thence to their office in Lisbon and thence by their own messenger service to Brussels.

don to put their government officials on the right track. They got as far as Lisbon, where it was reported to me that authorities in Britain refused them further passage to either London or the United States.

The President of the Norwegian Parliament, Dr. Carl J. Hambro, then in the United States, was Food Representative of the Norwegian Government. He had been loud in his praise of our efforts and had pledged in writing two million dollars for food to Norway if we were able to get permission to pass the blockade.

After conferences with our State Department, he arrived in New York and on January 29, 1941, addressed a Chamber of Commerce meeting. Mr. Edgar Rickard, who attended the meeting, reported to me that Dr. Hambro stated:

> . . . the Hoover Committee was taking initiatives which they had not been authorized in any way to assume. . . .
> . . . their attitude at times was pro-German.

The Norwegian Ambassador called upon me no more.

The Dutch Government in Exile, confident that it could make arrangements with the British to open the blockade, informed Mr. Gibson verbally that it could no longer go along with us.

On April 18, General Sikorski, the Prime Minister of the Polish Government in Exile, accompanied by the Polish Ambassador, Jan Ciechanowski, called upon me. They stated that the British were pressing them to disavow our activities. The Polish Prime Minister urged that we continue. He said that they would not be intimidated by London or Washington while their people were starving. Five days later, the Polish Minister of Foreign Affairs in London added his pleas that we continue our crusade.

During the summer of 1941 (the United States was not yet in the war) the Government of Turkey, distressed over widespread starvation in Greece from the German invasion a few months earlier, applied to the British Government for permission to take food through the blockade to the Greeks. After this was refused, the Turkish Ambassador in London appealed to Mr. Gibson for advice from our organization. Based on his full knowledge of the situation in the Middle East, Gibson gave the Turks succinct advice: "Send your ships, they will not dare stop them." The Turks sent their ships. They were not stopped. The blockade was relaxed for Greece. Co-operation was secured from both Britain and Germany.

I suggested to the Greek Relief Committee in New York that it would be well if they would request the Swiss or Swedes to supervise the distribution of food in Greece in order to avert criticism. The Greeks did so. We were prompt to point out to the American public that this was approval of the same program we had proposed for the small democracies in Western Europe.

In July, we issued a report on the food situation in Belgium made by Dr. E. J. Bigwood, a professor at the University of Brussels and an official of the Belgian Health Department. He quoted on the condition of school-age children from February and April reports of Professor Jacquemyn of Brussels University:

1. PHYSICAL CONDITION.

Kindergartens—33% of the children were in a definitely weak physical condition in May 1940; 47% in January 1941.

Primary schools—48% of the children were in a definitely weak physical condition in May 1940. 63% in January 1941.

Higher class schools—The same figures are respectively 20% and 42%.

2. GROWTH RATE.

From 6 to 14 years of age, growth rate has fallen in 51[%] to 84% of the children.

3. ALL MEDICAL REPORTS WITHOUT EXCEPTION DESCRIBE THE SITUATION AS A TRAGIC ONE FOR ADOLESCENTS FROM 14 TO 18 YEARS OF AGE.

The absolute loss of body-weight in 4 months time may amount to 5 to 6 kilograms (11 to 13 pounds), whereas in normal conditions there is an average increase of body-weight of 9 kilos from 12 to 14 years of age, of 11 kilos from 14 to 16 years of age, and of 8 kilos from 16 to 18 years of age. Pathological signs of deficiency diseases are reported—cases of children fainting at schools are becoming more and more numerous particularly between 13 and 18 years of age. In younger children cases of vomiting are chiefly reported.

Despite all the evidence of great suffering, Messrs. Churchill and Roosevelt continued their pressures on the Belgian Government to disavow any appeals for relief.

I made a nation-wide broadcast on Sunday, October 19, in which

I again reviewed our proposals for relief and the current situation in the occupied democracies. I emphasized the action taken by Turkey with respect to Greece, pointing out:

The British have themselves relaxed the blockade in important ways. For instance, Britain is furnishing food to some 40,000 British prisoners of war in Germany. Thus our British friends themselves open their own blockade to their countrymen. . . . British officials state it is distributed with fidelity. . . . If it is practical to feed captive British soldiers, is it not practical to feed captive women and children . . . ?

Also the blockade has been relaxed for Sweden. . . . But by what logic or humanity can neutrals be given supplies and peoples who have fought and died in the Allied cause be discriminated against?

And the blockade has been relaxed for Greece. Within the last month the Turkish Government, with no great reserves of food, has agreed to large shipments to save the Greeks. They have secured cooperation from both Britain and Germany. It will be partly paid for by Americans. That food is permitted to pass the British blockade. The Turks are Mohammedans; they are not Christians. I wish that Belgium, Poland, Norway and the others had a friend as compassionate as Turkey. . . .

The dead children of last winter and spring are gone. Whatever our bitterness may be for their useless sacrifice, they are past help. Our problem now is to look to saving the millions of others. . . .

I have recently read many statements by American and Allied leaders that large stocks of food will be accumulated with which to relieve these people after they are free from German domination. When that day may come no man can tell. But these promises sound hollow in my ears. Food for dead people has little consequence. I am in favor of providing food with which to fight the inevitable famine which will follow this war. I trust it is not being offered these people as a substitute for action now. It is not necessary to give such promises to people who are suffering and dying. That does not offer hope to them. It adds bitterness to their fate. . . .

. . . last spring a number of the members of our Senate and House of Representatives became interested in this question. Jointly Democrats and Republicans introduced a resolution into both Houses, making a simple request of our Government that it should initiate negotiations for international action on this question. . . .

We have been engaged in much discussion over the freedom of religion in foreign countries. I learned at my mother's knee that compassion and responsibility for my neighbors was a part of our American faith.

Has hate so entered our souls that we are indifferent to innocent suffering? Have we lost our way entirely? I do not believe it.

We talk much of our responsibility to the future of civilization. Is not the preservation of these children also a part of this responsibility? Hitler cannot be defeated with armies of starving children. . . .

Our Government should make an effort with every influence in its power. If its effort should fail, its duty is to develop publicly who is responsible for failure. The Administration of Woodrow Wilson did find the solution. It can be done again if there is the will to do it. Our Government has a grave responsibility today.

My countrymen, unless this effort is made our failure to act will some day come back to fill this nation with grief and remorse.[2]

WE GO INTO TEMPORARY RETIREMENT

The Japanese attack on Pearl Harbor on December 7, 1941, brought the United States into the war. Our relief organization had been repudiated by the exiled governments. Now at war, we could not act without the approval of our own government. Our National Committee on Food for the Small Democracies decided to suspend activities, but to resume if opportunity came. We sent word to the exiled governments that, now free from any embarrassment from us, they should secure permission directly to relieve their people at home.

But they got no relief.

It was not until three and one-half years later, when Mr. Truman became President in April, 1945, that American Government policies changed and became compassionate about relief of famine.

[2] Herbert Hoover, *Addresses Upon the American Road, 1955–1960* (Caldwell, Idaho, The Caxton Printers, Ltd., 1961), pp. 393–404.

CHAPTER 13

THE JAPANESE ATTACK ON PEARL HARBOR BRINGS A REVOLUTION IN WORLD FOOD SUPPLIES

The loss of American fighting ships at Pearl Harbor and those of the British in the Battle of Malaya was a great shock to Allied military strength, but it was also a severe setback to the Allies' food supply. The loss of sugar and vegetables from the Philippines and Dutch East Indies precipitated early rationing among all Allied populations. There was also a reduction in supplies of hemp, tin, rubber, zinc, lead, and quinine; immense sums were spent on the creation and production of synthetic substitutes.

At the news of Pearl Harbor, I at once publicly supported Mr. Roosevelt's declaration of war. Through Secretary of War Henry L. Stimson, I offered my services to the Government in any capacity in which I had some experience. There was no response.

However, Senate and House committees repeatedly requested my advice on many subjects. I was called upon by farm and other national organizations to sit in or address their conventions on the problems of food. During the war, when President Roosevelt called international conferences to consider postwar measures of relief, a number of foreign delegates repeatedly sought my advice.

The lessons learned by the Allied nations in World War I were ignored. There were heartbreaking blunders. However, I offered no criticism of Administration action for a year. But on November 2, 1942, I sent a letter to the *Farm Journal* on the problems of food organization. It appeared as a front-page editorial in the December issue of that magazine and was reprinted by the daily press. I said in part:

About a year ago I advised the Senate Committee on Banking and Currency that the functions of production, distribution, governmental purchases, prices, and rationing of food cannot be conducted under separate commands without confusion and disaster. The lack of co-ordination and the conflict between government bureaus are now limiting, and will even reduce, rather than increase, our animal products.

. . . At the present time the agencies under the Department of Agriculture control [only part of] production policies. . . . The Office of Price Administration fixes retail prices. . . . The regulation of processors and dealers in food is now partly under the Department of Agriculture and partly under the OPA. The War Production Board, through its requirements committee, apparently determines the needs of the Allies, and also formulates some production policies. That Board controls the production of farm machinery. The Army and the Navy independently compete in the markets for their supplies. The Draft Director and the War Manpower authorities are, in effect, determining the labor supply of agriculture. The Federal Employment Service of the Labor Department and the Farm Security Administration of the Department of Agriculture are competing with each other in recruiting labor for farms. The Board of Economic Warfare . . . determines import questions in relation to food. The Economic Stabilization Office also determines policies that affect food supply.

. . . a squeeze of the farmer has been going on for some months between the price systems of the Department of Agriculture and the OPA. . . .

The conflicts of manpower policies, by forcing wages up and draining men from the farms, are compelling farmers to sell dairy cattle. . . . Another of the consequences is that the increase . . . [of] hog production . . . [by] the Department of Agriculture has so far been disappointing.

. . . severe shortages are already developing. In addition, considerable ground crops are going unharvested in the Southwest for lack of labor. Of even more importance, without immediate assurance of labor many regions will plant less next year. The first answer is more production.

I outlined the setup required and recommended the transfer of about eight units exercising food authority to the Department of Agriculture.[1]

At the joint request of the press associations, I prepared a series of articles dealing with the situation on the home fronts in different countries, including the situation in food specifically. They were widely published from January 11 to January 16, 1943. Again, I set out the principles, learned in the First World War, of proper organization of the home front and concluded:

All nations in that war, Britain, France, the United States, and even Germany—had to pioneer the way to total civilian organization. In the end, they all arrived at certain common principles of organization. Our initial and continuing mistake in this war was ignoring this experience and these principles. . . .

The first principle in organization of the home front distilled by all nations from the last war is that civilian activities must be directed by single-headed responsible administrators. The second principle is that all functions and authority in respect to a particular activity must be concentrated into the hands of one administrator. We can no more administer civilian activities in war with committees, boards or commissions than we can direct a battle with a committee. And we can no more have divided authority over one function than we can have independent generals in command of a battle.

. . . That there is delay and confusion and enormous bureaucratic interference needs no proof. It lies all around the landscape.

There are some policies that should be determined at once. . . . We have two bottlenecks; one is manpower and the other is ships. . . .

. . . We will be short of ships for another year. . . . We are endangering the food supply to ourselves and our Allies by excessive drafts of manpower from agriculture. . . .

. . . [There is] the widespread conviction that the purposes of our administration are not alone to win the war, but to use the war to change fundamentals of [the] American [way of] life without submission to the people or their representatives.[2]

[1] Herbert Hoover, *Addresses Upon the American Road, World War II, 1941-1945* (New York, D. Van Nostrand Company, Inc., 1946), pp. 265-68.
[2] *Ibid.*, pp. 189-91.

Since it was evident that our policies on food administration not only were failing to provide for our immediate needs, but also were without vision of the impending postwar famine, I again discussed the food problem in a nation-wide broadcast, on January 21, 1943, saying in part:

. . . I believe I can speak not alone from some experience but in entire detachment from any group interest. It is not a problem to be dealt with in emotional terms. Nevertheless its ultimates are victory and peace, the loss of millions of human lives or the saving of them. . . . nor do I believe in the doctrine of—I told you so. We need to face the hard facts and secure a remedy. And at once.

Food supply has now become secondary only to military operations in determining the outcome of the war. And it will take first place in saving the world from anarchy after the war. . . .

There is today an acute [world] shortage, especially in meats . . . and edible oil products. . . .

And every householder knows there is a shortage already in the United States. And we are confronted with the fact that our shortage of labor, of machinery and methods of price control are limiting the vitally essential expansion of this production and the flocks and herds upon which production depends. . . .

Our difficulties are increased because American livestock has decreased. . . .

At the end of . . . [the First World] war we had 26% more beef cattle [and hogs] for each 1,000,000 of human population than we had twenty-three years later. . . .

The demands upon us today call imperatively and without delay to build up our flocks and herds and thus increase their production. And, further, we must increase our production of vegetable oils. . . .

. . . We did it during the last war. Over the whole period of that world war our hog population increased by 22%, our beef cattle by 27%, our milch cows 10%. It was this increase in production that enabled us to supply our Allies and prevented hardships on our own home front. And it was the salvation of Europe last time [from famine]. . . .

That the progress we are making today is not satisfactory can be demonstrated. In January, a year ago, the Secretary of Agriculture gave to the country an admirable victory program of increased herds and increased production [of ground crops]. The climatic conditions during the year were most favorable. . . . And now the Secretary warns us that production for 1943 may be less than that in 1942 in several directions.

I listed as the causes of this dilemma: the draft of farm boys beyond our ability to transport them overseas; price controls which put the farmers' return below the cost of production; and a 75 per cent reduction in the manufacture of farm machinery. I added:

. . . We still go on [with New Deal] subsidizing the farmer to restrict production. . . .

A Congressional Committee reports that millions of dollars' worth of crops in the Southwest were lost last year because they could not be harvested.

. . . The news comes daily . . . that the farmer is sending his dairy cows to slaughter for lack of labor. . . . For the four months ending November 1, 1942, the inspected slaughter of female cattle increased 30% over the same period in 1941. In the same period the increase in the slaughter of steers was only 5%. The increased slaughter of female cattle in this four months' period was nearly 40% greater than the same period in the average of the three previous years. . . . Also the cattle coming into the market during this four months ending November 1, 1942, were an average on different calculations from 30 to 40 lbs. per animal lighter than for the same period the year before. . . .

During this four months the number of sheep slaughtered has increased nearly 200% over the year before. Our national flock is less today than a year ago and will apparently be still less a year hence. There also seems to be some disturbance in the hog world, for sows have been coming to slaughter [faster] during the last four months. . . .

This undue slaughter of cows, ewes and sows gives a temporary increase in meats, but it is an illusion as to supplies for the future. That is "eating the seed corn." . . .

. . . The farmer must be given men and tools if he is to perform his part.[3]

I made other addresses and published more articles to the same effect.

On February 8, 1943, as a result of my statement that farm boys

[3] *Ibid.*, pp. 295–300.

were being called up unnecessarily rapidly, I was called to meet with the Senate Committee on Appropriations in executive session. The hearing lasted over two hours, during which time some thirty Senators were in and out of the room. In answer to questions, I pointed out that the military authorities were in the process of mobilizing eleven million men and women into uniform; that they could not, on their own statement of what shipping would be available, transport a quarter of that number overseas during the next twelve months; I also pointed out that they were manufacturing munitions faster than they could train men to use them and at the expense of needed farm machinery. I furnished statements supporting my views from the statistics made public by military authorities. I suggested that an investigation of the shipping bottleneck alone would show the possibility of relaxing the shackles on the farmer and farm labor without in any way imperiling the maximum military action at the front.

On March 15, I responded to an invitation from the Midwest Governors to speak at their conference in Des Moines, Iowa. I discussed their problems and raised the question of inevitable postwar famine, saying in part:

. . . I have discussed the question from our immediate point of view of winning the war. But food must also win the peace.

When firing ceases we will be faced with . . . [hundreds of millions of] starving people. . . .

To save these millions of people after the war is not alone a transcendent act of compassion. It is the only road to peace. Unless we stop the degenerative forces on our own food front we will have no supplies for this purpose.[4]

[4] *Ibid.*, p. 340.

FOUR YEARS OF FRUSTRATION
1942–1943

CHAPTER 14

THE CREATION OF THE UNITED NATIONS RELIEF AND REHABILITATION ADMINISTRATION

The British had recognized the inevitability of postwar famine and established an Inter-Allied Committee on Postwar Requirements. This was before Pearl Harbor. The Committee, represented by fifteen governments, met on September 24, 1941, at St. James's Palace to establish the preliminary machinery for postwar relief in Europe. Foreign Minister Anthony Eden presided, and the United States Government, which had been consulted previously, sent a message of encouragement. On October 4, Secretary Hull delegated Ambassador Winant in London to send an American representative to the meeting as an observer.

After the United States came into the war on December 8, 1941, the leadership in this international committee apparently transferred to the American Government under the direction of Assistant Secretary of State Dean Acheson.[1] Mr. Acheson was an able man, but without experience in food administration or relief of famine.

On January 13, 1942, the Soviet Ambassador to Great Britain, Ivan Maisky, sent a note to Mr. Eden demanding that all decisions of the Inter-Allied Committee be by unanimous vote of all the representatives.

[1] George Woodbridge, UNRRA: The History of the United Nations Relief and Rehabilitation Administration (New York, Columbia University Press, 1950), Vol. I, p. 12.

The Allied governments now held conferences in Washington. Those participating at the outset were, in addition to Mr. Acheson, limited to the Ambassadors of Britain, Russia, and China—not one of whom had had any experience in food administration. The Chinese representatives sought my advice from time to time and furnished me with documentation as to the steps being taken. I pointed out some weaknesses, and I especially warned against the political consequences involved in the unanimous vote—a polite way of reserving the veto right. Thus any member nation would be empowered with a veto right on every action taken in any part of the world.

On May 4, an informal meeting of the Inter-Allied Committee was held. On May 7, Secretary Hull made some proposals for the formation of a United Nations Relief Council. On July 10, a draft was drawn up, and on July 11, Assistant Secretary of State Acheson submitted a new draft which included the Russian demand of the previous January and took in all members of the United Nations.[2]

A draft agreement revised in some particulars (but keeping the unanimous vote) was again submitted to the Committee in August. This time the Chinese delegate, after consultation with me, objected to the unanimous vote and suggested a directorate with majority rule. The British sided with the Chinese at this particular time. The Chinese delegate suggested that I be called in, but the Roosevelt Administration was adamant against it.

On December 29, the Soviet Embassy notified the State Department that:

"1. The activities of the Relief Administration under Article I should be based on the consent of the government of the state receiving relief as regards the forms these activities may take in a given state. . . .

"3. All decisions of the Policy Committee should be unanimous." [3]

Hoping that some guidance might be given to these negotiations, I had written two articles which appeared in *Collier's* on November 28 and on December 5, 1942. In them I discussed the methods by

[2] Department of State, *Foreign Relations of the United States, 1942*, Vol. I, p. 118.
[3] *Ibid.*, p. 159.

which our country had met these problems during and after World War I, and I made some forecast as to what would be needed to do so again.[4]

Suddenly, on November 21, only a few weeks before his term expired, Governor Herbert Lehman of New York resigned and was appointed by Mr. Roosevelt to the post of Director of the "Office of Foreign Relief and Rehabilitation Operations." This was understood to be an interim organization.

Governor Lehman asked to have lunch with me in New York on December 3 and requested my advice. I warned him of the weaknesses in the proposed UNRRA organization as far as it had developed at that time. He asked for, and I gave him, the name of a man with experience in the First World War Relief who might serve as his principal assistant. I recommended General William N. Haskell, who had conducted large relief operations during the First World War. I urged the Governor to organize immediate relief for the children and destitute in the occupied democracies. He stated, however, that his organization was intended only for postwar purposes, and he could do nothing until hostilities ceased.

After lunch, about twenty reporters flocked around and demanded to know what we had discussed. I could not violate the Governor's confidence, but I did give them a talk on the immediate and urgent food needs of the suffering small democracies.

The drafting of the final charter of the United Nations Relief and Rehabilitation Administration (UNRRA) dragged on with further meetings. Belgian, Dutch, and Italian representatives in these discussions sought my advice. They, however, had little influence in the matter.

THE ADOPTION OF THE UNRRA AGREEMENT

On September 25, 1943, Mr. Roosevelt announced a conference to be held at the White House on November 9. At this meeting, with

[4] The full text of these articles appears in *Addresses Upon the American Road, World War II, 1941–1945*, pp. 269–94.

great pomp and circumstance, the agreement setting up UNRRA was signed by forty-four nations, after which the delegates adjourned to Atlantic City on November 10 to perfect the organization. Assistant Secretary of State Dean Acheson again presided. Governor Lehman was elected Director General.

My colleagues and I were glad that preparatory action for the inevitable famine had been undertaken. We hoped it might do something for the starving people in the German-occupied democracies in the meantime.

I may well recall some essential principles of the setup of the Relief Administration after the First World War:

(a) There was a single administrator, termed the Director General of Relief and Rehabilitation, with complete administrative authority, acting directly under the Supreme Economic Council. It was felt that command in relief could no more be undertaken by a committee than could command in battle.

(b) As most of the financing came from the United States, the Director General was an American.

(c) The Allied Council consisted of five members: representatives of Britain, France, Italy, and the United States, plus a nonvoting chairman. The majority ruled. Committees were formed for advice, co-ordination, and co-operation.

(d) No political pressure could be applied to the Director General regarding the distribution of supplies.

(e) The food was sold by the recipient nations to those persons who could pay. The destitute were provided for from sales receipts.

(f) The Director General could stop supplies to any nation failing to comply with the regulations.

(g) Any grievance was taken up with the Supreme Council of the Allies.[5]

Some of UNRRA's weaknesses stemmed from the following:

(a) The Director General of the United Nations Relief and Rehabilitation Administration was required to act through committees.

---

[5] A full description of the negotiations and conclusions in establishing this organization can be found in Section III of Volume II of this series.

(*b*) The Central Committee of UNRRA consisted of representatives of China, the U.S.S.R., the United Kingdom, and the United States, with the Director General presiding without a vote. The passage of proposals required the unanimous vote of the Central Committee, plus a majority vote of the Council (represented by each member government of UNRRA). UNRRA had no powers of its own superior to those of any single member nation.

(*c*) The UNRRA setup required that internal distribution of supplies be controlled by the recipient nations. All UNRRA supplies, upon landing at dockside or crossing the frontier of the recipient country, became the absolute property of that country. Therefore, UNRRA supplies in some areas were distributed under the authority of military leaders and politicians.

(*d*) The quantities of food provided by UNRRA as charity comprised about 20 per cent of the world's cereal needs, while nations representing 80 per cent were being financed by the importing countries themselves.

(*e*) Countries able to pay for supplies were not eligible for UNRRA aid. Just because the occupied democracies of Western Europe (such as France, Belgium, Holland, and Norway) could pay for their food did not mean they were less hungry than the destitute.

As during the First World War, the United States was again by far the largest supporter, carrying well over three-fourths of the burden of relief expenses, with Great Britain carrying the major part of the balance. The administrative expenses of UNRRA, however, were shared by the forty-four member nations.

Some comparisons of dimensions and results of our own American relief organization of the First World War period with UNRRA during World War II are of interest.

The former, under the organizations which I directed during the First World War, supplied some 42,366,066 tons of overseas food, seed, clothing, and miscellaneous supplies roughly valued at $7,101,-224,848.

During UNRRA's existence, its total shipment summary of food, clothing, medical supplies, and agricultural and industrial equipment amounted to 24,106,891 gross long tons valued at $2,903,412,000.[6] (It is of interest, in the light of the changing political picture of the world, that the first and major recipients of UNRRA aid were China, Poland, Yugoslavia, Italy, Greece, Czechoslovakia, and Russia.)

The principal officers of the American Relief Administration were volunteers. The officials of UNRRA were paid substantial salaries.

In his *Memoirs,* Mr. Truman has this to say about UNRRA:

The role of the United Nations Relief and Rehabilitation Administration—UNRRA—was negligibly small in western Europe, although it was doing a big job in Greece. A major difficulty was that when UNRRA had been established in Atlantic City in 1943 its purpose was not clearly defined. While it was organized to meet the needs of countries unable to provide their own relief and rehabilitation, there was no fixed limit of the field of rehabilitation into which UNRRA was entitled to go. And there was no clear distinction as to the scope and functions of its combined food boards. In addition to this, congressional appropriations for use by UNRRA were delayed and, with the United States being the largest financial supporter of the organization, its operations were obviously limited until funds could be made available.[7]

In the meantime, while the negotiations on UNRRA were going on, Mr. Roosevelt called together the United Nations Conference on Food and Agriculture at Hot Springs, Virginia, in May, 1943. The conference was conducted in strict secrecy, with guards around the grounds to keep the press out. After this meeting was over, the Belgian, Dutch, and French delegates who had attended gave me a detailed account of what happened.

The representatives of the small democracies occupied by the Germans had come with portfolios bursting with details on their desperate and immediate need to provide relief to their women and children. They were told that subject was not on the agenda.

The official report of this conference issued to the public glowed with such phrases as:

[6] *UNRRA: The History of the United Nations Relief and Rehabilitation Administration,* Vol. III, pp. 428–29.

[7] Harry S. Truman, *Memoirs,* Vol. I, *Year of Decisions* (Garden City, Doubleday and Company, Inc., 1955), p. 466.

All men on earth are consumers of food. . . .

Men cannot eat more and healthier food unless this food can be obtained from the land or the seas in sufficient quantities. . . .

. . . malnutrition was a leading cause for the high level of child mortality.

The conference was very firm that there should be "freedom from want." That phrase recurred seven times in the 2,500-word report. The specter of the postwar famine and the need for purposeful organization to combat it, however, were scarcely mentioned in the report.

The conference passed many resolutions. No. 13 called for "all the governments in the shortage period to prevent unrestrained competition and speculation in scarce supplies of foods, production materials and transport facilities." [8] Another resolution was to hold another conference.

Mr. Roosevelt, in a speech to the departing delegates, said in Washington on June 7:

. . . The Conference . . . has succeeded even beyond our hopes. . . .

You have surveyed with courage and with realism the magnitude of these problems, and you have reached unanimous agreement. . . .

He said that, in consequence, in the future:

. . . The better use of natural and human resources must be assured to improve the living standard; and, may I add, the better use of these resources without exploitation on the part of any Nation. . . .

You have demonstrated beyond question that free peoples all over the world can agree. . . . You have brought new hope to the world. . . .[9]

I prepared a derisive summation of the conference for the press, but concluded that such a statement would not bring food to the hungry people, and it would be tilting at a windmill anyway.

[8] United Nations, *A Start Toward Freedom from Want: The Story of the United Nations Conference on Food and Agriculture* (United Nations Information Office, 1943), p. 15.

[9] *The Public Papers and Addresses of Franklin D. Roosevelt, 1943: The Tide Turns* (New York, Harper & Brothers, 1950), pp. 238–41.

CHAPTER 15

WE RESUME OUR EFFORTS TO SECURE FOOD FOR THE OCCUPIED DEMOCRACIES

Since pressure upon the small democracies' exiled governments in London had prevented their co-operation with us and since our own country was at war, in December, 1941, we decided to dissolve the National Committee on Food for the Small Democracies (which was officially closed the next March). That, however, did not dissolve the responsibilities which my colleagues and I considered we still held to the mass of people in these nations.

The exiled governments had not after two years realized any of the promises which had been made to them. Reliable reports disclosed that starvation in these countries was becoming steadily more terrible. We continued to receive imploring messages for help from the people inside those countries.

An incident in January, 1943, seemed to indicate that there was a more favorable chance to open the blockade. Captain Victor Cazalet, a former member of Parliament in Great Britain, informed us that a few days before the relief question was revived he had met with British Ambassador Lord Halifax. He declared that the Ambassador now privately favored our relief proposals and would like very much to discuss the matter with us.

Therefore, on January 8, 1943, I arranged a luncheon with Lord Halifax, Hugh Gibson, and Captain Cazalet. Lord Halifax repeatedly avoided any talk about relief. I dictated a record of this discussion immediately after the interview. It was:

I said [to Lord Halifax] word had been passed around by our government officials to the exiled governments and others that I, personally, and our committee were an obstacle to relief and that it could be more easily arranged if we were not in the picture. Accordingly, we had withdrawn all our activities for . . . [about two years]. But not one step was taken in response to the continued . . . [appeals] of France, Belgium, Holland, Norway or Poland. During this time the Allies were carrying out aid for Greece on exactly the plan we had urged . . . [and had] stated publicly that the Germans were getting no benefits. [I told him that] as the American people were greatly concerned over the situation I did not propose to withhold agitation of the subject any longer and I proposed to begin in about a month.

Lord Halifax said that their policies had not been changed. Apparently, Captain Cazalet had been mistaken as to any change in Halifax's position.

Another ray of hope appeared early in 1943 when, under the leadership of the Archbishop of Canterbury and others, a movement in support of our ideas sprang up in England.

Meanwhile, as a beginning of our renewed activities, I contributed an article to the *Christian Advocate* on February 11, 1943, which was also released to other religious journals. And, jointly with Hugh Gibson, I contributed an article to *Collier's* on February 20. Both went over the whole ground and especially emphasized the fact that relief was successfully going to German-occupied Greece with no military damage to the Allied cause—and with Allied approval.

During our period of quietude, a number of organizations had been formed in the United States which were agitating for relief for special countries and for particular groups. The most important was the Temporary Council on Food for Europe's Children, under the devoted and intrepid leadership of Howard E. Kershner, who had been an important member of our National Committee on Food for the Small Democracies. We gave him our support.

In February, 1943, my old colleagues in the Committee on Food

for the Small Democracies and I took steps to bring these different efforts together by staging a mass meeting at Carnegie Hall in
New York on February 20. I made the chief address. Among my remarks, I said:

In this tragic world there are a multitude of military fronts and home
fronts. But if civilization is to be saved, there must be another front behind
these fronts. That is, the front of human decency. That front is the front of
ideals, of aspirations, of religious faith and humane purpose. It is the front
of honor among nations and men, of sacrifice, of kindliness, of helpfulness,
of fair play and sportsmanship. It is the front of justice and of compassion.
It is the front of saving human life and suffering. The present leaders of
Germany, Italy and Japan are stamping out such expression. It is to establish the front of decency in the world for which we are fighting.

The front of decency will survive only through deeds as well as words.
Action on this front must often be expressed through governments, but it
must arise from the people. Upon their thousands of organizations, religious and otherwise, rests the responsibility of making life better, happier
and less bitter. From them must come the insistence upon amelioration of
the hardships and spiritual destruction of war, and of upholding the front
of decency. And we are here today to demand an action on that front. . . .

I wish to make absolutely clear in the simplest terms exactly what we
are proposing, why we propose it, both that it be understood and that it be
not misrepresented. . . .

I reviewed our efforts and our proposals of previous years and continued:

Food has now been going through the blockade into Greece for over
nine months. It is being distributed under the supervision of the representatives of these neutral governments. The amount is inadequate but
it is saving thousands of Greek lives. Our Government now certifies that
the operation is successful and that the Germans receive no advantage
from it.

. . . We now ask that these neutral governments be authorized to
spread the same service to the other occupied democracies.

. . . The Swedes have idle ships that they will not risk in belligerent
service. They are, however, ready to charter them for use in humanitarian

service. Thus the question of depleting Allied shipping does not arise. There is ample food in South America which cannot be transported [such a long distance] by the Allies and therefore there need be no deprival of food to the Allies, including the United States.

. . . Most of the occupied democracies have funds with which to pay for the food. It is not, therefore, a drain upon the American taxpayer.

. . . This service is long overdue. . . . The rations these people receive are pitiful. Starvation is rife. With their vitality lowered, disease is claiming the children and the weak in thousands. The modern pestilence which first comes with famine is tuberculosis. Reports show whole districts in which 35% of the children react to tuberculosis tests and in some districts as high as 60%. If the child life of these democracies is to be saved it must be saved now.

. . . It is a hollow promise that these people will receive food after the war is over. It means little to a mother who sets her table only to watch her children wilt.

. . . These democracies have held the torch of free men for centuries. If we want the foundation of free men to survive in Europe, it must survive in these democracies. And it will not survive in bitter, frustrated, physically distorted or dead children.

. . . I ask you if in these dimming lights of civilization, it is not worth while that the lamp of compassion shall be kept alight? Can religious faith survive without it? Are we sustaining the front of human decency if we take no action? [1]

The meeting resoundingly passed resolutions demanding action by the Government to relax the blockade sufficiently to save these starving, suffering people.

We followed this up with a nation-wide program of public meetings, conducted by the local heads of our old committee. Leading citizens and churchmen participated in the meetings in more than eighty towns and in every large city. Resolutions went to Mr. Roosevelt, to the Secretary of State, and to Senators and Congressmen demanding action by our Government to relieve the blockade on food to the small democracies under the safeguards we had long since proposed.

[1] *Addresses Upon the American Road, World War II, 1941–1945*, pp. 324–28.

We repeatedly cited the precedent of Greek relief, which was proceeding smoothly along the exact lines we had proposed for the other democracies over two years before. The State Department finally undertook to explain itself, and on April 19, 1943, issued the following statement, which vindicated our proposals for the other occupied democracies:

> . . . this Government and the British Government have received regular reports through the Swedish Government . . . that the foodstuffs sent into Greece are being distributed to the Greek population without . . . diversion of these supplies to the enemy. Furthermore, these reports indicate that the Axis authorities have entered into agreement with the Swedish-Swiss Relief Commission . . . that Greek native produce would be reserved solely for . . . residents of Greece except in so far as local foodstuffs consumed by the armed forces . . . are replaced by equivalent foodstuffs imported from Axis sources. . . .[2]

We spread this news over the country—and to every Senator and Congressman. Our recurrent theme was that since our original plans were succeeding in Greece without benefiting the enemy, why not try them in the other starving democracies?

Senator Elbert D. Thomas of Utah introduced into the Senate a resolution calling for action in "formulating a comprehensive program of international economic cooperation." On the same day, Senator Guy Gillette of Iowa (for himself and for Senator Robert A. Taft) introduced a resolution requesting that further steps be taken "to extend the Greek experiment." On November 4, 1943, at the request of a subcommittee of the Senate Foreign Relations Committee, I appeared before the Senate Committee again. In reply to a question by Senator Thomas, I made a statement, the essential parts of which were:

> Senator, I do not believe there can be any doubt as to the general starvation amongst women and children in the occupied democracies. I do not believe there can be any doubt that relief could be given to those people, because of the experience in Greece and the fact that we are now deliver-

[2] Department of State, Press Release No. 147, April 19, 1943.

ing packages to prisoners in Germany under proper safeguards; and indeed, we are delivering packages to French, Belgian, Dutch and Norwegian military prisoners. At the moment, we are denying food to the children of those very prisoners. It seems to me they are as much in prison as are soldiers. . . .

. . . I proposed a plan of procedure [three years ago] and that plan was adopted as to Greece. The State Department has on numerous occasions certified that the Germans are receiving no benefits from the Greek relief and that it has saved the lives of millions of Greek women and children. . . .

There is no large military question involved in feeding the women and children of those areas. In the ordinary course of handling relief I do not presume we would have in excess of 75,000 tons of imported foods in stock in the whole group of western European democracies at any one time, and, if the Germans should violate their agreements and seize it all, it would not amount to 12 hours' food supply for Germany; so that the military question is a perfectly trivial one. . . .

I am told, and I think the committee could confirm it at any time, that both the Swedish and Swiss Governments would be glad to undertake this. The Swedes have ample tonnage, which they cannot put into use. The food supplies are available from outside the United States if we did not believe we could furnish the quantities needed, and most of these governments concerned have funds with which they could even pay for it. . . .

I have no idea what the attitude of our military leaders is upon this question. I do know that General Pershing, who had to deal with this very same problem in the last war, was not only its staunch supporter during the war, but was its constant defender after the war; and he has himself made an extraordinarily strong pronouncement as to the necessity of doing it during this war. Likewise has Admiral Pratt, who was second in command of our naval operations in the last war.

In order to bring some public opinion into focus on this matter we created some time ago a committee called the Committee on Food for the Small Democracies. That committee . . . [includes] some 12 or 14 men who have been ambassadors and ministers; it [includes] some 50 or 60 leading public men of all kinds from over the United States, including such men as General Pershing and General Dawes and Admiral Pratt. It includes over 600 leading ministers and prelates from every religious body in the United States. It includes some 200 university professors and educational leaders, and it includes several hundred writers and editors and publishers. That at least would indicate there is a great American public opinion in support of the proposal, that at least we should make an effort.[3]

In December, Mr. Kershner's committee got together a few thousand dollars to take full-page advertisements in leading newspapers, setting forth our proposals and in a footnote asking for contributions to pay for another advertisement. This form of presentation largely supported itself and was quite effective in keeping this humanitarian cause before the public.

On February 15, 1944, the Senate adopted the following Taft-Gillette resolution favoring extension of the "Greek experiment" to provide food for the starving in occupied nations:

Whereas the small democratic countries of Belgium, Norway, Poland, the Netherlands, Greece, Yugoslavia, Czechoslovakia, and others have been invaded and occupied; and

Whereas these small countries which are allied with us in the cause of democracy resisted to the limit of their strength the onrush of invading forces; and

Whereas the usual economic processes of these small countries have been completely dislocated as a result of being occupied by invading forces; and

Whereas the food supplies of all these nations are dangerously exhausted due to requisition of native food supplies by the Germans, and inability to secure their usual imports through the blockade; and

Whereas no relief can be brought to them unless there be international action through which their native supplies can be protected and imports be made through the blockade; and

Whereas starvation has already begun; and

Whereas a plan for feeding the people of Greece has been in effect for several months in Greece under supervision of the Swedish and Swiss Governments and the International Red Cross; and

Whereas after 6 months' trial this relief has been certified by the State Department as working satisfactorily and without benefit to the Germans; and

Whereas the Governments of Belgium, Norway, Poland have requested that their people be given relief; and

[3] *Addresses Upon the American Road, World War II, 1941–1945*, pp. 353–56.

Whereas there are food surpluses available in the United States and in South America; and

Whereas many of the small invaded countries have money with which to purchase the food needed to keep their people alive and have signified their desire to use funds for that purpose; and

Whereas the Swedish Government has ships not available to the Allies which could be used for transportation; and

Whereas the specter of mass starvation among friendly and noncombatant women and children is a tragedy that the compassionate heart of America wants to avert; and

Whereas Belgium, Czechoslovakia, Norway, Poland, Greece, Yugoslavia, and the Netherlands and others have lived in friendship with the United States during our entire national existence, and have sent us millions of our most useful and helpful American citizens, and now have no means whatever of securing the necessary agreements by which this disaster can be averted: Now, therefore, be it

Resolved, That the Senate of the United States does express the conviction that immediate steps should be taken to extend the Greek experiment and thereby prevent this impending tragedy of mass starvation heretofore named; and be it further

Resolved, That the Senate of the United States respectfully urges that the Government of the United States, through the Secretary of State, endeavor as quickly as possible to work out, in cooperation with the British Government and the Governments of Sweden, Switzerland, and the accredited representatives of the other governments concerned, the setting up of systematic and definite relief for all stricken and hungry countries where the need is now the most acute; this relief to be based on agreements by the belligerents for the protection of the native and imported food supplies, with rigid safeguarding of such relief so that no military advantage whatever may accrue to the civil populations or armed forces of the invading nations.[4]

The adoption of this resolution had no apparent effect on Churchill and the Roosevelt Administration. However, devoted men were demonstrating that compassion was not dead in America.

[4] *Congressional Record,* Senate, 78th Congr., 2d sess., February 15, 1944, p. 1652.

MR. TRUMAN BECOMES PRESIDENT

CHAPTER 16

THE RELIEF SCENE SHIFTS

The whole scene as regarded the relief of starving people shifted when Mr. Truman became President on April 12, 1945. Mr. Truman believed in relief—he had demonstrated this as Senator and I relate in these pages his role in relief activities as President.

In the meantime, the Allied armies had liberated Italy, France, Belgium, and Holland. The German armies had retreated to within Germany's borders. Except for food furnished by the armies, the people of the liberated countries would be starving. The Russians had followed this retreat by establishing Communist governments in Poland, Bulgaria, and Yugoslavia, and had annexed Estonia, Latvia, and Lithuania, part of Finland, and also Bessarabia and Bukovina. By early 1945, Rumania and Hungary also had Communist governments. Two countries became Communist shortly after Mr. Truman's inauguration. Czechoslovakia was Communist controlled by May, 1945, although Beneš was still President. Albania was officially Communist controlled as a result of its December, 1945, elections.

Except for Greece and Italy, UNRRA was barely present in Western Europe. It was concentrating its efforts on Communist-dominated nations in Eastern Europe. The Allied armies, knowing that disease goes with malnutrition, wanted no starving people in their rear, so they were furnishing limited food in some of the liberated countries. However, it was unorganized and inadequate. And no effort was being made to save and rehabilitate tens of millions of debilitated children in Western Europe. The degeneration and disease among children had reached appalling dimensions. My colleagues and I were flooded with more appeals from old associates in Western Europe. We took no satisfaction that our repeated warnings over the years had come true.

My colleagues and I again arranged a meeting to be held in Carnegie Hall, New York City, on May 8, 1945. The Bishop of Chichester, a leading British prelate, attended the meeting. He had made an on-the-ground inspection of the desperate plight of the civilians, especially of the children in the liberated countries. His address was moving, but I have no record of the many poignant facts he related. I myself said:

I propose in this 15 minutes to give you some evidence of the food situation in liberated countries, to recite a little history and make some constructive suggestions.

One of the most terrible and the most lasting of the hideous list of Hitler's brutalities is this starving and stunting of the bodies and minds of the children of the democracies.

Archbishop Spellman has recently returned from France, Belgium and Italy. You may have read his report in *Collier's*.

I quoted from his article as follows:

". . . The long denial of adequate food has so arrested brain-tissue development in children that mental growth has been stunted. . . .

". . . peace will not thrive among nations with a world half well-fed and half starved. To millions of children, democracy is still a word and a promise only. They have been exposed to hatred, hunger and a hopeless future, and if they are denied the right of taking their places in a world of personal security, they will form the underground army for the next war, and take by stealth and force what they cannot enjoy by right.

". . . Since the [German] occupation, over a million children subsisting at famine level have died in France, and three-quarters of the children in Belgium are pre-tubercular from lack of food.

"Poland's tragedy has been the greatest, for more than half of her eleven million children under fifteen years of age have been liquidated by starvation or enslavement. . . ."

To this statement of Archbishop Spellman I may add a few sentences from a multitude of recent official reports upon the situation of the children in the industrial areas.

The French Ministry of Public Health says: "In industrial areas three-quarters of children are underweight, nutritional diseases rampant. Children's growth diminished 70% to 80%. . . . 54% of children under 2 suffer from rickets. Death rate increased 37% due to debilitation during the war. . . ."

Belgium [Ministry of Health Reports]: "33% of the children are tubercular. . . . 6 out of 10 children under normal weight. . . . Children's death rate increased 44%." . . .

We have two separate problems before us today.

One of these problems is to save the working classes in the great industrial centers of France, Italy, Belgium, Holland, Norway and Poland from the starvation which marches upon them. None of these countries has produced enough food since the last harvest to carry them over until the harvest of next August [1945]. . . .

We Americans should not be misled by the descriptions of American trippers to Europe of luxurious meals they are able to buy from $10 and up. Working people could not buy but one such meal with a week's wages.

In the twelve months after liberation during the last war [World War I], we organized the delivery of 23,000,000 tons of overseas food into Europe and Britain. Only a trickle of food has been supplied since the liberation of eight months ago. We dealt then with starvation, not power politics.

You may well ask: Do we have the supplies for this great task?

We have 450,000,000 bushels of wheat in North America which we can export without reducing our own bread consumption one atom. Sixty per cent of the normal diet of the working classes in Europe is cereals. We have the resources to supply them with bread. If we could give all the bread they can eat, plus what margins they have of their own supplies, it would carry the adults in the industrial areas through. Release from restricted bread rationing would be a great step in liberation. It would be a great step toward political stability. . . .

. . . [First] the United States War Department . . . [should] take over the whole problem. They control the agencies of transportation in the United States, they control docks and wharves here, they control overseas transportation, they control docks and interior transportation in Europe and they have the personnel. If they start a great stream of food flowing within two weeks' time, they can do the job in time. It is now 11:59 on the clock of starvation. . . .[1]

---

[1] *Addresses Upon the American Road, World War II, 1941–1945*, pp. 357–61.

I followed this speech with a national broadcast on May 16 from New York to give emphasis to my previous statement, saying:

A week ago I stated that the time was rapidly approaching when the United States Army should take over the whole job of food relief to the liberated countries of Western Europe. That statement received such favorable response that I propose to amplify and clarify the subject further. . . .

Apart from every humanitarian reason, food must be provided for the liberated countries if there is to be order and stable government. We cannot have our American armies of 3,500,000 men involved in starving populations on their communication lines.

A week ago I expressed the belief that the only agency in the world which can save this situation now is the American Army. They have the administrative ability, the personnel and the energy; they can control the transport of wheat to the American seaboard; they control the ships; they control transport in Europe; they know how to act quickly. They could do the job.

Of course Europe needs meats and fats, but we also have a shortage of those things. . . . But their children must have some meats and fats. . . . We could tighten our belt a little and supply this comparatively small amount. . . .

And this is not a question of feeding Europe next winter. After they get their harvest three months from now there will be time to organize that.

I repeat, this is a problem of the next ninety days; it is urgent. It is urgent as a matter of humanity. It is urgent as a matter of preserving order. It is urgent in protection of our boys in Europe. It is a job so long delayed that only the American Army can solve it.[2]

The next day, as a result of these statements, Secretary of War Henry Stimson, who had been Secretary of State in my Administration, asked me to see Assistant Secretary of War John J. McCloy and discuss my proposals. I met with Mr. McCloy and several Army officers and government officials who accompanied him. They were understandably reluctant to undertake relief work by the Army, but in the end they agreed there was no other way during the emergency.

Then, into the scene came another break for relief.

[2] *Ibid.*, pp. 362–64.

CHAPTER 17

PRESIDENT TRUMAN REQUESTS MY ASSISTANCE

At Mr. Truman's request, I called upon him at the White House on May 28, 1945, six weeks after he had become President. He asked my advice on several subjects, including the possibility of peace with Japan, our domestic food administration, and the food situation abroad. Among other things, I urged emergency action by the Army in the liberated countries. The President at once directed the War Department to undertake my recommendations regarding emergency relief in the liberated countries. During the months of June, July, and August, 1945, it furnished about one million tons of food per month to these countries.

Our discussion of food problems and their solution can be shown best by a memorandum which I prepared at the President's request and sent to him on May 30. The memorandum is in some respects a repetition of my previous public statements, but I introduce it to make the record complete.

MEMORANDUM FOR PRESIDENT TRUMAN

The lack of regularly organized overseas supplies in the ten months since liberation and the exhaustion of the insufficient last harvest of European peoples have projected an emergency which, entirely aside from humanitarian questions, must be solved or it will seriously jeopardize the

105

stability of these nations and may embarrass our armies. The exhaustion of the [1944] harvest will have its main impact upon the workers in the industrial areas as the farmers and villagers will take care of themselves.

The method of UNRRA organization from the start, with the dominance of power politics and the lack of authority, made this organization incapable of administering the larger economic problems of Europe.

1. The peoples needing help can be considered in three groups:

   a. The new Russian sphere comprising probably 170,000,000 people.

   b. Northwestern Europe—that is, France, Belgium, Holland, Denmark, Norway, and the area of Germany occupied by the United States, Britain and France—comprising altogether perhaps 90,000,000 people.

   c. The Mediterranean area comprising the area of Italy, Greece, etc., of perhaps 50,000,000 people.

The Russian sphere is not included in this discussion because there is no adequate information as to their situation.

A minor amount of food and other supplies has gone into Northwestern Europe and into Italy during the past ten months which has been furnished partly by the Army and partly by Lend-Lease. Some supplies have reached Greece and North Africa through UNRRA.

2. The problem in Northwestern Europe and the Mediterranean areas falls into two stages:

   a. The emergency stage—until the next harvest ninety days from now [August, 1945].

   b. The longer view stage—until the harvest of 1946.

If these peoples [in the liberated countries] can be carried over until the next 90 days there will be time to develop a considered organization. . . .

4. The American food supplies to this Northwestern European area can probably be paid for by these countries. If not, Lend-Lease and Army funds should help out, but only where absolutely necessary. Italy is a separate financial problem and more difficult.

5. A program should at once be provided for undernourished children by feeding from soup kitchens and canteens, many of which already exist over these areas. The 50,000,000 pounds of surplus Red Cross Prisoners of War packages already in Europe could be most useful in such work.

6. The long-view organization program of supplies and finance after September 1st should be worked out during the next three months while the Army is looking after emergencies. Proposals for this involve careful study on the ground by men of experience and skill in such matters.

President Truman had also requested my recommendations on solving the chaos in our domestic food administration. Therefore, on May 30, I sent another detailed memorandum, the essential parts of which were:

When the War Food organization was set up in 1941–42 the experience of every nation in the last war [World War I] was discarded or ignored. Not only was the form of organization wrongly based, but the economic principles adopted were fatal. Unlike the last war, the country is today rampant with black markets and there are dangerous local famines of animal products and sugar in the large cities which are proof of a breakdown in distribution.

The production of ground crops has been maintained by the unparalleled seven years of bumper crops although cultivated acreage has not been restored to World War I levels.

The production of fats (the greatest essential after bread in time of war) has decreased . . . through the fall in hog population by nearly 35%. The production of range cattle has increased, but the amount of meat produced has decreased [due to inadequate feed].

If black market prices and subsidies are included, the public is paying higher average retail prices for food than even in the . . . [rampant] inflation period of 1920. . . .

The consumption of animal products and sugar is higher per capita under this elaborate [compulsory] system of rationing than it was in the last war with voluntary rationing.

The number of paid employees handling war food questions is probably over 120,000 compared to under 10,000 in the last war and the administrative cost is nearly 100 times greater.

The men who founded this system were removed some years ago. The present men in its direction inherited an impossible legacy and are not to be condemned for all its faults. . . .

The appointment of a new Secretary of Agriculture [Clinton P. Anderson] and the transfer to him of the functions of the Food Administrator is an admirable step.

My view is that the following further organization steps be taken:

1. The whole of the price functions of O.P.A. and its policing as to food should be transferred to the Secretary of Agriculture, leaving the O.P.A. only the [temporary] mechanical job of rationing food.

(Price is the greatest factor in both production and distribution. Freezing prices is like freezing the water mains in a city. Prices must be controlled but can be better controlled and more effectively stabilized if the experience of the last war be adopted of fixing prices by agreement with the farmers at points nearest the farms, guaranteeing them where necessary, and then adding proper mark-ups to the various stages of processing and distribution. . . . In any event the people will pay less under the method I have proposed than under this plan of trying to catch an economic force with a policeman.)

2. The Secretary of Agriculture should control or approve of all purchases by the Army, Navy, Lend-Lease, UNRRA and any other government agency . . . [which] should be represented on an advisory board to him.

3. The Food Administration [regulating activities] should be decentralized as much as possible into state, county and municipal food administrators. The Agricultural Department already has state and county rural organizations which could do this job. Through local organization far more effective appeal can be made to the patriotic cooperation of both the trades and the consumers.

The President, in my meeting with him on May 28, requested me to aid the Secretary of Agriculture in the reorganization of the food agencies. Secretary Anderson was quick to welcome my services. He was an able, forthright, energetic, and co-operative man. We at once jointly recommended to the President that six or seven conflicting agencies, each dealing separately with segments of the food problem, should all be transferred to the Secretary of Agriculture. We urged that there must be an increase in the price of wheat relative to corn. This was to stop the excessive feeding of wheat to animals. We also recommended a readjustment of the price of fats in relation to meat in order to secure fat recovery at the packinghouses, instead of having it sold with the meat and thus lost. Secretary Anderson expressed the hope that I would publicly stir up these questions.

Therefore, on June 20, 1945, I took the opportunity to reply to an inquiry I had received from Congressman Thomas Jenkins, a member of the Agricultural committee of the House. My statement about food was:

. . . Let me say at once that this is not a partisan question either domestically or internationally. Not only does the well-being of our own people rest upon successful handling, but at least for the present we are unable to furnish the volume of meats and fats required for the restoration of undernourished children in the liberated countries of Europe. Therefore, we need full cooperation on all sides in finding solutions. . . .

The Department of Labor reports that, in April, 55% to 80% of the retail stores dealing in meats and fats in 56 large cities had no supplies.

. . . The existence of black markets in meats and fats except milk in every city of the country is sufficient evidence of a breakdown in control of both distribution and price. A large part of the civilian consumption is in fact being dealt with at prices up to 100% above the supposed ceiling prices. A survey within a week by the New York Board of Trade states that from 50 to 85 per cent of the meat and fat supplies in the city are in effect black market operations. An economic force like that cannot be caught by a policeman. . . .

The causes of all this lie broadly in the method of organization where the control of food has been divided over six or seven agencies, where the whole price control machinery is based upon ill-advised concepts and where the organization has considered coercion more useful than cooperation with producers, distributors and consumers. . . .

I made twelve detailed recommendations covering the reorganization of our food policies. The concluding paragraph was:

Without reform our domestic difficulties will increase, and the hope of aid on meats and fats to women and children abroad becomes hopeless.[1]

[1] *Addresses Upon the American Road, World War II, 1941–1945*, pp. 365–71.

THE GREATEST FAMINE IN ALL HISTORY

CHAPTER 18

WE BEGIN WORLD ORGANIZATION
TO MEET THE FAMINE

By September, 1945, the results of the Northern Hemisphere harvest were clear. The harvest had proved most disappointing. The causes reached into the war years with the diversion of farmers to armies; of the manufacture of farm machinery to munitions; and of nitrate fertilizers to explosives. But beyond all these limitations of production, unusual droughts had struck the Mediterranean states, India, and China, and partial droughts struck South Africa and the Argentine.

Little actual progress had been made by President Truman and the Congress on the recommendations of Secretary Anderson and myself. No adequate organization had been set up to meet the impending disaster. The President and the Congress cannot be blamed for this. They had the burden of the continued war with Japan; the Potsdam Conference of July–August, 1945; the military and reparations settlements among the great powers; the liquidation of a large part of the administrative agencies set up during the war; and increasing strains with the Soviet Government in carrying out the agreements made at Tehran and Yalta. As a result, little attention could be given to food matters, and I decided to go fishing in Florida and to await developments in Washington.

Early in February, 1946, Secretary of Agriculture Anderson telephoned me in Florida saying that the world was rushing into a food panic, that nations were grabbing food for themselves everywhere, and that it was imperative that something be done. This was no surprise to either Secretary Anderson or to me. He again asked for advice. I replied that each of the different nations of the world must be rationed in proportion to overseas supplies available in the world; that he should seek from the President the powers that would make him Food Administrator in fact; that he should put on a consumer conservation program across the country to increase the exportable supplies; that there must be some regulation of the food trades to prevent waste; and that the huge waste of human food down the gullets of animals due to maladjustment of prices by the OPA must be stopped.

The Secretary secured from President Truman an appeal for the voluntary saving of food, which I supported in a statement issued to the press on February 8.

On February 25, while I was out fishing, my secretary, Miss Bernice Miller, received another telephone call from Secretary Anderson saying that he was speaking for the President, that they wished me to come to Washington at once to advise on the crisis, which was steadily worsening. He stated that they proposed to form a national committee of citizens to cope with the emergency. Part of Miss Miller's stenographic record of the conversation contains these words:

Mr. Anderson said that Mr. Hoover had always been very helpful to him, had given him the best advice he had ever received last . . . [spring] and that everything Mr. H. had told him at that time had worked out as Mr. H. had said it would.

I replied that the crisis could not be handled by any committee of citizens; that while such a committee would be useful to stimulate saving of food in the homes and eating places, the world crisis must be dealt with by all governments, with single-headed leadership from Washington. I stated that my experience proved that it was pointless for me to give advice unless it was agreed by himself and the President that my advice would be heeded. Otherwise, I would fail in a great responsibility for lack of authority. Secretary Anderson reported back that he and the President agreed to this stipulation and the President announced to the press that he had requested my services. I arrived in Washington on February 28.

On the afternoon of March 1, a preliminary meeting was held at the White House to organize a national committee for domestic food conservation. It was called the Famine Emergency Committee. I was made Honorary Chairman, and Chester Davis, a leading banker from St. Louis, was made Chairman. There were speeches over the radio by Mr. Truman and others. I confined myself to the following:

Mr. President, the inevitable aftermath of war is famine, and with famine civilization itself is jeopardized. The last great reservoir from which starvation can be halted is the United States. There is thrust upon us one of the greatest obligations of these troubled years. It is my belief that the American people will respond again, as they did after the last war. And we cannot fail.[1]

Members of the Committee [2] fell into an argument about the merits of reduction of food consumption by compulsory card rationing as against an appeal for voluntary saving. President Truman, during the previous summer, had abolished the card-rationing system of the Roosevelt Administration. Governor Lehman insisted upon card rationing. Anderson, Davis, and I held it would require two months to print new cards, set up a new central organization and rationing boards, with inspectors all over the country, and our only hope for more supplies was through organized voluntary action. We prevailed.

The same day, March 1, I also met with President Truman privately. I told him that Secretary Anderson's preliminary statistics of available food supplies and of the needs in the world were appallingly far apart, that if the figures were right, the world was faced with a gigantic catastrophe. Based on our Government's statistics,

[1] *New York Herald Tribune*, March 2, 1946.
[2] The members of the Committee were: Chester C. Davis, Chairman; Herbert Hoover, Honorary Chairman; Eugene Meyer; Clarence Francis; Justin Miller; George H. Gallup; Sheldon Clark; Henry Luce; James W. Young; Mrs. LaFell Dickinson; Miss Anna Lord Strauss; Eric Johnston; and Dr. William I. Myers. Alfred D. Stedman was named Assistant to the Chairman, and Harry W. Henderson was detailed to the Committee to serve as Secretary.

our only hope would be to minimize the loss of life. I said that the extent of salvation would depend upon our securing the co-operation and co-ordination of all the nations in the world to fight the famine. I stated that I would restudy the specific steps that could be taken and advise him on what international machinery might be available to manage the situation. I would also re-examine the statistical information and, with Secretary Anderson, report to him.

The only possible international organizations which could be used quickly to stem the famine were UNRRA and the Combined Food Board. When I examined the famine areas supplied by UNRRA, I was astonished to find that they were providing for less than 20 per cent of the world's needs. The largest part of UNRRA food supplies in Europe was going to the Ukraine (U.S.S.R.) and to the Communist puppet states of Poland, Czechoslovakia, and Yugoslavia. Of the non-Communist areas, only Greece and a small area in China had been supplied by that organization. A short time before, it had taken over from the American and British armies the job of providing supplies to Italy and Austria.

The seat of Western civilization is west of the Iron Curtain. Except for Greece and belated help to Italy and Austria, Western Europe held little interest for UNRRA. Upon examining the financial support given to UNRRA, I found that as of December 31, 1945, there were forty-five member nations in the organization. Apparently, up to that time these nations had agreed to subscribe to contributions totaling $2,937,624,676. Of this latter amount the United States had agreed to contribute $2,100,000,000, or 71.0 per cent; Great Britain and her dominions $791,433,964, or 26.9 per cent; and the U.S.S.R. $1,750,000, or 0.1 per cent. However, some of the funds contributed by various nations were derived from Lend-Lease borrowings from the United States. Conceivably, this might have increased the American contribution to as much as 90.0 per cent or more.

Only a few had contributed to the major problem of actual food or other supplies. The Soviet Union had contributed to the cost of administration, but avoided any direct participation in the financial burden of relief, although she was the beneficiary of a large part of the supplies.

In any event, there was no hope that UNRRA would be able to unify and galvanize the whole world to action.

I agreed with Secretary Anderson that the only possible existing organization which could effectively control food distribution among nations was the Combined Food Board, which was composed of American, British, and Canadian representatives, with Secretary Anderson as Chairman and an American, Dr. Dennis A. FitzGerald, as U.S. Executive Officer. The Board had been set up during the war to allocate overseas shipments of food from the United States, Canada, and other sources. The United Kingdom, of course, had no overseas exports whatsoever.

Dr. FitzGerald had been the Director of the Office of Requirements and Allocations, Department of Agriculture. He is a man of great abilities and good fellowship. He and I at once went into session to re-examine the available data. We estimated that there was a world shortage of roughly eleven million tons of cereals and three million tons of fats before the next harvest in 1946. We classified the nations in the world as either "deficit," "self-sufficient," or "major surplus" countries. We came up with forty-five "deficit," fifteen "self-sufficient," and four "major surplus" nations. We included the former enemy countries—Germany and Japan—as "deficit" nations in our calculations.

Secretary of War Robert P. Patterson warned:

If food riots and disturbances occur in the occupied territories we may have to call for additional troops. . . .[3]

The military argument was not necessary with me, as I was prepared to take the responsibility on humanitarian and future peace grounds alone. I had taken a similar responsibility in 1919 and had found no consequential public opposition.

Dr. FitzGerald's and my further classification of the situation in the world was as follows. Seventeen European nations with a population of about 305,000,000 people were classified as "deficit":

[3] *Washington Post*, March 8, 1946.

Great Britain	Italy
France	Austria
Holland	Poland
Belgium	Czechoslovakia
Spain	Finland
Portugal	Yugoslavia
Germany	Greece
Norway	Albania
Switzerland	

Of the population in these countries, perhaps a third were farmers who would supply themselves in any event.

We classified Sweden, Denmark, Rumania, Bulgaria, and Hungary —some 38,000,000 people—as "self-sufficient."

Because of their drought, we placed in the deficit category the French Provinces in North Africa and the Union of South Africa. This made a total of about 30,000,000 people who were affected by the drought and required large supplies.

Of "self-sufficient" nations in Africa, we classified Egypt, Ethiopia, Liberia, and Somaliland, with a total population of perhaps 35,000,000 people. Central Africa had never imported much overseas food, and since there were no reports of drought, we classified this area as "self-sufficient." There were no reliable statistics as to its population.

In Asia, there were seven nations of the "deficit" category with a total population of about one billion. These areas were:

India	Korea
Ceylon	Japan
Malaya	The Philippines
China	

We classified Thailand, Iraq, Iran, Afghanistan, and Indo-China —with a total of some sixty-five million people—as "self-sufficient." They possibly had a small surplus.

In Latin America, there were nineteen countries with a population of about 100,000,000 which had hitherto normally imported overseas food. They were:

Mexico	Chile
Guatemala	Costa Rica
Nicaragua	Paraguay
Honduras	Panama
El Salvador	Colombia
Venezuela	Cuba
Ecuador	Brazil
Peru	Haiti
Bolivia	Dominican Republic
Uruguay	

We classified only the Argentine as a "major surplus" country of grain and meat. A few of the Latin-American nations could export some amounts of beans, rice, and corn, but these exports were less than their food import requirements.

While we could classify the Soviet satellite states, we could not classify Russia proper, for that country gave out no information. However, we knew what the Russian ration was in most cities and that the Russians had seized huge amounts of food in their invasion of Eastern Europe, Mongolia, and Manchuria. We believed that Russia proper was in no critical need, and even hoped that, in view of the gigantic amounts they had plundered, they might help out with some supplies for the hungry world.

Thus the major surplus countries were:

Canada
United States
Australia
Argentina

They had a total population of about 175,000,000.

The net result of our computations was that approximately 313,000,000 people were confronted with the problem of providing overseas food for some 1,400,000,000 hungry people in "deficit" countries. The Washington representatives of these countries were clamoring at the Departments of State and Agriculture and the Combined Food Board for commitments of supplies. And the American Army was demanding food for the former enemy countries it occupied.

Ours were only rough estimates for the purpose of visualizing our problems and the organization needed to solve them. The compilation of these demands showed that from January 1, 1946, to the harvest in August, the needy world was asking for 26,000,000 tons of cereals. The supplies in sight from the evident "surplus" countries were about 15,000,000 tons, leaving an apparent gap of over 11,000,000 tons. The statistical shortage in fats was over 3,000,000 tons. We made no attempt to estimate the shortage in any of the less-important foodstuffs.

The estimated surplus of bread grains for export from the United States alone from January 1 to the 1946 harvests appeared to be about 5,100,000 tons. From our wealth of experience, Dr. FitzGerald and I knew that the food intake must be a minimum of 1,500 calories per person, and that it would have to be varied for different groups, from children at the minimum level and hard workers at the maximum. We assumed that by and large the farmers or peasants would hold back enough for their own families. The situation looked almost hopeless. On the basis of these statistics, it now appeared that we could not prevent mass starvation among over 800,000,000 people.

Secretary Anderson, Mr. Davis, and I worked out details for a system of voluntary conservation in the United States largely based upon the experience of the First World War, and we prepared some rules for the trades. We were confident that the nation-wide appeal based on these principles would substantially increase the available supplies from the United States. At the next meeting of the Famine Emergency Committee (on March 11), Mr. Davis requested that I make a short statement in the press urging support of the Committee's conservation measures:

The world faces the gigantic emergency of famine among . . . [eight] hundred million people due to war exhaustion of agriculture and drought.

A great human cry has come to us to save them over a terrible four months until the next harvest. . . . A heavy part of the burden falls upon the United States.

These people can survive if we provide a minimum of bread and fats to them. Of breadstuffs, wheat can best be transported and used in the famine countries. Therefore, we are asking our citizens to make a voluntary sacrifice of 40 per cent of their consumption of wheat products and 20 per cent of food fats and oils during this next 120 days. . . .

In order to avert hunger, we cannot fail to meet this call. If we fail we shall see a world of disorders which will paralyze every effort at recovery and peace. We shall see the death of millions of fellow human beings. Guns speak the first word of victory, but only food can speak the last word.[4]

[4] Herbert Hoover, *Addresses Upon the American Road, 1945–1948* (New York, D. Van Nostrand Company, Inc., 1949), pp. 165–66.

CHAPTER 19

WE UNDERTAKE TO CO-ORDINATE
THE WORLD IN BATTLE AGAINST
FAMINE

In my discussions with President Truman, Secretary Anderson, and Secretary of War Patterson, I stated that I saw no way to get this situation under control unless a strong mission was sent by the President to the governments of all important nations to enlist them and co-ordinate them in a solid world front in this fight against world disaster.

The State Department proposed that, instead of such a mission, a conference be called in Washington of all countries to determine the major actions. Secretary Anderson and I insisted that there was no time for an international convention with all of its protocols, proposals, wrangles, and logrolling by mere agents, who would perforce have to "bring home the bacon." I insisted also that such a mission, to win a race with the famine, must deal with the heads of states and their food officials on the spot—and quickly—to determine the facts and if possible come to agreements on their minimum needs. Also, it would aid the conservation programs if such a mission reported the seriousness of the situation through the press in each country. Moreover, only such a mission could pave the way among the former Allies to recognition of the grim necessity for their reducing their own supplies to feed a recent enemy.

As a result of these discussions, President Truman requested that

I take on the job, at least in Western Europe. I accepted with reluctance, since I was seventy-one years old and my time was committed to administer several educational, scientific, and charitable institutions at home. However, it was pointed out to me that I could have more influence with other countries because of my having directed the relief of the great famine which followed the First World War—a service which had been applauded by all the nations concerned. I also had many old friends in the various governments.

I arranged with President Truman that he instruct our representatives and American civilian agencies in every country to place themselves at our service and that the Combined Food Board, unless other necessities intervened, would accept our recommendations with regard to the allotment of the food which it controlled. He agreed that I choose the members of the mission and that the Army provide me with the best air service it had.

For this mission I secured the voluntary membership of former Ambassador Hugh Gibson, Captain Hallam Tuck, USN, Maurice Pate, and Perrin C. Galpin, all of whom had served with me in World War I famine relief. I also had the valuable services of Frank E. Mason, a long-time foreign correspondent in Europe and former President of International News Service, to handle our relations with the foreign press. And I especially valued the services of Dr. Fitz-Gerald, not only for his abilities, but also because his recommendations would assure Secretary Anderson and the Combined Food Board that our allotments of the supplies would be fairly distributed, insofar as was possible with the world situation.

All of the men on this mission knew Europe, and among them were competent linguists in French, Italian, German, Spanish, Portuguese and Polish. We borrowed the services of Hugo Meier, an accomplished secretary. On our journey to Latin America, we had the help of Dr. Julius Klein, a former Department of Commerce commercial attaché in those countries, who later became Undersecretary of Commerce.

The Air Transport Command furnished their largest plane, a C-54, with a splendid crew under Major Douglas N. MacOdrum, a flight surgeon, Captain Delbert F. Rey, Captain John A. De Wolfe, and a personal military aide, Captain Ivey T. Westmoreland. They also provided a second plane to accompany us for emergencies and to carry material for repairs.

The thirty-eight countries and states we visited were: Great Britain, France, Italy, the Vatican, Germany, Austria, Belgium, Holland, Switzerland, Denmark, Norway, Sweden, Finland, Yugoslavia, Czechoslovakia, Poland, Greece, Egypt, Iraq, India, Thailand, the Philippines, China, Korea, Japan, Hawaii, Canada, Mexico, Panama, Colombia, Ecuador, Peru, Chile, the Argentine, Uruguay, Brazil, Venezuela, and Cuba. We flew a total of 50,711 miles.

In order to expedite our work, we had requested that the Embassy and Legation staffs assemble, prior to our arrival, data on food conditions in each country. This was not a difficult task, since information was readily obtainable from most governments as to estimated stocks of supplies still in the hands of farmers, distributors, and governments, the amounts en route from overseas, as well as the amount of food required to meet the existing daily rations. We sent word in advance that our mission—in the midst of this starving world—wanted no social entertainment, but that if it were unavoidable, only the simplest food should be served.

I might add here that in almost every discussion in the non-Communist countries, their officials raised the problems of Communist conspiracy. In addition to our information on food problems, we were able to draw some conclusions as to the advance of Communism in the world up to this time.

We were also able to secure data on the amount of physical destruction from the war. Building up the documentary history of the world in the Hoover Institution at Stanford University since the beginning of the First World War had been one of my preoccupations. We therefore, with the help of many officials, added to those collections as we went along.

We took off from New York in bright sunshine on March 17, 1946, and the sun continued to shine upon us at every take-off and every landing except one. The exception was Athens, where we landed in the rain. However, almost the second word from the officials who met us there was, "You have brought us good cheer; this is the first rain in months." It is a monument to Air Transport Command efficiency that we were never more than five minutes late in forty take-offs or twenty minutes late on the landings.

This account is not a travelogue of journeys, of hotels good or bad, of people intelligent or apathetic, or of the dramatic incidents of such an unusual mission. As far as we were concerned, it was a race with a ghastly famine and every minute of every day, except for seven or eight hours of sleep, was filled with work and anxieties. My colleagues have recorded some of their experiences and their appraisals of many foreign officials—with much wit and good humor, but these observations are not the point of this memoir. However, they are part of our documentary collections.

I cannot speak too gratefully of these men who, holding responsible positions, left them to accompany me, and without pay. It was the only American official mission that had been sent abroad for years that cost our Government nothing except transport and hotel bills, where we had them.

Before leaving, at Mr. Davis' request, I had made two public nation-wide radio addresses, describing the world situation and our mission. The first was on March 14, 1946. The pertinent parts were:

The stark facts of the world famine problem are these: The inevitable aftermath of six years of war in Europe and Asia is terrible famine. It is inevitable because men are taken from the farms, animals and machinery are destroyed, the crops are less and less. . . . The amount of breadstuffs now visible to supply these people from the surplus countries is about 450,000,000 bushels, but that is about 400,000,000 bushels short of enough to maintain their present meagre rations until the next harvest comes. . . . we also have a great gap in supplies of fats.

The major burden of bridging this gap is by consuming less and making available more food from the Western Hemisphere and the heaviest part of the burden falls upon the American people if hundreds of millions of lives are to be saved from disease or death.

I fear it is now so late that there are many thousands who cannot be saved. But we must relax no effort to minimize the loss.

These stark facts point our path. The war's end closed a horrible era of the killing of millions of men, women, and children. Today we must transform the world from this era of killing to an era of saving of lives. The dawn of a new era can be made to glow with new faith and new hope to all the world if we are willing to make the sacrifice now.

We talk about starving people—but the word "people" is too indefinite. People are, in majority, youth and children. From them the future of civilization must be built. If they are to die or to be stunted in body and distorted in mind all hope of peace and progress is lost.

This is also an issue of religious faith and morals which affects not only our country but our individual selves. Saving of human life is a moral and spiritual duty. If your neighbors and their children were hungry, you would instantly invite them to a seat at your table. These starving women and children are in foreign countries, yet they are hungry human beings—and they are also your neighbors. Could you not imagine one of these helpless women or children as an invisible guest at your table? By following the voluntary rules for saving food you give life to that starving person just as surely as if he sat at your table.

To whatever extent we succeed in this task, we shall have given that much health, courage and faith to a despondent and discouraged world.

We must realize the calamity that has befallen . . . [mankind]. I have no desire to relate the horrors of starvation. I can only appeal to your pity and your . . . [compassion]. I know that the heart of the American people always responds with kindliness to suffering. Will you not take to your table an invisible guest? [1]

Mr. Davis urged me to broadcast again the day before we left. The important parts of this statement, made on March 16 over a national network, were:

Two weeks ago I was asked by President Truman and Secretary of Agriculture Anderson to advise upon what measures and what sort of organization should be set up to cope with the famine which now stretches over . . . [800] million in foreign lands. . . .

There are some matters which I hope our people understand. . . .

2. The number of lives that we can save depends upon the extent to which the American people will comply with the Famine Emergency Committee's rules and their appeal.

3. It also depends upon the extent of measures by the Washington Ad-

[1] *Addresses Upon the American Road, 1945–1948,* pp. 167–68.

ministration to reduce livestock consumption of bread grains and to increase the available fats.

4. It further depends upon the extent to which Latin-American states will cooperate by reducing their consumption and waste of breadstuffs and fats to the end that they also send us the last pound and that they import the very least amount.

5. Even with success in these measures, we have insufficient food for all the millions of women and children and every atom of increase means life and hope somewhere.

I could discuss at length the repeated warnings and recommendations that I have made during the past five years—that effective organization and preparation of world supplies should be made against this inevitable after-war famine. But this is a time for cooperation and not controversy. Our duty is to serve starving people.

. . . I leave tomorrow morning by plane. I am accompanied by a number of men who were associated with me in relief and rehabilitation during and after the first world war. . . .

And I should like, in leaving my country, to repeat to this different audience part of what I have said elsewhere.

This is an issue of religious faith and morals which affects our country as a whole and each individual. Saving of human life is a moral and spiritual duty. If your neighbors and their children were hungry, you would instantly invite them to a seat at your table. These starving women and children are in foreign countries, yet they are hungry human beings—and they are also your neighbors. Could you not imagine one of these helpless women or children as an invisible guest at your table?

I can only appeal to your pity and your mercy. I know that the heart of the American people will respond with kindliness and . . . [compassion]. Will you not take to your table an invisible guest? [2]

[2] *Ibid.*, pp. 169–71.

CO-ORDINATION OF THIRTY-EIGHT NATIONS IN THE BATTLE AGAINST FAMINE

CHAPTER 20

FRANCE, ITALY, AND THE VATICAN

FRANCE

We landed at Paris on March 19, 1946, and were met by American Ambassador Jefferson Caffery and representatives of the President and Minister of Foreign Affairs. We arrived with anxious minds. This was to be our first test of whether we could get the co-operation for necessary self-denial among thirty-eight different nations to save hundreds of millions of lives. Constantly with us was the seemingly unfillable eleven-million-ton statistical gap in world cereal supplies and the three-million-ton gap in fat supplies. Because France was our first stop, I go into our experiences there at some length.

Immediately upon our arrival, Mr. Gibson and I, in company with Ambassador Caffery, met with President Félix Gouin and Minister of Foreign Affairs Georges Bidault. The President recalled my service in the First World War and exclaimed that it was a great blessing for the world that I had undertaken this new task. Therefore, we had no need even to mention the world crisis; they were already greatly alarmed at both their own situation and the reports from over the world. They reviewed France's desperate situation and assured us of their full co-operation.

We immediately went into a huddle with our American officials to analyze the French food data they had collected. We then made the necessary appointments for our staff to meet with the French

Agricultural and Food Ministers and their technical advisers. The French Ministry included seven Communists who came up from the wartime underground. The French Minister of Agriculture was a Socialist who knew nothing of agriculture. However, the Minister of Food was Henri Longchambon, an honest, skilled, and experienced man.

Our staff checked and rechecked the data with the French technicians; we found that their statistics agreed with our own. Those on our staff who were not engaged in the technical sessions went out on investigations for direct checking themselves. We also used the American Army, the Red Cross and other agencies in these independent inquiries. Maurice Pate collected data on the situation of the children and the aged, as well as information on the spread of certain diseases which invariably accompany malnutrition. He not only collected this from various bureaucratic sources but went himself to homes in the slums and talked directly to the people. Hallam Tuck and Perrin Galpin went in person to the rationing agencies and public feeding institutions and talked with industrial and labor leaders.

The French had already decreased the food rations to 1,500 calories. Further decreases in the bread and fat ration had been announced, which would reduce the daily sustenance to 1,200 calories. The stocks on hand, en route, and possibly some from peasants, if evenly distributed until the harvest, would provide only about 700 calories per day per person to the urban population. Neither a government nor a people could survive on such a regimen.

After thoroughly digesting all the data, Dr. FitzGerald and I drew up a tentative table of what we believed were the minimum required overseas supplies for France, month by month, from April through the coming critical months until the harvest. We based these calculations on a minimum average requirement of 1,500 calories per person per day—a drastic regimen. Nevertheless, when I presented this proposal, the French officials accepted at once. Their only remark was that it would be tough going for a people whose prewar consumption was about 3,000 calories. They would do it. But, they asked, could we do it?

Prior to our visit, Stalin had telegraphed the French Communist

leader Maurice Thorez, Vice Premier and Minister without Port-
folio, that he would supply France with 500,000 tons of cereals
before the next harvest if France, the United States, or Great
Britain would furnish the ships. The Soviets would make available
400,000 tons of wheat and 100,000 tons of barley at Odessa, Batum,
and Novorossisk. This might be either charity or a political propaganda maneuver to influence the forthcoming French election. In
any event, 500,000 tons were a considerable amount of food, but in
our calculations we reduced this possible source to 300,000 tons.
Our estimate proved to be correct. The French secured ships from
the United States and Russia in addition to their own.

Dr. FitzGerald flew to French North Africa to make an investigation on the ground. Normally these provinces exported food to the
mother country, but their previous harvest had been devastated by
droughts and locusts. Instead of being a help, the North Africans
themselves required the importation from abroad of large supplies
before the next harvest. However, the new crop for 1946 would be
harvested earlier than in France. The French authorities stated that
they could borrow 300,000 or 400,000 tons from early harvesting for
use in France during July and August, and, if necessary, it could be
replaced after the French harvest.

The remaining problem was to agree on a month-to-month program of supply from the Combined Food Board sources, if world
supplies permitted. We agreed with the French Ministry upon a
program sufficient to maintain the minimum requirement of 350,000
tons of cereals per month for each of the five months from May to
September, along with 5,000 tons of fats per month if we could find
them. And for French North Africa, we agreed upon a total of 100,-
000 tons until their harvest in June. This brought the French needs
to 1,850,000.

Before our visit to Paris, the French representatives in Washington,
supported by elaborate dietary documents and statistical statements,
had made to the Combined Food Board a minimum estimate of over
4,000,000 tons of overseas cereals and 500,000 tons of overseas fats
to meet their needs for the period from January 1, 1946, to the 1946
harvest. Thus the minimum French requirements turned out to be

smaller than their original estimate to the Combined Food Board by more than 2,000,000 tons in cereals alone, fully gratifying my insistence upon an on-the-spot check. On the basis of this experience, I began to have hopes that we could greatly narrow that 11,000,000-ton cereal gap.

The French officials were most insistent that I personally explain the world situation to the French people and thus ease the drastic regulatory tasks of the Government. For this purpose we suggested a press conference, during which, in answer to a question, I took occasion to state our satisfaction over the offer of Russian supplies, but said that these would comprise only about 10 or 15 per cent of the amounts needed from the free nations. On this occasion we learned a lesson about foreign press conferences. A dozen orators, with as many different philosophies or political objectives, were on their feet at once, delivering lectures which wound up with demands that I answer yes or no.

At an official austerity luncheon tendered the mission by M. Bidault, Minister of Foreign Affairs, I replied to a gracious address from him as follows:

MR. MINISTER:

I am greatly honored by your generous references to my many years of cooperation with the people of France.

These rooms awake many recollections of friendly association with a long list of your able predecessors. And you, Mr. Minister, are also carrying forward the great tradition and contribution to world peace which has given this office a century of distinction.

I return to France to find grievous contrasts with other visits over the past forty years. I am greatly saddened by the continuing evidences of the deep injury and suffering of the French people. Even the streets proclaim the stilling lack of the vivaciousness and gaiety of other days. The people are lethargic and silent. It is profound expression not only of the shortage of food, but the effect of six long years of war, of German occupation and strain.

You have referred to my associations with France during the first World War. I was young in years at that time, but today I find myself, like the old family doctor, called from retirement to consult again in a most grave illness of the world. I have indeed been called in late in the crisis.

The spectre of starvation rises among . . . [800] million people in many nations. It haunts our every thought. But there is one satisfaction, if we can find satisfaction in it. We know that the wolf at the door will go away after 120 days. We will then be released from his siege and the bondage of the fears he brings. If we can carry on during that short time to the harvest, the wolf will be gone, I hope forever.

And by our joint efforts we will carry through this last supreme effort, for this crisis is a moral and spiritual crisis, in which the world must serve to save human life. That is a command from the depths of our religious faith.

Mr. Minister, we are in that last stage of seven years of an era of appalling killing of men, women and children, and their barbaric reduction to starvation. It has been the most terrible era of all human history. But today the Four Horsemen are exhausted. A new era dawns. And in that era France will rise from her sufferings to that high place in civilization to which she has contributed so much over so many centuries.[1]

Since I had promised the French Food Minister I would deliver a radio address to the French people after our visit to Rome and Switzerland, I returned to Paris on March 27 for this purpose. On that day, I delivered the address in English. Each paragraph was followed by a French translation. I reviewed the world food situation and the imperative need to support the government measures. Then I added one item for Americans:

The American people should not be misled by reports of American travelers who judge the food supply of tens of millions of people by the kind of a meal that can be bought in a black market restaurant. Such meals cost from $2 to $5 per person. Even white-collar and skilled workmen in Italy and France earn less than $60 a month. Their entire pay for a month would support a family of five for only one or two days from such sources, and many of them are unemployed and without income. If our people are misled by such reports into slackening their efforts, it will be interpreted into the loss of from thousands to millions of human lives.[2]

[1] *Addresses Upon the American Road, 1945–1948*, pp. 172–73.
[2] *Ibid.*, p. 177.

ITALY

Upon arrival in Rome on March 22, we were lodged by the Government in luxurious apartments in the Grand Hotel. Mr. Gibson opined that the hotel menu was just sufficient for a robust canary.

Mr. Gibson and I met with Crown Prince Humbert, Premier Alcide de Gasperi, and Dr. Bergami of the Ministry of Agriculture. All of them were greatly alarmed at the world food situation, and assured us of their full co-operation. Also present at this meeting were Admiral Ellery W. Stone, head of the Allied Control Commission in Italy, and Lieutenant General John C. H. Lee, who commanded American forces in the Mediterranean. The Communists were represented in the Ministry by Minister of Agriculture Fausto Gullo, Minister of Justice Palmiro Togliatti, and Minister of Finance Mauro Scoccimarro.

UNRRA had very recently been placed in charge of food imports into Italy and was under the direction of one of our old hands from the First World War, Spurgeon M. Keeny. He was able, experienced, most co-operative, and accurate in his information.

We again applied as our measure a minimum daily requirement of 1,500 calories, subject to world supplies. To do this, we tentatively advised the Combined Food Board to allot 225,000 tons of cereals for each of the three months of May, June, and July, plus 100,000 tons for August, a total of 775,000 tons. We also allocated some fats —provided we could find them.

I made a statement on March 25, mainly for the American press:

The food story of Italy is that of decreased production from war and drought, exhaustion of stocks before harvest four months hence and increasing difficulties of distribution. The government cereal ration, which was about 10 ounces per person per diem, has been reduced to about 7 ounces. The stocks of cereals on hand and supplies en route will hold this reduced ration about 30 days, and it is urgent that further supplies be loaded at once. Otherwise the cereal ration will need to be further reduced.

The fat ration is 6 ounces and the sugar ration is about 4 ounces per month per person. . . .

I again warned against reports of American tourists who were eating at black-market-supplied restaurants. I said:

. . . Those with money can go to the restaurants where such food is served, and live luxuriously, but Italians with average skilled wages of about $40 per month, and of clerical wages of about $50 per month, could not buy four meals a month for their families at black market restaurants.

Italy has hopes that the Argentine and Brazil may realize her plight and join the United States and Canada in the burden of their urgent supplies.

If the present Government rations are lowered as the result of failure of imports, it will be a disaster to white-collar and working classes. Starvation does not start until supplies cease coming. The problem here, as everywhere, is to prevent starvation during the next 120 days until the harvest. That fate will fall on the lower income groups and children in the cities soon after arrivals of overseas food stop.[3]

CO-OPERATION BY THE VATICAN

An important part of our problem all over the world was to convince every individual of the need for self-sacrifice in order to save food. Therefore, a primary objective of our mission to Italy was to enlist the co-operation of the Vatican to secure this sacrifice among all Catholics and especially to aid us in Latin America.

Mr. Gibson and I spent an hour with Pope Pius XII. As is well known, he was a man of high intelligence and great spiritual dignity. He spoke English fluently and was anxious to know about the famine in every part of the world and the measures we were taking to meet it. While we related the need of support from Catholic authorities, His Holiness said repeatedly, "Willingly, willingly," and stressed over and over his determination to aid in every way possible.

In reply to his questions of what the Vatican could do specifically, we suggested that he could be of great aid in enlisting the co-opera-

[3] *Ibid.*, pp. 174–75.

tion of Latin America, since it was now obvious that we would be dependent upon large supplies and much individual sacrifice from that quarter. Mr. Gibson suggested that the Vatican make a short-wave broadcast to the Latin American states and arrange that it be rebroadcasted in those countries on their standard wave lengths. I suggested that this appeal emphasize the situation among the children in Europe; that His Holiness recommend to the Latin-American states, which imported food, that they reduce imports and increase exports where possible. He asked what more he could do. Mr. Gibson hoped that he would urge Catholic prelates, from Cardinals down, to take part in explaining the world situation and world needs. I further suggested that His Holiness might make a personal appeal through the Cardinals and the Papal Nuncios to every government in the Latin-American states. He agreed at once and asked, "What more?" [4]

[4] Fifteen years afterward in an address I related an incident at one of our interviews at the Vatican which illustrated the kindliness and understanding of His Holiness. I quote:

". . . [In 1946] President Truman requested me to undertake the co-ordination of all the nations in the world to meet the greatest famine in all human history. In that undertaking . . . [former Ambassador] Hugh Gibson and I went to the Vatican on various occasions to enlist the influence of His Holiness the Pope in our efforts. . . . Just before leaving for one of our interviews at the Vatican, the Captain of one of the crew of our planes came to me stating that there were four devout Catholics among the crew and asked if I could arrange for them to receive the blessing of His Holiness as that would be the greatest event that could come into their lives. I told the Captain to bring the boys along and to sit in the anteroom and I would ask His Holiness if a chance arose.

"When Hugh's and my conference with His Holiness was over, I presented the Captain's request. His Holiness at once sent for the crew members. To my astonishment when they filed in, there were not four but sixteen! At that time Rome was occupied by the American Army, and these extras were MPs who just attached themselves to our group and came along. I started to apologize, but His Holiness waved this aside and requested that I present all of them to him. The Captain knelt and received the blessing, the others followed, and all went well until we came to Number 14. He jerked back and exploded: 'I am a Protestant. I am a Baptist'—and retreated to the back end of the room. His Holiness motioned to the boy to step nearer, and said to him: 'Young man, any young man is the better for the blessing of an old man, and I extend it to you.'

"Later on, when we arrived in Cairo this young man asked me to get a substitute for him as he was being guyed as a 'Baptist and a Protestant.' I agreed to do so but asked him how he came to do that thing in the Pope's presence. He said: 'My Mother and Father believed that the Pope was the devil himself and would never have forgiven me if I had knelt before him.'"

The next day, a Vatican official called upon us to explain that, while their knowledge of religious and political matters was considerable, their technical knowledge of food-supply matters was deficient. Did we have someone who could help draft the statements we had asked for from His Holiness? Mr. Gibson undertook this chore. As a result, when we later visited Latin America, we found our path made easier.

CHAPTER 21

SWITZERLAND, CZECHOSLOVAKIA, AND POLAND

A PROGRAM

From our experience in France and Italy, we decided to apply to each country a rough routine, which was:

1. To telegraph in advance requesting the American Ambassador or Minister to arrange a meeting with the top authorities in which we could discuss the world food situation in general.

2. To have the American Embassy arrange a time of meeting for our staff with the local American staff to secure the data which they had compiled in advance for us.

3. To arrange a time for our staff to meet with the food authorities of the country.

4. For Dr. FitzGerald and me to formulate a *tentative* program of monthly imports for recommendation to the Combined Food Board as a provisional supply.

5. To base this on a minimum of 1,500 or 1,550 calories per diem per person of the urban population. (We assumed that the agricultural population would provide for itself in countries where there was no great drought.)

6. To submit the tentative import program to the food authorities of each nation for their views but without commitment until we could scan the larger picture of the world situation.

140

SWITZERLAND

The American Minister, Leland Harrison, had arranged a meeting with the Swiss authorities on March 25, 1946. We proposed a tentative program to supply 30,000 tons of cereals in each of the months of July, August, and September, or a total of 90,000 tons, and so advised the Combined Food Board and the Swiss authorities. The Swiss had a small surplus of meats and fats, which they agreed to supply to their neighbors France and Italy.

CZECHOSLOVAKIA

We arrived in Prague on March 27. The American Minister, Laurence A. Steinhardt, had arranged a conference with President Eduard Beneš, Prime Minister Zdenek Fierlinger, Foreign Minister Jan Masaryk, Supply Minister Vaclav Majer, and himself. Nine of the Cabinet members were Communists. I had known Beneš and Masaryk for over thirty years. They were not Communists, but they were now helpless in the midst of the forces which surrounded them.

Gibson, Pate, and Tuck had many old friends in various legations in Prague. From them we learned much about the political forces in motion.

UNRRA had furnished some relief during the previous nine months. Our American officials informed us that the Director of UNRRA for Czechoslovakia was a Russian Communist named Peter I. Alekseev. The trains carrying North American food had been dressed with Russian signs.

After our investigation of the situation, we proposed a tentative program to the Combined Food Board to supply 60,000 tons of cereals for each of the months from June to August and 50,000 for September, plus some fats if they were available—for a total of about 300,000 tons. This would maintain a minimum food intake of about 1,500 calories.

We gave the following statement to the fourteen American press representatives who now accompanied us on their own plane:

Our report on Czechoslovakia can be stated very briefly, although brevity and statistics do not express the human picture of these people.

Their food is vigorously rationed and in different quantities, from children to heavy workers. . . . The farmers take care of themselves. There is practically no black market. The ration is badly deficient in fats, which average only about 20 ounces per month per person. The Czechoslovak ration is already one-third below normal and cannot be fully maintained until the next harvest without some further overseas breadstuffs and fats. Czechoslovakia has the additional background that the country has been short of food ever since the German occupation which began over seven years ago. Without UNRRA, the Czechoslovaks could not have carried on thus far. . . .

The food shortage has its worst expression in the children. They need additions to lift the ration above the danger level, where it now is. . . . The whole child question urgently requires vigorous reorganization to provide an extra meal a day for the subnormal cases, in the same way we did it after the last war.

The American Red Cross, the American Relief for Czechoslovakia and the American Catholic Welfare Association are endeavoring to extend special feeding of children. But with all their efforts, no more than a third of the need is covered for lack of supplies.[1]

POLAND

We arrived in Warsaw from Prague on March 28. The Government of Poland, with one exception, was Communist.

We were lodged in the Mysliwski Palace, which had recently been restored for a visit by Prime Minister Tito of Yugoslavia. Ambassador Arthur Bliss Lane warned us that the place was wired with recording microphones.

Accompanied by Ambassador Lane, Gibson and I made formal calls upon President Bolesław Bierut and Premier Edward Osóbka-Morawski.

[1] *Addresses Upon the American Road, 1945–1948*, pp. 179–80.

Herbert Hoover and a group of Polish friends in Warsaw.

Herbert Hoover and President Harry S. Truman discussing world food needs.

Acme Photo

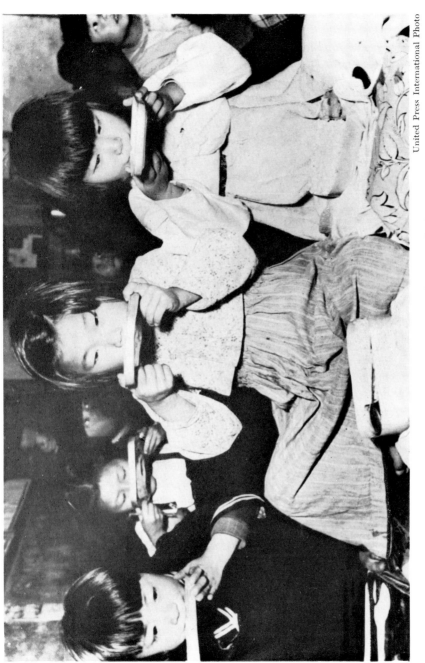

Korean schoolgirls sipping American milk provided by UNICEF.

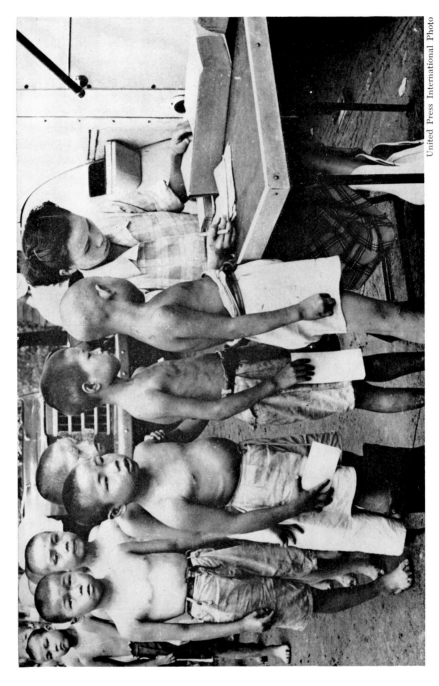

Schoolboys lined up for chest examinations in Formosa.

We went into the usual huddle with our American officials over their appraisal of the food situation. UNRRA was furnishing relief. The American and British Ambassadors had protested at discrimination in food distribution in favor of the Communists and had secured the removal of the UNRRA chief in Poland, Mikhail A. Menshikov, a hard-core Communist from the Soviet Union. They substituted Brigadier Charles M. Drury, a Canadian administrator, as a condition of more imports by UNRRA.

Ambassador Lane arranged a meeting for our mission with Vice Premier Władysław Gomulka at the Council of Ministers Building, where the Premier presided over some fifty or sixty officials. Elaborate reports were made to us by the Ministers of Food and Public Health and by Stanisław Mikolajczyk, who was Vice Premier and Minister of Agriculture. (Mikolajczyk had been Premier of the Polish Government in Exile in London during the war.) He was the only non-Communist in the Ministry and had been retained by demand of the Americans and British under agreements previously settled with Stalin. I made a short statement on the world situation. The Ministers insisted that UNRRA imports were insufficient.

As we were filing out of the meeting, Mikolajczyk whispered to me that I should arrange a meeting where he could inform me on both the food and political situations. Ambassador Lane arranged a dinner, where we had a long conversation. Mikolajczyk disclosed that he had warded off various attempts at assassination; he gave Gibson some tender messages for his family in England, whom he did not expect to see again. (He subsequently escaped from Poland in disguise.)

Gibson, who had been the first U.S. Minister to the newly created Poland of 1919, and Pate had many old friends in Warsaw from whom they received many accounts of the terrors of the Communist regime. We also received from them and from Mikolajczyk some documents of historical importance for the Hoover Institution on War, Revolution, and Peace at Stanford University.

Pate arranged for a Mrs. Victoria Winnicka, who had benefited from our children's canteens in the First World War, to accompany me on a tour through Warsaw. The city was a horror of vengeance.

The Germans had systematically destroyed the city by demolition regiments prior to their retreat from Poland. My guide had personally witnessed the destruction of the Jewish ghetto by aerial bombardment and artillery. It was now a pile of rubble—the tomb of more than 200,000 Jews. My tour of it was a shattering experience which haunted my dreams for years.

In reply to questions by the American press representatives, I tried to present to the American people a picture of Poland:

This is the worst situation we have seen so far in every respect. It is lightened only by the hope and gallantry of the Polish people. They are digging themselves out of the greatest physical, political, intellectual and moral destruction ever known. But my Mission has no part in political, economic or social matters. It is solely concerned with food.

Armies have four times swept over Poland, living on the country, and she had five years of German occupation. The population of new Poland, about twenty-four million, will be about eleven million less than old Poland, of which probably 5,000,000 were killed. A Polish woman remarked to me today, "We are weary of dying."

There has been enormous destruction of housing, amounting to 90 per cent in Warsaw alone. Most of the people in the destroyed areas are living in hovels without adequate clothing, furniture, or heat.

Compared to pre-war, the horses remaining are stated to be only 45 per cent; cattle, 33 per cent; sheep, 36 per cent; swine, 17 per cent; and they are mostly underfed. But of even more importance has been the intellectual destruction and physical weakening of the human beings.

The food situation has become sudden and heartbreaking due to miscalculations. The breadstuffs and potatoes in stock and enroute from overseas will theoretically last only until May 7th on a reduced ration. The bread ration is a theoretical average of seven ounces per day per person, and two cities, Cracow and Lodz, have already been without bread for three weeks at a time. The fat ration, when you can get it, is 16 ounces per month per person. The average caloric intake, including hospital inmates, is perhaps 1,500 (mostly starches), but inability to create effective distribution makes any estimate unreliable. Examination by American experts shows over 2,500,000 children are estimated to be terribly sub-normal from under-nourishment. Dairy products are practically unknown to the great majority of city children. Samplings indicate an infant mortality of 20 per cent per annum, with a huge increase of tuberculosis and other under-feeding diseases among all children and adolescents. There are 1,100,000 orphans and half-orphans. Five million children should have more food and more appropriate food at once. Children cannot wait for their reconstruction until some other time; their future is being made now. Unlike after the first World War, there has been no over-all organization to care for and rebuild the children. There are gallant efforts by Polish women in local areas, conducted under unbelievable difficulty. They are receiving some assistance from the American Red Cross and the American Catholic Welfare.

Added to all the other problems is the migration of some millions of Poles westward from the territory annexed by Russia, and the expulsion of Germans west from the territory annexed by Poland. Both migrations add to the already disorganized food situation.

It is a forbidding picture. . . .[2]

FitzGerald, Pate, Tuck, and I, with the aid of the American officials, concluded that we had enough information to make a tentative recommendation to the Combined Food Board. It was that for Poland UNRRA should be supplied with 85,000 tons of cereals for each of May, June, July, and August, or a total of 340,000 tons, plus such condensed milk and fats as could be obtained for children. With these margins, we believed there would be no starvation.

Pate, who had administered relief for millions of Polish children from 1919 to 1923 and in 1939 with ability and devotion, had gone to Poland in advance of our mission to examine the situation among the children. His report reads in part:

WARSAW, March 30, 1946

In the estimated total population of Poland of 23,000,000 are approximately 7,000,000 children and young people up to 20 years of age. Of these, 1,100,000 are orphans or half-orphans, 660,000 being fatherless, 330,000 motherless, and 110,000 without parents. . . .

Children with their parents in the bombed areas are living in bad physical conditions. It is estimated, for instance, that in the ruins of Warsaw are 80,000 children, exclusive of babies. There is serious overcrowding, sometimes in buildings that collapse; many dwell in cellars that are dark, damp

[2] *Ibid.*, pp. 183–84.

and unhealthy. Thousands of homes are without light or heat, and water must be carried. In one destroyed province, Kielce, 6,600 children live in dugouts and shacks. In both city and country many dwellings are rat-infested.

Food of many children of poor families is little more than soup carried from a nearby soup kitchen. In some sections of the country, where supplementary food cannot be given, families are living on potatoes and potato soup. In Kielce, for instance, are small towns where the women walk miles each day begging and foraging for food. Children are too poorly clothed to go out in winter, and thousands are without shoes and cannot attend school.

. . . Height, weight, age ratio [of children] in Poland is said to be worse than any other country in Europe. . . . Mortality of children from 0–1 year now runs for the city of Warsaw approximately 20 percent.

In view of the disorganization of war and the great poverty now existing in Poland, organized efforts to aid children are sporadic. Hundreds of women volunteers are struggling to do what they can. For example, in the city of Warsaw about one-quarter of the children attending schools are receiving soup each day. This amounts to only 300 calories and is principally starches. After the last war, every child in the city of Warsaw (as well as all other industrial and needy communities in Poland) received, with American help, a school meal of 625 calories daily . . . as compared with the pitiful soup served today, and served to only a small fraction of the needy children.

The night before we left Poland, President Bierut gave an elaborate dinner to our mission and some fifty Communist dignitaries. The preliminaries of *zakąski*, vodka, and cocktails were heaped on tables and repeatedly replenished. The dinner was in seven huge courses with various drinks. The whole show was a depressing scene in the midst of a hungry people. The President made a long but amiable speech, to which I made a cautious reply. A paragraph from it was:

. . . Mr. President, I can echo the sentiment you have expressed as to the imperative need of lasting peace in the world. . . . Twice in a lifetime we in America have been called upon to intervene with our military strength to secure the liberation of Europe, at huge sacrifices to ourselves.

Twice in a lifetime we have been called upon to rescue the world from famine as a result of war. We know we cannot have peace in the presence of the spectre of famine. . . .[3]

There were few satisfactions to be had from witnessing the reality of Communism in Poland.

[3] *Ibid.*, pp. 181–82.

CHAPTER 22

FINLAND, SWEDEN, AND NORWAY

FINLAND

On March 31, 1946, we flew from Warsaw to Helsinki. The other Baltic States, having been annexed by Russia, were not open to us. Half of our mission was put up in the American Embassy, where we were met by a large, cheering crowd.

American Minister Maxwell M. Hamilton had arranged a meeting with President Juho K. Paasikivi, Prime Minister Mauno Pekkala, and Foreign Minister Carl J. H. Enckell. Meanwhile, we had gone into the usual conference with the local American Embassy staff, who had prepared the data we wished.

The Finns were most hospitable. The President and the Cabinet gave us a dinner. The Foreign Office and the Finnish press gave a dinner to our accompanying press representatives, and the Finnish Army gave one to our two air crews. The menus were simple, as befitted our surrounding of hungry people. A touching incident was a letter from the amateur boxing champion of Finland, who sent me the championship medal he had received. I returned the medal with a note of appreciation.

The Government of Finland was menaced by Soviet Russia, and one-fourth of the Parliament was composed of Communists. The Russians had plundered the country on their invasion, but the Finns were receiving a small monthly shipment of wheat from Russia—in exchange for an extensive list of Finnish products. They had no consequential exports to exchange for overseas food. The situation was complicated by the Finns, who, in order to attack their arch enemy, Russia, had fought with the Germans against the Allies. American Quakers and Lutherans, with the American Red Cross, were giving some aid.

The gist of Pate's report on the condition of Finnish children was:

There are roughly 500,000 in bracket 0–7 years. These are best-off category, because by law they receive first cut on national milk supply.

Tuberculosis: Present annual general mortality per 10,000 inhabitants:

Finland 16	Norway 6
Sweden 6	Denmark 3

Finland makes an heroic effort in the care of children. Over 75 percent of the elementary schools serve a modest noon soup to children; 83 percent of the children of the country receive this soup; thanks to Quaker and other encouragement, the figure will soon be raised to 88 percent. By already enacted law, 100 percent must be fed as soon as the backwoods communities can be organized. The State and municipalities join to pay for this noon meal, which is free to the children.

Average value of noon soup is 355 calories, plus average of 50 grams (about 1.7 ounces) (115 calories) dark bread which child usually brings from house. The soup is a milk gruel 4 days weekly; a little meat or fats is put in vegetable soup 2 days weekly. There is no sugar in school feeding.

The need is for more fats, proteins, sugar, for children and expectant and nursing mothers, and items like cocoa for morale, and to relieve a very drab, unchanging diet.

In addition to Pate's report, I gave this statement to the American press representatives who were among us:

The food administration in Finland is so efficient that our report can be made brief.

Her major supplies in sight to maintain the Government ration will be exhausted at the end of June. Finland is so far to the North that the harvest does not come in until the end of September. . . .

There are three groups in great distress. [First,] there is a deficient

food supply in the lower-income groups of the cities. The second are
400,000 people in the areas devastated by the Germans and by battle.
The third group is the 400,000 refugees from the areas transferred to
Russia. Thus, there are, in addition to the lower-income group of the
cities, 800,000 people in especial distress out of a total population of
3,800,000. Further provision of food outside the Government ration is
urgently needed. . . .

The situation among children is that priority in milk supplies . . . [is]
given to infants under two years of age. But there are in all groups about
500,000 children above this age, and adolescents, who are badly undernourished. The usual diseases from undernourishment are serious among
the children of these groups. The American Quakers, the Lutherans, the
Red Cross and UNRRA are giving service to the children and adults in
these distressed areas and to the refugees. But it is insufficient. They need
greater financial support and supplies. All this is besides provision to carry
the major Government ration over the gap. Finland has a fine determination to help itself. The Finnish people are working to their utmost capacity.

The removal of the 400,000 people from the area transferred to Russia
amounts to about twelve per cent of the whole population being re-settled
among the remaining 3,400,000, of whom 400,000 in the devastated areas
of Finland are in distress. This is a burden on a people already short of
housing from destruction, and upon farms already small. It is a situation
comparable to moving all of the people in the three Pacific Coast States
onto the people East of the Rockies.

If the Finns are to be re-established to their place in the world, they
must be helped, and quickly.[1]

After our visit and the published press reports, we learned that a
loan in the amount of $35,000,000 was made to Finland by the U.S.
Export-Import Bank.

SWEDEN

On April 1, we flew from Helsinki to Stockholm. The members of
our mission and I had opportunity to discuss our problem with King
Gustav V, Crown Prince Gustav Adolf, Prime Minister Per Albin

---

[1] *Addresses Upon the American Road, 1945–1948*, pp. 185–86.

Hansson, Foreign Minister Bo Östen B. Undén, Agriculture Minister Per Edvin Sköld, Supply Minister Axel Gjöres, and Chief of Food Commission Ake Hovgard, as well as the American Chargé d'Affaires Christian M. Ravndal. They were most co-operative.

I urged upon the Swedish Ministers the plight of the Finns and explained the reasons why we could not thus far secure relief. They undertook to help the Finns and did so.

The Swedish officials informed me that the Government had purchased about 80,000 tons of grain in the United States and the Argentine which had not yet been shipped. As a contribution to our mission, they canceled the orders, thus making it available to the Combined Food Board.

Maurice Pate gave me his report on the children's condition, the major conclusion of which was that they were in good shape. Milk was unrationed and school feeding was general. It was a great satisfaction to visit a country where children were being cared for.

The Minister of Foreign Affairs gave a parting luncheon to all of our mission—with an appropriately modest menu. The conversation was mostly directed to the dangers of the Communist conspiracies.

NORWAY

On April 2, we flew from Stockholm to Oslo. We were met by the American Ambassador, Lithgow Osborne, Crown Prince Olaf, and some members of the Norwegian Ministry.

Mr. Osborne, Mr. Gibson, and I made calls upon King Haakon VII, Premier Einar Gerhardsen, and Minister of Foreign Affairs Halvard Lange. We discussed with them the critical world food situation and the purpose of our mission.

We held the usual huddle with the Embassy staff, who had prepared for us an excellent analysis of Norway's outstanding food problems. During the war Norway had been plundered by the Germans, who carried off everything they could get loose, including much railway rolling stock and many farm animals. However, UNRRA had given them no help.

Ambassador Osborne arranged a meeting at the Embassy with the full Norwegian Ministry to discuss the situation. The Ministry members were young in years—all under forty—and young in experience; they were strongly Socialist. These "frozen men of the North," as Mr. Gibson described them, were a bit stiff at the start, apparently fearing we represented some capitalistic purpose. However, as I explained the world situation and the object of our mission to save human lives by co-ordination of the efforts of the whole world, and the fact that we were seeking to help them and for them to help us, they began to thaw out and became quite human and very co-operative.

Norway had a need for wheat only. Dr. FitzGerald and I recommended a tentative program to the Combined Food Board of 30,000 tons a month for August and September.

The Norwegians had resumed whaling operations and now had an increasing surplus of whale oil, which was in demand by European countries for oleomargarine. We suggested that in its distribution a priority be given to Finland (on credit), to which the Norwegians agreed. We suggested they exchange their major supply of whale oil with Germany, if they could get goods or money in return. To this they also agreed. (Later we arranged this barter with the American authorities in Germany.)

The Norwegians had a current surplus of 200,000 tons of fish and could readily increase it to 500,000 tons if they could get salt with which to preserve it. We arranged to secure the salt through the American authorities in Germany. We suggested they ship fish to Finland on credit, since the Soviet Government had seized the Finnish fisheries. To this they also agreed.

Maurice Pate reported to me his investigation of the children's situation, which in substance was:

Children under insufficient wartime diet are less resistant to illnesses. In 1945 adolescent children ran 4 to 5 pounds underweight.

There are 350,000 school children 7–14 years. There is no school feeding legislation, and none pending.

In Oslo, a free breakfast (paid by municipality) is offered to all at 8 a.m. About 95 per cent of the children come for breakfast, which is under their needs.

Dr. FitzGerald, while on a field trip, made a new discovery in animal nutrition. He witnessed the Norwegian farmers, who had little protein feed for their animals but a surplus of fish, feeding their dairy cows with herring. We confirmed it by the flavors in a lunch given to us.

The King tendered a parting luncheon to our mission at which the entire Royal Family and the Ministers were present. They gave many expressions of good will to us and to the American people.

CHAPTER 23

GREAT BRITAIN

We arrived at a London airport from Oslo on April 4. Mr. Churchill had been retired as Prime Minister and was succeeded by Clement R. Attlee, the leader of the Labour Party.

On arrival at Claridge's, a messenger brought me a formal invitation to speak the next morning to the "Emergency Conference on European Cereal Supplies," comprising some twenty-two countries, which had been called by the British Government. British Minister of State Philip J. Noel-Baker gave me a most gracious introduction. My address was a description of the food situation on the Continent, with special emphasis on the plight of subnormal children. The more important paragraphs were:

. . . The very character of the Conference is based on the knowledge that the few months until the next harvest are the most critical food period in all modern history. With the coming harvest, world food problems are by no means ended, but with favorable weather conditions, the situation after the harvest will be much easier. We shall have a breathing spell. The hungry wolf now at the door of the world should then go away. . . .

The apprehensions which I entertained before beginning this journey have not decreased. They have increased. Hunger sits at the table thrice daily in hundreds of millions of homes. And the spectre of possible starvation haunts equally the halls of government and squalid hovels in the ruins of war.

The world uses the words "starvation" and "famine" very loosely. Some travelers glibly report there is no widespread death-dealing famine on the Continent of Europe. . . . [These] casual observers do not realize that famine would have already struck great groups . . . were it not for past overseas supplies, and that it is inevitable unless we land, for the next months, every ton of overseas food that we can summon. And nothing is more preposterous than the opinions of travelers on the Continent who live on black market food at prices out of reach of ninety-nine per cent of the people.

And let me say at once that . . . [press] reports do not convey the information or give the basis for conclusions that come from personal investigation on the spot. Only by personal contact with officials, and especially by intimate discussions with the leaders of the many different relief agencies who are working intimately among the people, can information be checked and cross-checked. Only by judgment upon this information on the spot by men experienced in food problems does the picture become clear.

I then briefly described the food situation on the Continent and gave our findings that many in the city populations were receiving no more than 1,250 calories per capita per day and that unless immediate increased overseas supplies were furnished, starvation was certain:

. . . On any definition, millions are today at the danger level.

But even that is not the whole story. The stocks in hand and supplies en route with which to maintain the meagre government rations will not last, in many countries, beyond the end of May, and in some of them only to the end of April.

Nor is even this the whole story. The predominant diet of these city masses is very short of protein and fats. Adults can stand this for long stretches of time, but the effect upon children is disastrous. The first expression of famine is to be found among the children. Infant mortality in some cities exceeds 20 per cent a year. . . .

It would not be an immoderate estimate that from the Russian frontier to the Channel there are today twenty millions of children who are not only badly undernourished, but steadily developing tuberculosis, rickets, anemia, and other diseases of subnormal feeding. There may be a much larger number.

If Europe is to have a future, something must be done about these children. Unless they are better fed, many will die and others will grow up with stunted bodies and distorted minds. They will furnish more malevolents in the world.

I stated that there were only sporadic efforts to aid the children:

. . . They have only touched the fringes of the problem.

It is a matter of profound regret that the experience of the last World War was not followed and an effective organization set up to give one extra meal of 400 or 500 calories a day to all undernourished children and certain classes of mothers. Experience shows that the normal recuperative powers of children is such that, if not too far gone, a few months of food of the right kind could recover much of the losses of years of privation. There is abundant proof of this in the handling of . . . fifteen million subnormal children in this way in 1919 . . . [to 1923]. Strong bodies and clear minds were created in the vast majority of those served.

The rehabilitation of children cannot wait. It cannot be postponed until some other day. They are not like a bridge or a factory. They lose ground every day that is lost. Already almost a year has been lost. The world cannot hate children, even of the enemy. Our children must live in the same world with them. Nor is this a question of vast quantities of food; such an extra meal a day would not involve the import of more than four thousand tons a month for every one million children.

It is not too late to expand this work at once, and it is imperative to prepare for its continuance over the next twelve months. . . .

I then spoke of the necessity for a world-wide organization for distribution of the coming harvest of 1946 and continued:

Had such a central organization been really functioning in the world last September, with a realistic appraisal of European production, the crisis would have been realized then, instead of five months later. Larger supplies could have been had if both surplus and importing countries had taken more extensive steps earlier to conserve food. Some of the present suffering and physical degeneration would have been lessened. . . .

. . . The first voice of victory is the guns. But the first voice of peace is food. The world has organized to maintain peace. Surely it can organize to maintain life. . . .[1]

[1] *Addresses Upon the American Road, 1945-1948*, pp. 187-92.

Prime Minister Attlee gave our mission a dinner at which the guests included members of the Ministry Herbert S. Morrison, Tom Williams, Ben Smith, and others. I presented to them a food problem in which they could co-operate.

As a protection during the war, Great Britain had built up some one million tons of a food reserve which was either in stock or in their transportation pipeline. It was double their prewar reserves. I stated that they could well reduce the reserve to prewar normal and thus partly solve the problem of India and other spots. I stated that our advance reports showed that great areas in India were receiving only 1,200 calories and could not even sustain that level without greatly increased overseas supplies. I also said that India was demanding huge quantities of food from the United States, with all the waste that such long voyages implied, instead of diverting Australian cargoes. I made no headway with this idea at that time.

The British had done a magnificent job for their children, as is indicated by some paragraphs from Maurice Pate's report:

(1) England has the most advanced, extensive, and generous system of supplementary child feeding of any country in the world.

(2) For supplemental feeding of school children, originally an allowance of 1,000 calories, including generous portions of meat, cheese, and fats, was made each day. Actually, the children are able to consume only 600 to 900 calories daily.

(3) Of 4,500,000 school children:

(A) 1,850,000 receive the above-mentioned supplementary meal each day.

(B) 3,200,000 receive milk, in the amount of either one-third or two-thirds pint per day.

(4) More children would be served but either their parents prefer to have them eat at home or there is lack of locales or local initiative. . . .

(5) All officials confirmed to me that in the history of the country the health of English children has never been higher; and their weight and height measurements are now at an all-time high.

In visiting the schools during the meal hour, in a working man's district, I found the children all looking unusually well and round. The meal served to them is balanced and attractive. . . .

. . . Every child is allowed to consume all he can eat. . . .

Dr. FitzGerald and I estimated that Britain's needs for cereals from overseas would require about 400,000 tons for each of the five months from May up to and including September, or a total of 2,000,000 tons. We recommended it to the Combined Food Board. However, we were greatly disappointed at British unwillingness to apply their excessive pipeline supply in order to effect a reduction of these requirements.

CHAPTER 24

BELGIUM, HOLLAND, AND DENMARK

BELGIUM

On April 6, 1946, we arrived in Brussels, where we were met by the American Ambassador, Admiral Alan G. Kirk. He provided an opportunity for discussion of the food problems by giving a dinner which included as guests the Belgian Prime Minister, Achille van Acker; the Minister for Foreign Affairs, Paul-Henri Spaak; the President of the Senate, R. Gillon; the President of the Chamber of Representatives, Frans Van Cauwelaert; Burgomaster of Brussels Friedrich Joseph Van de Meulebroeck; and our mission.

I explained the world situation and made an appeal that sacrifice was the necessity of the times. Their spokesman informed us that, having laid their requirements before the Combined Food Board, they felt they should await its decision. However, we canvassed the situation with our old colleagues from the Belgian Relief during the First World War, checked all data from our American officials with the information we brought from Washington, and as a result, Dr. FitzGerald and I made a tentative recommendation to the Combined Food Board of 60,000 tons of cereals per month for each of the next five months.

The rehabilitation of children was going slowly, and Maurice Pate urged the Belgian Government to resume the children's feeding program of the First World War.

HOLLAND

On April 9, we arrived in The Hague, where American Ambassador Stanley K. Hornbeck had arranged our usual meetings.

At the time of their liberation the year before, the Dutch representatives had asked for my advice on the food outlook. I had recommended that they secure their cereal supplies before the inevitable famine overtook the world. They had done so.

The Dutch expressed their appreciation for my advice and were most co-operative in their wish to reduce their demands to the very minimum. Although they had been plundered by the Germans, they informed us that they could and would fill their own requirements for meats and fats. As for grain, they said they might need 80,000 tons of cereals in September, and that only if their harvest proved late. We so informed the Combined Food Board.

DENMARK

We arrived in Copenhagen on April 10, 1946, and were met by Gustav Rasmussen, the Danish Foreign Minister, and his staff, together with Garret G. Ackerson, Jr., the American Chargé d'Affaires.

The Danes had offered no resistance when overrun by Hitler and thus were not plundered. Moreover, the Germans had set aside the plenteous dairy and fishing areas of Denmark and Norway as food reserves, but events had moved too fast, leaving these regions largely unpillaged. They had sufficient supplies to last until the next harvest. Our visit was one of courtesy at the urgent invitation of the Danish Government: the Danes were considering a program of relief to children in Germany and Austria, and they were most interested in the work of our mission.

Mr. Gibson and I called upon King Christian X, at his request. He wanted to know all about the world food situation and expressed to us his admiration and good wishes.

Maurice Pate made his usual investigation into the condition of the children. He reported that they were in excellent shape and that they were offered a 400-calorie meal in the schools, but 70 per cent of them brought their own lunches. His final paragraph read:

As Denmark is a country of relatively plentiful food resources, and as the sense of care of children is highly developed, one need have little concern for the health of children there. I visited the section of the town where the most modest workers live. There the children were energetically playing games in court yards and appeared to be in generally good shape.

CHAPTER 25

GERMANY AND AUSTRIA

GERMANY

General Lucius D. Clay, as Deputy Military Governor for the American Zone of Germany, also had the food responsibilities for the British Zone. He had come from Berlin to meet me upon my arrival in Brussels on April 6 and to outline his urgent food problems.

During our interview, General Clay confirmed that the German people in the American, British, and French Zones were much worse off for food, medical care, clothing, and housing than they had been at the surrender ten months before. The Russians, having taken in their zone the breadbasket of Germany, gave a ration to those people barely sufficient to prevent mass starvation and confiscated the remainder for export to Russia.

General Clay told me that in the American Zone the food ration had been cut from 1,550 calories per capita per diem to 1,275, effective April 1. He predicted that unless supplies could be imported at once, he might be compelled to reduce the ration to 1,000 calories. The British had already done this in their zone. He said the French Zone was even worse, for they were providing about 900 calories except for unrationed foods, which added a little to the total. Human beings could not survive on such a diet.

General Clay made a strong plea for the Germans, to which I replied that feeding the former enemy peoples required no debate with me, since it must be done for many reasons. I urged him to restore his 1,550-calorie ration level and promised to do my best to arrange immediate help. But the General apparently determined to take no risks and held to the reduced 1,275 calories—which was below the endurance level.

The plight of Germany was, of course, due fundamentally to Hitler's wars of aggression and to his defeat amidst a Germany exhausted of supplies. The methods of disarmament and reparations, the spirit of the Morgenthau Plan of "pastoralization"—all combined to stifle any internal recuperation. This may have been just retribution for the Nazi sins against humanity, but no man with a vision that the world would have to bury the hatchet sometime if civilization were to survive, had sat in on these decisions. The result was that mass destitution and prevention of sheer starvation had become the burden of the victors.

We landed at Tempelhof in Berlin on April 11, five days after the Brussels interview. We were met, with military honors, by General Joseph T. McNarney, Commander of U.S. Forces in Europe and of the German occupation forces; Ambassador Robert D. Murphy, U.S. Political Adviser for Germany; and General Clay.

On the evening of our arrival, I assigned investigation of the general food situation to Dr. FitzGerald and myself, the situation of children to Mr. Pate, and directed Messrs. Galpin, Gibson, Mason, and Tuck to find something of the immediate problems confronting General Clay.

The General assembled the Allied food officials in the three zones; he also organized separate conferences with the newly appointed German officials. Dr. FitzGerald and I devoted every working hour to these conferences, the end result of which was that we agreed upon a tentative program of imports which would support a 1,500-calorie base of food supply. It was obvious that the British and French could furnish no substantial supplies, and the burden of their zones would therefore fall upon the United States.

After the conferences and the investigation by our staff, Dr. FitzGerald and I recommended a tentative program to the Combined Food Board: *for the American Zone:* in May, June, and July, 50,000 tons of cereals per month; for August, 65,000 tons; and for September,

60,000 tons, or a total of 275,000 tons; *for the British Zone:* we recommended 180,000 tons of cereals per month for the five months from May to September, or a total of 900,000 tons; *for the French Zone:* we suggested 30,000 tons for May; 45,000 tons per month for June, July, and August; and 30,000 tons for September, or a total of 195,000 tons. This all came to the staggering total of 1,370,000 tons of cereals alone. All this was in addition to our arrangements for fish and whale oil from Norway.

Mr. Pate personally inspected many sections of Berlin and also journeyed to other German cities, where he collected information from the Allied military, civil authorities, and the charitable agencies. He himself went into many homes to talk with the people. He showed that the general mortality rate in Berlin had increased from about 13.2 per 1,000 population in 1938 to about 41 per 1,000 early in the year of our visit. The children's mortality rate was apparently somewhat higher. The military authorities had reserved the scarce milk supplies for children under three years of age. In the few localities when food was provided for school meals, it contained only about 124 calories, compared to a minimum need of over 500 calories. The net of this report was that the condition of the children was appalling.

We settled a minor question about food packages from CARE (Co-operative for American Remittances to Europe, Inc.), the organization whose creation I had been largely responsible for. These gifts, sent by donors in the United States, although small in proportion to the over-all need, did contribute to hungry people. The spirit of the Morgenthau Plan had invented the warning that these packages would all go to the "upper classes," so our military authorities had refused to allow the distribution of CARE packages in Germany on the ground that it would be discriminatory. With General Clay's help, however, we arranged that CARE packages should be admitted. Our military also agreed that the packages would be given free railway and postal transport.

In all of our dealings with food questions, we were greatly indebted not only to General Clay but also to General Hugh Hester, who was chief of food and agriculture in the American Zone. We were similarly obligated to Ambassador Murphy.

Some samples of the Allied actions are an indication of some of the postwar causes of the situation. The Allies had completely destroyed the nitrate plants, since they were denominated as munitions works. As a matter of fact, the making of explosives was a war use of the great nitrate plants which before the war produced mainly fertilizers. By destroying the plants, the Allies destroyed the production of fertilizers, which were vital, not only to German food production, but also to food production in other parts of Europe.

Because the plants making petroleum products from coal had been destroyed by the Allies, I sustained General Clay in recommending shipments of American lubricants, gasoline, and other petroleum products if the wheels were to be kept going on the railways. This was necessary to sustain both German life and the American Army of Occupation.

Since I had the job of preparing the Western world for the shock that Germany must have vast supplies of food, I secured statements from General McNarney and General Clay, which we issued to the press. Fortunately, there had arrived in Berlin at this time a group of about thirty important American publishers. I spent an evening with them discussing world and former-enemy food situations. They were unanimous in their support of General Clay's program.

I saw little of Berlin, but I did take time out to visit Hitler's chancellery and the dugout where he committed suicide, as well as the yard where his body was cremated. I had talked with Hitler in his newly built chancellery in 1938, when he strutted at the height of his pomp. I had thought it a massive stone structure. I talked with him in his immense office, paneled with marble and its marble ceiling studded with chandeliers. I now found the stone and marble were only ersatz. Allied bombs had made great gaps in the ceilings, and the plaster of paris, ersatz marble, was hanging down on the twine which had been used to hold it together. The massive chandeliers were scattered over the floors, sparkling in the heaps of rubbish.

Having seen the results of Hitler's vengeance on the Poles and remembering the millions who had died in his rape of Europe and those who were still dying from the aftermath of famine, I, like the rest of the world, had no pity for his ending.

AUSTRIA

We arrived in Vienna on April 14, accompanied in our plane by Ambassador Robert D. Murphy and Supreme Court Justice Robert H. Jackson. We were met at the airport by General Mark W. Clark, Commander of U.S. Occupation Forces in Austria, and State Department representative Jack Earhardt; the Austrian Chancellor Leopold Figl; the Vice-Chancellor Dr. Adolf Schaerf; and Dr. Karl Gruber, the Minister of Foreign Affairs. There was a large American guard of honor with salutes.

General Clark took us at once to his office, where he made a detailed and most intelligent summary of the Austrian Government and its food situation. I had long been convinced that Clark was one of the greatest generals of the war, but as he spoke, my impression of him at once expanded to include the fact that he was also a great statesman.

The General's review of the economic situation of Austria was the same as it had been twenty-seven years before, when Austria came out of the grinding of the Versailles mill. Then and now, Austria was a country with a capital city of approximately two million people. Its trade was cut off and its agricultural area was unable to support Vienna for four months a year. I had protested at Versailles and took part in Austria's continued relief for more than three years after World War I. Therefore, I was not at all unfamiliar with the problems which lay ahead.[1]

For the most part, since the liberation in 1945 the Austrians had been fed by the American, British, and French occupying armies in their respective zones. The Russians, again, as in Germany, having

[1] After the Austrian Peace Treaty was signed in 1955 and all occupation armies withdrawn, including the Soviets, Austria made a remarkable economic recovery and is now fully self-supporting, with an improving standard of living.

seized the breadbasket of Austria as their zone, had plundered it of food. Now even the meager ration given the people was about to end. Shortly before our arrival, they had joined the other three armies in handing the feeding job over to UNRRA.

From General Clark's information and that of his able staff, we had no difficulty in arriving at the conclusion that in order to maintain a minimum 1,500-calorie supply we would need to recommend to the Combined Food Board a tentative program of 30,000 tons of cereals in May; 55,000 tons per month for June, July, and August; and 30,000 tons for September, a total of 225,000 tons. As the Austrians had some domestic meat and fat supplies and were trading with Hungary and Switzerland for more, we did not recommend any of these items from overseas. However, our cereal recommendation was the highest per capita of any country we visited.

Mr. Pate made his usual thorough investigation of the condition of the children. Parts of his report follow:

. . . the condition of children in Vienna and other Austrian industrial and urban communities is one of the most serious in Europe. The Austrians are doing their best to struggle with this problem. In spite of the general lack of food . . . the school administration in Vienna gives a daily soup to all, or approximately 90,000 children in the Vienna schools. However, this is a very meagre soup. . . . The total caloric content . . . runs from 250 to 300 calories. This should be contrasted against the meal served to school children . . . after World War I, which . . . had a caloric content of 625 calories.

The Swedes and the Swiss are sending some supplies [for children] . . . the Swedes are specializing on children from 3–6 years of age . . . a total of about 55,000 children in Vienna in this age category. As their supplies are limited, they are feeding only 20,000 children at a time, in rotation, for periods of two months. . . . The children who receive this meal benefit greatly by it, but the tragedy is that each child is benefiting from these meals only for a period of two months, and the program will cease in mid-Summer.

Each one of the 55,000 children in the 3–6 year category, and each one of the 90,000 school children above 6 years of age, should be receiving daily and for a longer period a balanced supplemental meal of at least 600 calories.

Various foreign relief organizations—American, Swedish, Swiss, Danish —are doing sporadic relief work for children in various parts of Austria. At a meeting of eight foreign agencies called during our stay in Vienna, it was agreed that the matter of real child needs in the country was actually covered [by] only somewhere between 10 and 20 percent of the volume of work that should be done for them to maintain normal health.

We urged the directors of UNRRA to inaugurate a full system of child feeding and rehabilitation. Nothing was done.

We took time off to look at the terrible destruction in the city of Vienna, including, to my mind, the most beautiful cathedral in all Europe—St. Stephen's.

General Clark gave a dinner to the Austrian Ministry and our mission, at which I sat next to Chancellor Figl. He described freely the events of previous years and his precarious situation with the Russian occupying forces. To illustrate the situation, he told me a parable.

American Secretary Byrnes, British Minister Bevin, and Russian Foreign Minister Molotov were in conference. Byrnes took out his plain silver cigarette case and passed it to each of the others. Bevin noticed there was an inscription on Byrnes' case and read it:

> To James F. Byrnes, Secretary of State
> From his devoted friends in the South Carolina Legislature.

Bevin produced his plain silver cigarette case and offered a cigarette to each of the others. Byrnes asked to see the case and read:

> To Ernest Bevin
> From his devoted friends of the Labour Party.

Molotov produced a jewel-studded gold case and helped himself alone. Bevin asked to see the case and read:

> To Prince Esterhazy
> From his devoted friends of the Vienna Jockey Club.

CHAPTER 26

HUNGARY, YUGOSLAVIA, GREECE, AND EGYPT

HUNGARY

We did not visit Hungary because we had received reports from our American officials there that the country had sufficient supplies to prevent starvation until the next harvest.

YUGOSLAVIA

We arrived in Belgrade on April 16. The American Chargé d'Affaires, Harold Schantz, arranged a meeting with the Embassy staff to check the data collected by them. We met with the UNRRA officials and with Yugoslav food officials. The Director of UNRRA was Michail A. Sergeichic, a Communist sent from Russia.

The Yugoslav Ministry gave a luncheon to our mission. There were speeches. One speaker stated that he would not be living but for my relief activities after the First World War.

We consolidated the information from our own files, the Embassy staff, reports of a former American and a foreign member of the UNRRA staff, and reliable American press representatives. From it we concluded that with the shipments already made by UNRRA

169

added to those en route, Yugoslavia had even more supplies than necessary to get her adults through until the harvest. Indeed, supplies were being distributed without any control, and we could buy American food freely in the shops.

Tito had created an army of 750,000 men which constituted a military link with the other Russian satellites from the Baltic to the Adriatic. Our Embassy officials informed us that cloth for the uniforms of this army were provided by UNRRA. Embassy officials informed us the supplies were proclaimed to be coming from Communist Russia. However, the record showed the United States was carrying, either directly or indirectly, 90 per cent of the burden.

Mr. Pate's report on the condition of children read in part:

> The combination of war and internal upheavals have left 120,000 complete war orphans and 450,000 half-orphans in Yugoslavia. . . . The mortality of children from 0–1 years is estimated at 21 per 100 for the entire country. For Belgrade alone, the figure is 25 per 100. . . .
>
> . . . out of approximately 40,000 children in public schools only 2,900 . . . of the children in Belgrade are receiving supplementary feeding.
>
> There has been a vast increase in tuberculosis in the children . . . the rate of increase . . . has been such that only a fraction of the children affected may be segregated in institutions.
>
> Out of a total population of 14,500,000 in Yugoslavia, it is estimated that at least 1,000,000 children seriously require supplementary feeding. Actually, in all parts of the country, the number helped by supplementary feeding amounts to only several tens of thousands.

Thus the Yugoslav situation was a sorry tale. The problem before our mission was: should we publicly expose this situation? We decided not to do so because it would dishearten the people over the world who were making great personal sacrifices to stem the famine. However, we stopped any further food shipments.

In a discussion with Secretary of State Byrnes before I left Washington, he had expressed to me great doubts with regard to UNRRA supplies to Yugoslavia. I cabled my New York office to inform the Secretary that he was right.

GREECE

We were met at the airport by Greek Prime Minister Panayotis Poulitsas; the Minister of Foreign Affairs, Constantin Tsaldaris; the Mayor of Athens; and the American Chargé d'Affaires, Karl L. Rankin. Hugh Gibson and I called on Archbishop Damaskinos, the Regent, who expressed high appreciation for the work of our mission.

We went into the usual conferences with the American Embassy staff, Minister of Agriculture John Theotokis, other Greek food officials, and Buell F. Maben, the UNRRA chief in Greece. We held a further conference with all the Ministers at dinner that evening.

Greece had been looted by two invasions during the war. The Germans, in their final retreat, had carried away livestock, farm implements, and railway rolling stock. They had blown up the bridges and destroyed the fishing fleet.

We listened to long accounts of the ineptitude of UNRRA from Greek food officials. In the early months their supply was in excess of need, but some months before our arrival, for some reason unknown to the UNRRA Director, Washington had reduced their supplies below the endurance level. At the time of our visit there were less than fifteen days' supplies for the towns and cities. The farmers' surplus had already been requisitioned.

Through Washington, we arranged a diversion to Greece of UNRRA cargoes that had been en route from Australia. We also secured a loan of some grain supplies from Egypt to meet the emergency.

Pate found it difficult to make a conclusive report on the condition of the children, for the Greek Government had been unable to restore fully its health services, and interior communications were almost totally demoralized. However, he reported that UNRRA had assigned 15,480 tons of food, especially for children, the previous month to a Greek philanthropic organization, which was thus able to give some service to child feeding.

We left Greece with the conviction that while there was a good deal of politics in motion, the people were nonetheless making an intelligent, devoted, and unified effort to reconstruct a nation which had been brought to nearly complete ruin.

While we were in Athens, a newspaper published a story to the effect that President Truman was recalling our mission.

EGYPT

Our prior information revealed that Egypt had sufficient food supplies to maintain her very low standard of living. However, we hoped to get a little rest and deliver a radio address to the United States, which Mr. Mason had arranged with an American broadcasting company. Our main objective was to learn from the Egyptian authorities the food situation in the other Arab states. Also, I needed to communicate with President Truman.

We arrived in Cairo on April 18. We were met at the airport by American Ambassador S. Pinkney Tuck, brother of Hallam Tuck of our mission. The Egyptian Government was represented by Ismail Teymour Pasha, the Court Chamberlain. The airport, built by the American Army during the war, was under the command of Major General Henry S. Aurand, who gave us military honors.

Gibson and I made formal calls upon King Farouk I; upon the Heir Apparent, Prince Mohammed Aly; upon Prime Minister Ismail Sidky Pasha; and upon Minister of Foreign Affairs Ahmed Lurfi el Sayed.

King Farouk gave our mission a luncheon at his palace, where the Egyptian Ministry was present. I was astonished to find the table decorated with hundreds of *Herbert Hoover* roses. The King explained to me that he was a rose fancier and had raised them in the palace gardens for many years.

The Egyptian Ministers at once showed great interest in our mission and stated that they wished to be of help. Following up their expressions, Ambassador Tuck arranged a meeting for us with the Ministers of Agriculture and Economics at the Embassy. The Minister of Agriculture pointed out that their harvest would arrive before those of Greece and Italy and, if they could have an assurance of a later replacement, they could make a loan of food to those countries. We so informed the Italians and Greeks, subsequently learning that under this arrangement the Egyptians had advanced about 40,000 tons of cereals. The Minister also informed us that he was sure Iraq possessed a considerable surplus of food which could be of possible assistance to India. He surveyed for us the food situation in Turkey and the other Arab states, which confirmed our conclusions that they were self-sufficient for the present emergency.

I took time off to visit the Egyptian Museum in Cairo and inspect the astounding recoveries from the tomb of King Tutankhamun. In a discussion with the Director of the Museum, he reminded me that, contrary to the universal opinion of archaeologists, I had one time stated that the world possessed iron tools prior to the so-called Bronze Age but that the iron tools had disappeared because of rust, which did not affect bronze. He confirmed my view by showing me some iron implements, made before the Bronze Age, which had been preserved because of enclosure within dry, rock constructions.

I called President Truman by transatlantic telephone and told him of a statement saying it was desired in Washington that I come home. I told him Secretary Byrnes wished us to go on into the Far East, where our visit was already being anticipated. He replied that it had been reported to him that I was tired out but that if I could stand it, he would be glad for me to continue. I ended the conversation at that point, with the usual amenities. In a few moments the telephone bell rang, and an English girl's voice exclaimed: "Sir, you have a right to three minutes on the phone. You have used only two minutes."

In my broadcast, I determined not only to survey the results of our mission to date but also to speak my mind on the problem of relief and rehabilitation of the stricken children and to give some urgent recommendations with regard to the further actions by which governments could be of more help. The important paragraphs of the address were:

. . . We have now surveyed the [famine] problem in seventeen nations, to determine the minimum amounts required to sustain life. We have in-

directly established the position of four others. It has been possible to arrive quickly at sufficiently accurate conclusions through the advance work
of my colleagues, the officials of our Government and of the various nations visited and those of the various relief organizations. . . .

. . . The dimensions of the European part of the world food crisis as a
whole can be quickly summed up. There are about 300 million people on
the Continent of Europe from the Russian frontier to the English Channel. A few small countries on the Continent, comprising about 40 million
people, have enough food to last until the next harvest. Of the other nations, about one-third of the remainder are farmers who are [usually] able
largely to feed themselves. Thus, there are over 170 million people, mostly
in towns and cities, of whom perhaps less than 10 per cent can support
themselves from black markets and country relatives. The final remainder,
of 150 million, mostly the lower-income groups, must have overseas supplies during the next . . . [five] months if widespread famine is to be
prevented.

Hunger has placed three words every hour of the day on the tongues
of these 150 millions of people. The first is "bread." Bread has a reality as
the symbol of life as never before in history. To reduce the bread ration
is a symbol of calamity. It is now the symbol of the life of nations. The
second word is "fats," for which there is an insatiable craving and physical
need. The third word is "calories." That is the common denominator.
Calories are only a partial yardstick of food, but that word has become
everywhere the grim measure of the steps along the road from plenty to
hunger and to starvation. Europe has become a vast involuntary experimental laboratory as to different levels of calories which the population
are to have in their rations.

Do not forget that the caloric level of America is an average of about
3,200 per person per day. Britain has about 2,800. Experts say an average
level of 2,200 calories is the minimum at which public health and progress
can be maintained in a nation. There are thirteen countries where the city
populations have [at present] an average intake of less than 1,900 calories.
Of these, six countries are at or below the 1,500 caloric level. There are
millions of people below 1,000 calories. Somewhere down these various
levels starvation begins. And its immediate expression is the disease rate
in children and in death rates of the infants and the old people. . . .

To provide this minimum to the next harvest, there must be loaded
on ships for the Continent during each of the four months from the
first of April to the end of July a total of at least 5,300,000 tons of cereals,

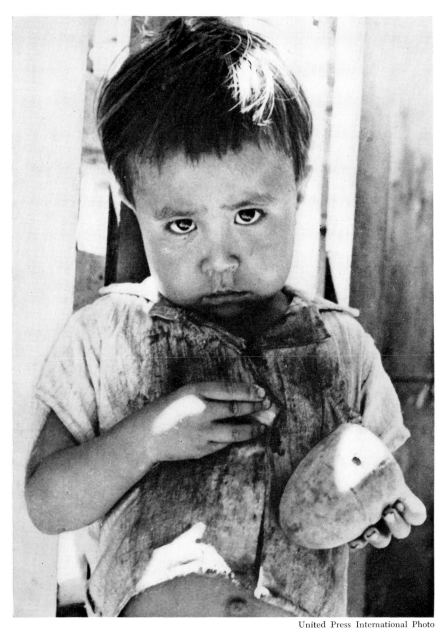

A shy, badly undernourished youngster waiting for food in Honduras.

Brightly clad Indian children enjoying a treat in Guatemala.

Three little Italian boys passing around a bottle of free milk from America.

A five-year-old girl in Honduras drinking milk served by UNICEF.

300,000 tons of fats, and an additional 100,000 tons of special food is urgently needed to restore subnormal children.

A few days ago I . . . [stated as] a rough estimate that there are 20 million subnormal or diseased children on the Continent. My able and experienced colleague, Maurice Pate, who has gone to the bottom of this . . . problem throughout Europe, insists that my estimate was too low. He points out that there are probably 11 millions of orphans and half-orphans alone. He also points out that the mortality among children under two is already over 25 per cent per annum in many cities. The reconstruction of the children is more precious than factories or bridges. They will determine the good or evil future of Europe.

The food supplied by UNRRA to the nations they serve has been an untold blessing. For various reasons, they do not cover much over 25 per cent of the total food problems of the Continent. . . .

After the most drastic scaling down, as closely as we can give a tentative estimate now, the total requirements of cereals alone for Europe and Asia during the next four months is a minimum of about 11 million tons. And, in addition, as much fats as can be secured.

As against this need, the grim fact is that in normal commercial supplies there is not much over 6 million tons available. The problem before us, if we would preserve millions of lives, is to make up this gap of 5 million tons of cereals. I believe this could be done by self-denial and cooperation of the people of the better-supplied nations in the world. There are seven substantial sources where these supplies can possibly come from. They are Canada, the United States, Britain, the Argentine, Russia, Australia and Siam.

To narrow this 5 million ton gap between supply and the minimum need to save life, I have six suggestions. I shall state them bluntly. With some experience in these matters, I say this is the only way by which millions of lives can be saved at this late date. At once let me say that these proposals are only my personal views. It is my duty to exhaust every possibility of saving these people. If there is criticism of the proposals, it should be directed to me alone. My suggestions are:

First: Our [American] Government has asked our people to voluntarily reduce their consumption of wheat products by 40 per cent and fats by 20 per cent. My proposal is that our Government do as they did during the war and acquire enough of our wheat and its products to assure an export to the famine areas of an average of 1,100,000 tons per month during the months of April, May, June and July. . . .

It will make the conservation campaign effective beyond any doubt. We need similar action as to fats. In making these sacrifices of bread and fats, the American people have a right to expect other nations also to cooperate to the full.

Second: By the American program above, the American consumption of wheat products will be reduced to an equivalent of about 200 grams per person per day in European terms. European nations need more wheat bread than we do because they have less substitutes or supplemental food. I propose that all nations in Europe who now exceed a cereal ration equal to 300 grams of bread per person per day, should reduce it to 300 grams. This would, I know, be a burden to such countries as Britain, Holland, Denmark and Yugoslavia.

Third: I suggest to the British that as they are carrying about a million tons of breadstuffs in their pipeline and stocks, instead of one-half this amount before the war, they could release half a million tons to the starving.

Fourth: My next suggestion is to the Latin-American States. The largest part of the Argentine exports are going to Chile, Brazil and other neighboring countries. Other Latin-American States, such as Cuba and Mexico, are drawing large amounts of wheat and flour from the United States and Canada. If the United States, Canada and the Argentine would reduce these exports by 40 per cent during the next four months, and if these Latin-American States would cooperate by accepting this reduction, it would furnish most valuable assistance. Their sacrifice would be no greater than we are asking from the United States. It would be a translation into action of the eloquent appeal of His Holiness, Pope Pius XII, a few days ago.

Fifth: My next proposal is in respect to Russia. At the request of the Soviet Government, I organized and directed the relief of the great Russian famine of . . . [1921]–1923. America made a gift of . . . [huge amounts] of food and overcame that famine. The Soviet Government expressed its warm appreciation to myself and my colleagues. I learned at that time of the sacrifice which millions of Russians made for their more helpless neighbors. I know full well the suffering of her people during this war. I am advised, however, that their food situation has somewhat improved since the war. She has been able to make available a generous supply of about 75,000 tons of grain per month to France. If her contribution to the general pool could be raised to 300,000 tons per month for each of the four months of the crisis, it would be a great human service.

By these methods, over 90 per cent of the gap between supply and minimum need of the famine areas would be met.

Sixth: I suggest that priority in supplies be given to the smaller liberated nations. They have suffered most. Their domestic resources are more limited than others. They comprise only 15 per cent of the whole European problem. . . .

The burden will be very heavy upon the United States and we cannot do more. Europe and other countries must look to the other sources for the balance.

The current world crisis is unique among all crises in history. This crisis has a definite terminal date. That date is the arrival of the next harvest. It is, therefore, a short pull.

If every source of supplies will do its utmost, we can pull the world through this most dangerous crisis. The saving of these human lives is far more than an economic necessity to the recovery of the world. It is more than the only path to order, to stability and to peace. Such action marks the return of the lamp of compassion to the world. And that is a part of the moral and spiritual reconstruction of the world.[1]

[1] *Addresses Upon the American Road, 1945–1948,* pp. 193–98.

CHAPTER 27

IRAQ, INDIA, THAILAND, AND THE PHILIPPINES

IRAQ

Because of the information we had obtained in Cairo, we flew to Bagdad on April 21, circling over Jerusalem en route for it was Easter Sunday. Along the way we looked down from the air at the ancient irrigation works in the Tigris and Euphrates Valleys. The crew flew our plane a thousand feet above what was now a desert, and the marks of the old irrigation canals were still plainly visible; the works had been destroyed by the Mongols six hundred years before. The area was said to have supported twelve million people. Some years before our visit a group of able British engineers had examined these works and reported that the ancient fertility could be restored. I have since often urged that consideration be given to the settlement in this area of the Arab refugees from Palestine as a solution to this sad problem of many years' standing.

The American Chargé d'Affaires, James S. Moose, Jr., had arranged a meeting with the Embassy staff to compare their information with that we had already obtained. They confirmed that Iraq had a substantial supply of food for export.

Mr. Gibson and I called upon Prime Minister Hamdi Al-Pachachi. He stated that Iraq had about 400,000 tons of surplus dates and grain which she would be glad to export to India if paid a reasonable price but that the Indian Government did not seem to be interested and that I could fix the price. We took up this important discovery when we arrived in New Delhi.

INDIA

We arrived at Karachi on April 22. In the morning a distinguished official called on us in behalf of the Governor of the Northwest Provinces, Sir H. Ramaswami Mudaliar. We learned from him that the Governor estimated that three provinces had a surplus of about 600,000 tons of grain.

At Karachi we were met by Dr. Binay Ranjan Sen, a distinguished Indian Civil Service official, representing the Indian Food Minister at New Delhi, who accompanied us during our whole stay in India. Dr. Sen was a man of fine integrity, trained in his profession, and a most agreeable companion. In later years he rose to high positions, and I have been proud of his continuing friendship.

The Viceroy and Governor-General of India, Lord Wavell, generously insisted upon putting up our whole mission in the luxurious viceroy's palace. The night of our arrival, Lord Wavell gave a dinner for a large number of dignitaries, including Sir Robert H. Hutchings, Secretary of the Indian Government's Food Department, and Sir J. P. Srivastava, who was food head in the Nationalist Government.

The American Commissioner to India arranged a meeting for us with the American officials to review the situation. It did not take long for us to find that India's deep political problems affected our mission. She was in the white heat of the Nationalist independence movement against the British regime. The friction between the Moslems and the Hindus also entered into all our problems. The British were still in control of the Government, but seemed numb from the forces arising around them.

Our difficulties loomed quickly. Some months previously, there had been sent to Washington a delegation of Nationalist leaders who claimed that they were promised 4,000,000 tons of cereals and 500,000 tons of other foods from the United States by our State Department. This had been announced to the Indian press prior to our arrival.

There was no such record in the files of the Combined Food Board. Even if someone in the State Department had made the commitment, this was far beyond India's minimum needs, and would have starved hundreds of thousands of other people.

The Moslem League of the Northwest Provinces was willing to sell its surplus to the Nationalists, but I was informed by the British that the Nationalists were refusing to buy it until they had effected some political ends.

I had a conference with Pandit Jawaharlal Nehru, the Nationalist leader, who insisted that they had already arranged matters with the State Department. A British official on the Viceroy's staff suggested that if I invited Mohandas K. Gandhi to call and explained the situation to him, he might be helpful in working out the situation. Gandhi responded to my invitation. He was most anxious over the creeping famine. He willingly agreed to use his influence with the other Nationalist leaders to settle the conflict over the supplies from the Northwest Provinces.

My meeting with Gandhi had some interesting details. He was clad in his usual loincloth and carried what was then known as a "dollar" watch. I showed him the "dollar" watch I carried and said they were a mark of our common humility. Gandhi was instrumental in obtaining the surplus grain of the Northwest Provinces.

Our next problem was to activate the Indian Government to purchase the Iraqi surplus of 400,000 tons. After we left India, we were informed that the Indian officials had arranged this satisfactorily.

The second great source of Indian supplies was Australia, where at this time there were about one million tons of wheat. The Australians, who were represented on the Cereals Committee of the Combined Food Board, were shipping wheat to South Africa, Great Britain, and, in small quantity, to India. I communicated with the Australian food authorities through the British officials in Delhi, pointing out the folly of shipping American food all the way from the Atlantic Seaboard through the Mediterranean to India while Australian food was going on the same route back to Europe. The Australians were most co-operative.

India was normally greatly dependent upon rice supplies from

Burma and Thailand. The British officials informed us that there was little hope for supplies from Burma, as the Japanese had plundered that country of both rice and work animals. Further, the country was in political chaos from Communist infiltration. Regarding Thailand, the officials said that nation had a surplus of about one million tons of rice remaining from the previous harvest of November and December, 1945. We undertook to visit the country and see what we could do in this matter.

In an effort to get the Indian Ocean supplies mobilized, I proposed to the Viceroy that he lead in the creation of an Indian Ocean Food Committee to administer the surplus food of each country of the area; that this committee comprise representatives of India, Iraq, the Malay States, Thailand, and Australia; and that the chairman have powers over food import and sea transportation. I stated that I believed we could secure approval of such a committee from the Combined Food Board. I proposed that they make no assignments in that area without the approval of this new committee. Lord Wavell was at first enthusiastic, but soon ran into difficulties with the Nationalists. In fact, the Viceroy no longer had command in India and was indeed a frustrated man.

We flew to Bombay on April 24, 1946. We were lodged in Government House by the Governor, Sir David Colville. The palace was not air-conditioned.

Dr. FitzGerald and I went at once into session with the Nationalist Cabinet, which in reality governed the Province. They made an intelligent presentation of their grave situation. The British Governor, at my suggestion, invited the Ministry to dinner in order to honor our mission. He had never met them before.

We decided to visit one of the most acute famine areas so that we might see the problem on the spot, confer with the local officials, and be able to make a more intelligent report to the rest of the world on India's needs. On April 25, we flew to Bangalore, in Mysore, where the famine was at its worst. We were lodged in the guest house of the Maharaja. Among delegations which called upon us was one from the Nationalist Ministry of Madras, headed by Sir S. V. Ramamurthi and accompanied by the British Governor of the Province, Sir Henry Knight. The Nationalist leader demanded to know whether the United States was going to deliver "the four million tons of wheat promised by your government." I explained that there could not have been any such undertaking by the responsible departments in Washington, because if there was to be an equitable distribution of our supplies, there was no such quantity available. I stated that most of the supplies needed by India were available in the Indian Ocean area, that we were endeavoring to co-ordinate them, and that I believed there would be help from the United States when these other resources were exhausted. He became very insulting to the American people, and I was compelled to make some "remarks" and remind him that it was my country. The Madras papers were subsequently venomous about my dark past life, and published cartoons of dying Indian people amid gluttonous American capitalists.

On April 26, we spent a long and unpleasant day motoring through village after village and town after town, where we made constant inquiry into the stocks of food and watched the rations being issued. It was a heartbreaking experience. Already the ration in some places was as low as 1,000 calories per person per diem. Without increased imports of food, death would sweep the area.

To urge aid from Australia, I had made a radio address from Bombay on April 24 which was broadcast to the Australians on short wave—I was informed that it was in part rebroadcast. It represents a partial appraisal of the situation in India. The more important of its paragraphs were:

I am glad to have the opportunity of broadcasting to India and particularly to Australia. . . . And in so doing, I recall many happy years spent in Australia and in abiding admiration for her people and her institutions which I received from those happy times.

This acute phase of the world crisis in food will continue until the August-September harvest in the Northern Hemisphere. . . .

I then described the world-wide statistical situation, the gap in world supplies, and continued with the special situation in India:

The enormity of the Indian problem can be shortly expressed. The total population of the provinces of India and Ceylon normally dependent upon imports, plus those provinces affected by the great drought, is about 240,000,000. Even after deducting certain localities which are self-supporting, other localities less affected, and the farmers who supply themselves, the number in jeopardy of life runs into tens of millions. Unless there can be a large and constant flow of overseas food, the loss of life will mount to numbers too horrible to contemplate. Due to able, careful administration, and drastic rationing, there is no stark starvation of the famine type in India yet. This is a job of prevention. Every ton of food received will lessen the loss of life from the gigantic danger which impends. . . .

. . . many of the children and the aged will drop by the wayside through increased disease which is always the result of lowered vitality. However, the overseas supply necessary to maintain even this level of food is not yet in sight.

I have no right to address the Australian people on what further measures they could take to aid in this situation. But the critical jeopardy of millions of lives should be my justification.

I pointed out that supplies from the next American harvest could not arrive in India for four months and said:

. . . It would be an immense help if delivery of Australian supplies could be . . . [increased] to cover these critical months.

And I repeated two paragraphs from former addresses:

. . . This food crisis has a definite terminal date. That date is the arrival of the next harvest in the Northern Hemisphere. It is, therefore, a short, hard pull.

If every supplying country will do its utmost, and if we can have full cooperation everywhere, we can pull the world through these most dangerous months. The saving of these human lives is far more than an economic necessity to the recovery of the world. It is more than the only path to order, to stability, and to peace. Such action marks the re-lighting of the lamp of compassion on the earth. And that is a part of the normal and spiritual reconstruction of the world.[1]

[1] *Addresses Upon the American Road, 1945–1948,* pp. 199–202.

The Indian harvest did not come in until October or November, but part of their needed supplies could be shipped from the new North American crops of June–August and thus relieve the strains elsewhere.

Dr. FitzGerald and I put together all of our ascertainable facts, including the possibility of delivering supplies to India during October from the early American harvest. Our final tentative recommendation, conditional upon India's securing the supplies available in the Indian Ocean area, was that the United States should ship about 1,900,000 tons of cereals to that country. We concluded that if our recommendations concerning other sources were acted upon by the Indian authorities, there would be no mass starvation.

On April 26, from Bangalore, I summed up the food situation in a statement to the American press. I said:

Indian Provinces containing about 230,000,000 people are involved in food difficulties . . . but figures are a poor vehicle with which to convey the extent of the danger and the human misery involved.

The causes of her food difficulties come from three directions:

First, India normally imports considerable food supplies, especially from Burma. This source has been largely curtailed for this year.

Second, South India has suffered from a disastrous drought; and

Third, the standard of living of the great mass of Indian people has always been low and a marginal group has always been on the borderline of what we in America would regard as starvation.

After making all of the statistical deductions by way of certain local parts of the Provinces which are self-supporting, other localities less affected, the farmers who supply themselves, the remaining people in jeopardy of life runs into tens of millions unless they obtain additional food from outside the short areas. . . .

I then spoke of the drastic rationing already in progress in certain areas, where the ration had been reduced to 1,400 calories and would get worse, and continued:

[We] have today motored through parched districts in Mysore where even this ration has begun to break down. About two-thirds of the cereal ration is [from] less nutritious ground nuts and cattle food.

. . . tragedy lies in the fact that large districts cannot, without outside supplies, maintain even the present reduced ration for more than 30 to 90 days. Many districts are on the edge of the precipice. It is impossible to hazard what the death rate might be if there were no imports into the deficit areas. It would be too terrible to contemplate. Every ton of food imported into these areas will lessen the loss of life.

I then reviewed the amounts needed and the Indian Ocean sources of supplies and continued:

. . . There needs to be more coordination of effort over the whole Indian Ocean area. When all this has been done, a large part of the solution must come from the Western Hemisphere.

The situation of these stricken people must appeal to every humane person in the world. It is not insoluble. But cooperation and devotion from every quarter is essential. The American people will stretch every resource to help.[2]

THAILAND

As Thailand was of vital importance as a source of rice to India and the Philippines, we flew to Bangkok on April 27. At the airport a Siamese band played the American and Thailand national anthems beautifully.

The American Chargé d'Affaires Charles W. Yost arranged a conference with King Ananda Mahidol; Premier Nai Pridi Phanomyong; Minister of Foreign Affairs Nai Direk Chaiyanam; the Minister of Agriculture, Nai Thawee Bunyaket; Prince Wiwatchai Chaiyan, Financial Adviser; Prince Wan Waithayakorn, Foreign Affairs Adviser; and other officials. They were greatly interested in the progress of our mission and at once assured us of their co-operation.

During the three years of Japanese occupation, Thailand had been looted of her railway rolling stock, her trucks, her carts, and hundreds of thousands of her work buffalo, which had been eaten by the Japanese. The Japanese Army had also looted almost all of the precious

[2] *Ibid.*, pp. 203–205.

objects in the kingdom, but since that army had to surrender on the spot, the Thais recovered most of the loot. They still held a large number of Japanese war prisoners, whom they had put to work cleaning things up.

From our meetings with American, British, and Thai authorities, we were soon to find several difficulties with regard to moving the rice. Because of a lack of transportation, only part of it could get to the seaboard. Little had been done to restore the railways. Moreover, Thailand's currency had been inflated by the Japanese until it was valueless, and Thai farmers would not give up their rice except for sound money—or goods, of which Thailand had very little. And besides, the British had demanded the rice surplus for "reparations." The result was that upon our arrival in Bangkok five months after the harvest, less than 190,000 tons of rice had been exported.

I cannot say that our mission solved all these problems, but at least we got all parties into joint sessions. The British officials in India agreed to buy the rice, and for Indian rupees, which were still in good standing in Thailand. But this was not the end of the trouble. The British Treasury officials in London still insisted that some rice must be given for "reparations." In the end, about half the Thai surplus was shipped out, mainly to India and the Malay States. We suggested that we would try to secure army trucks from the Philippines in exchange for some of the rice.

Pate reported that the children of Thailand were in good condition—by Asiatic standards. The people were well fed, and their women's cheery little bursts into song, day and night, were a relief from the gloom of India.

THE PHILIPPINES

We arrived in Manila on April 28 and were met at the airport by U.S. High Commissioner Paul V. McNutt and an old hand of the Commission for Relief in Belgium, Admiral Gilchrist B. Stockton.

On the morning of the twenty-ninth, Commissioner McNutt assembled a meeting of Philippine and American food authorities. By telegram, we had laid the groundwork for exchange of army trucks to Thailand for rice. Commissioner McNutt completed this transaction and made the same trade to Indochina for rice.

In the meantime, Dr. FitzGerald had discovered substantial stocks of rice in Northern Luzon, stored by speculators for future sales at famine prices. We included these stocks in our calculation of future needs. Our recommendation to the Combined Food Board was that a total of 60,000 tons of grain from overseas would be sufficient during the period until the next harvest, and possibly even this amount would prove to be unnecessary.

CHAPTER 28

CHINA, KOREA, JAPAN, AND OUR RETURN HOME

CHINA

We arrived in Shanghai on April 30, 1946. We were met by Dr. T. V. Soong of the Chinese Ministry; the American Consul General, Monnett B. Davis; and Lieutenant General Alvan C. Gillem, Commander of the American forces remaining in China. Since I had practiced my profession in China for three years and had dealt with Chinese problems for thirteen years as an American official, I was somewhat informed on the problems in China.

On arriving at our hotel, Consul General Davis informed me that there was gigantic corruption going on in UNRRA, which was supposed to be relieving famine in China. About 200,000 tons of cereals had been sold to speculators. And there were dreadful reports of famine. I set our staff to investigate the Consul General's statement and on confirmation jointly with him notified the State Department. The State Department advised Mr. Fiorello LaGuardia, recently made Director General of UNRRA. Mr. LaGuardia investigated, then discharged many of the UNRRA staff members in China—both Chinese and American. He recovered most of the food.

In the meantime, the members of our mission and I went into session with the Chinese Ministers of Food and Agriculture. Also present were Colonel R. L. Harrison, who had been sent by the Combined Food Board to investigate the Chinese needs, and Colonel

Paul E. Howe, a nutrition expert who accompanied him. Their reports were an appalling recitation of mass starvation, with only a trickle of overseas food reaching the famine districts. The major physical obstacle was the lack of equipment on the rivers and the railways—a hangover from the Japanese plunder of Central China.

General Gillem provided a meeting for our mission with the top American military officers. They gave us an extensive review of the military, political, and economic situations.

President Chiang Kai-shek had invited us to visit him at Nanking. On May 3, Gibson, FitzGerald, Mason, and I flew there, leaving our colleagues to explore food matters further with officials in Shanghai. At Nanking, General George C. Marshall (then the special envoy of President Truman) gave us full information on the political and food situations as he saw them.

The Chinese Minister of Foreign Affairs, Dr. Wang Shih-chieh, provided a meeting for us with most of Chiang Kai-shek's Cabinet. We called upon President Chiang Kai-shek and Madame Chiang. The President gave us an account of the situation in China regarding the transportation of food and also the military outlook.

General Marshall was endeavoring to amalgamate the Communist Government in the North under Mao Tse-tung with the Nationalist Government in the South under Chiang Kai-shek. He assured us that there was no greater difference between what he called the "agrarian liberals" of the North and the "conservatives" of the South than there was between the Republican and Democratic political parties at home. Although it was no part of my mission, my conscience would not permit me to appear even tacitly to agree with the General. Nor could Mr. Gibson. We observed to him that these two parties could no more be mixed than oil with water.

The General was making an effort to get the Yangtze River traffic re-established in order to reach the most acute famine areas. Dr. FitzGerald and I approved a tentative program of 200,000 tons a month (after the restoration of the stolen food), although it was improbable that there was sufficient transportation for these supplies to reach the famine spots. With a feeling of helplessness that such an amount of supplies would not reach the starving in the face of a wall of difficulties, I issued a statement to the press from Shanghai on May 3:

The food need of China is enormous. They have had eight years' war destruction and agricultural degeneration, to which both drought and flood have now been added. There are no adequate data upon which to accurately compute the tonnage of [food] needs. In any event, they are greater than the transportation facilities into the interior [can handle]. These will be fully taxed to distribute 200,000 tons of food a month during the critical months from May to September.

With the absence of all adequate statistical services . . . it is impossible to compute the numbers of people in a critical condition, but no doubt they run into millions, as several Provinces are involved.

Both Chinese and foreign authorities report that some death from starvation is in progress in interior Provinces and still more from lowered resistance to epidemics. The death of whole villages over wide areas has not yet taken place, but will no doubt occur within a few weeks unless supplies have reached the deficit spots.[1]

On May 3, we had a final meeting in Shanghai with Consul General Davis and the American military leaders; but depression from the UNRRA episode and the lack of understanding by General Marshall haunted everyone's mind. The only encouraging note was a report from Nanking that the American Navy had succeeded in getting a landing craft loaded with food up the Yangtze rapids and into the starving area.

KOREA

We arrived in Seoul at noon on May 4 and were met by Lieutenant General John R. Hodge, in command of the American forces. The Government of Korea had been divided between American and Russian military control. I was somewhat familiar with the country, for I had operated mines there in my engineering days.

At our request from Shanghai, General Hodge had arranged a

[1] *Addresses Upon the American Road, 1945–1948*, p. 207.

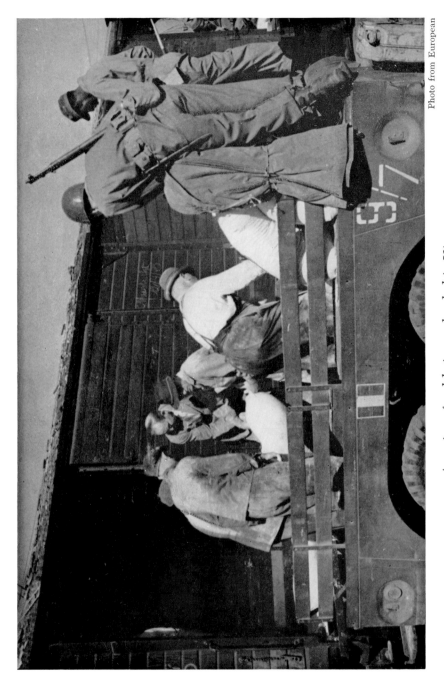

American food being unloaded in Vienna.

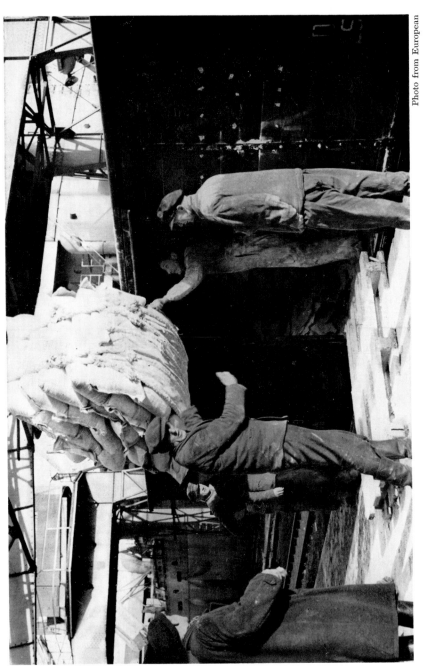

Unloading U.S. supplies to Germany at Bremerhaven.

Food for needy Greek children being unloaded from an American ship.

A refugee camp, with plenty of occupants and their belongings, in France.

meeting for us with all food officials in South Korea, both Korean and American. He also arranged a meeting of fifty or sixty Korean leaders and his military staff. We received quick and intelligent answers to our questions. The food and other problems revolved around the activities of the Communists in North Korea, with their constant threat of invasion of South Korea. A further difficulty was that Korea's normal supply of fertilizers came from prewar factories located in the Communist area. The Communists refused to comply with their agreements to furnish these fertilizers to South Korea.

Dr. FitzGerald came up with a tentative program of imports of about 110,000 tons' total for the five months until the harvest, which we recommended to the Combined Food Board. With this supply, there was no starvation in Korea.

JAPAN

We landed at the Tokyo airport on May 5. We were a day earlier than was expected, and General Douglas MacArthur was away from Tokyo. But he sent Major General William F. Marquat, with a full guard of honor, to welcome us. We were lodged at the old American Embassy, which had now been restored.

General MacArthur was an old and devoted friend of mine from the World War I days, and during my term as President, I had appointed him Chief of Staff, then the highest position in the U.S. Army. I had visited Japan often during my engineering days en route to China, and while in the White House, I had need to deal with the Japanese invasions of China.

We went into session with General MacArthur's food and economic officials, and they presented us with accurate statements of the entire food and economic situation. We had expected that there would be considerable need for food to carry Japan through until the harvest, but we were not prepared for the shock we received: the stocks of food in that country of more than 75,000,000 people would supply about 700 calories per diem per person during the remaining months until the harvest. Even worse, we learned that the harvest might supply only one-half of Japan's needs for the following year.

Before the war, the Japanese fishing fleets in the Pacific had provided a major source of food supply, but these had been largely lost during the war and their fishing grounds reduced to a fraction of the area covered in normal times. At one time, early in the war, the Japanese had the food reserves of Manchuria, Thailand, Indochina, Malaya, and the Dutch East Indies to fall back on. Now all these sources were either dried up or completely lost to them.

Therefore, we were confronted with mass starvation on a gigantic scale. If order was to be preserved and wholesale death prevented, there was only one course of action possible. We must undertake huge imports from overseas through the Combined Food Board. We could only hope that the conservation measures of the American people would exceed our estimates and that we could increase shipments to the common pool from Latin-American countries beyond our previous estimates. Our tentative recommendations to Washington for Japan were for the following minimum program, mostly of cereals:

May	50,000 tons
June	250,000
July	270,000
August	200,000
September	100,000
Total	870,000 tons

Mr. Pate had made an investigation of the condition of Japanese children. I urged General MacArthur to agree to a much more extensive program of rehabilitation of subnormal children, and we included special supplies in our tentative program for this purpose. Extensive child feeding in the schools and canteens was ordered by the General.

Chiang Kai-shek had stated to me that there was in Manchuria an enormous surplus of food given to Russia under the Yalta Agreement. He suggested that the American Government, because of its friendship with Stalin, could obtain the release of some of this surplus for Korea, China, and Japan. I had no faith in any American influence in the matter; however, I asked General MacArthur's aides whether they could get the facts from Japanese records concerning the amount of food surplus in Manchuria at the time of its surrender in 1945. They produced evidence that in the previous August, Manchuria had an exportable surplus of about three million tons of wheat, millet, beans, bean cake, and soya oil. But the Russians refused to give up one iota of these supplies.

One of our tasks was to prepare the American people for the shock of such a high diversion of food to Japan. I secured from General MacArthur a statement of the facts and followed it with my own brief statement, which summarized the situation as follows:

Japan must have some food imports. Without them, all Japan will be on a ration little better than that which the Germans gave to the Buchenwald and Belsen concentration camps. It is an impossible concept that the American flag fly over such a situation. Aside from any Christian spirit, food imports are required if the American boys here are not to be endangered by disorders and not involved in the sweep of epidemics that are inevitable from starvation. Moreover, unless there are food imports, the people will not have the stamina to work upon reconstruction or in the fields for the next crop.

. . . The whole situation would be greatly helped if Russia would release to China and Korea a part of the foodstuffs they have secured in Manchuria.[2]

I may well add here that General MacArthur was not only the outstanding general in the war, but also an outstanding statesman, as was proved so well in his administration of Japan. When he marched down their streets with his victorious army, the Japanese people turned their faces and spat at the walls, but when he marched the troops down the streets at his departure, they were in tears.

[2] *Ibid.,* p. 208.

CHAPTER 29

WE REPORT TO PRESIDENT TRUMAN
AND TO THE AMERICAN PEOPLE

En route from Japan to San Francisco, we prepared a draft of our report to President Truman on the world situation. This did not include Latin America, which we planned to visit later. I also prepared an address to the American people. Our report to the President, dated May 13, 1946, was necessarily factual and statistical. It contained very little description of the human side of the tragedy which we had witnessed:

DEAR MR. PRESIDENT:

We have completed your instructions to survey the principal nations affected by food shortages which have resulted, or may result in widespread famine; to evaluate the minimum needs of those areas until the next harvest; and to discover such additional food resources as possible. In accordance with your instructions, we have also presented the American point of view on the food problem to these nations and the interest and understanding of our people in their plight. Finally, we have constantly advised American officials and the American public as to the situation as we found it.

We have traveled some 35,000 miles, visited twenty-two countries which have a deficiency of food, and informed ourselves of the situation in several others. The only country of large reported deficiency we did not visit was the Union of South Africa. We visited five self-sufficient or surplus countries and informed ourselves of the situation in other consequential surplus nations.

The dominant need of the world in this crisis is cereals, particularly wheat and rice. There is great need of fats and special food for children, but as cereals can furnish 85 per cent of an emergency diet, we considered cereal requirements were the first concern, and the best indicator. If a foundation of bread can be assured, and as much fats and children's food as possible, mass starvation can be prevented.

At the time of our departure, the Combined Food Board's estimate of the available cereal supplies from surplus countries showed a deficit as compared with stated requirements of 11,000,000 tons, or 43 per cent.

REQUIREMENTS

. . . The . . . [following] programs represent a considerable reduction from the hitherto stated requirements of the various nations. The amounts have in most cases been agreed upon by their governments. In the case of China, we regret to say our program is less than minimum need but is all, or more, than can be transported inland to the famine areas.

The totals are:

Europe	8,390,000 tons
Latin America	1,000,000
South Africa and New Zealand	198,000
Middle East	100,000
Indian Ocean area	2,886,000
Pacific Ocean area	1,910,000
Total	14,484,000 tons

Of course, every country would be better off if more could be furnished.

SUPPLIES

We have found some increases in supplies possible during the crisis through development of certain new sources of supply; through additional loans of cereals from early-crop countries which may not themselves have annual surpluses; through substitution of other cereals for wheat and rice; and as a result of conservation up to this time.

Our estimates (Table II) of Probable Supplies as of May 1st to September 30th are:

From
United States	4,220,000 tons
Canada	2,300,000
Australia	992,000
United Kingdom	200,000
The Argentine	2,375,000
Brazil	200,000
Other Western Hemisphere states	40,000
Burma	75,000
Siam [Thailand]	195,000
Russia to France	300,000
Total	10,897,000 tons

Therefore the gap in supplies between May 1st and September 30th can be reduced to about 3,600,000 tons, as against an 11,000,000 tons gap in the earlier appraisals.

In addition to the above supplies there is a "possible" about 1,500,000 tons more . . . [to be had].

We are confident that if until the end of August, there can be further vigorous conservation in surplus countries, mainly wheats and fats, and more energetic cooperation between nations, the remaining deficit can be largely overcome. The cooperation of Russia and the Latin-American states would greatly aid in meeting the problem. If mass starvation is to be prevented it will require constant effort.

It is of interest to note that the quantities which are provided by UNRRA as charity comprise about 20 per cent of the world's cereal needs, whereas nations representing 80 per cent are being financed by the importing countries themselves. But the need in these latter is no less urgent.

You will recognize that these statements are estimates. They, however, comprise a reasonable basis upon which to formulate policies.

We wish to express our especial appreciation of the unfailing aid and courtesy of the Secretaries of Agriculture, State and War, and the American officials abroad. We are also deeply indebted to Generals George and

Saville of the Air Transport Command, their efficient crews, and for their provisions for our comfort and safety.[1]

Yours faithfully,
HERBERT HOOVER
D. A. FITZGERALD
HUGH GIBSON
W. HALLAM TUCK
PERRIN C. GALPIN
MAURICE PATE

On May 17, 1946, at Chicago, I gave my report to the American people over a nation-wide broadcast. I was introduced by Secretary Anderson in glowing terms. At that time we were still in the midst of a hungry world, a long three months away from the coming harvest. I said:

This is my report to the American people upon the world famine situation [in 25 countries]. Three weeks ago I broadcasted from Cairo our report upon the situation in Europe. Since then we have examined the food problems in Egypt, Iraq, India, Siam, the Philippines, China, Korea and Japan, thus compassing most of Asia. . . .

Along the 35,000 miles we have traveled, I have seen with my own eyes the grimmest spectre of famine in all the history of the world.

Of the Four Horsemen of the Apocalypse, the one named War has gone —at least for a while. But Famine, Pestilence and Death are still charging over the earth. And the modern world has added four more to this evil brigade. Their names are Destruction, Drought, Fear and Revolution. This crisis is not alone due to war destruction of agriculture. On the top of that calamity has been piled drought in the Mediterranean, drought in India, drought in China and partial drought in South Africa and the Argentine. Never have so many evil Horsemen come all at one time.

[Despite all we have done, Hunger still threatens] . . . the homes of more than 800,000,000 people—over one-third of the people of the earth. Hunger is a silent visitor who comes like a shadow. He sits beside every anxious mother three times each day. He brings not alone suffering and sorrow, but fear and terror. He carries disorder and the paralysis of government, and even its downfall. He is more destructive than armies, not

[1] *Addresses Upon the American Road, 1945–1948,* pp. 210–13.

only in human life but in morals. All of the values of right living melt before his invasions, and every gain of civilization crumbles. But we can save these people from the worst, if we will.

In our Mission through Europe, I have had the devoted co-operation of my six colleagues, all of them with long experience in famines. We secured independent investigations in advance of coming; we consulted at length with the heads of state and with the food and agricultural experts of each government; we checked and cross-checked all information with American officials in those countries. . . . And above all, my colleagues and I have gone into the byways to see for ourselves. I am confident our conclusions are close to reality.

On this journey I have seen much which I could criticize as to the management of the famine relief. I criticized such matters to many officials in the world frankly. I could criticize them bitterly. But, after every boiling of inward indignation at men and at nations, I come back again and again to the fact that millions are in grave danger of starvation. To explode into public criticism in this crisis would only weaken the amount of support and diminish the fcod they will receive. Criticism can wait for history. I only want to record that all has not been perfect in the world that I have witnessed. It all adds emphasis to the fact that today the vital need is unity and cooperation now, so that we may master this crisis.

In appraising the world situation, I could give you reams of figures of rations, of calories, of tons of this and that, for every country and each district. I could give you their stocks of foods on hand, in transit, and the further need of each famine area. I could give it by the month, or for the crisis. I could give the time required for ship transport with details of port, railroad and truck capacities for distribution. This sort of detailed information would convey little to you, but it is full of meaning in the lives of men, women and children [and] to my colleagues and myself. For in these figures lurks the certainty of hunger to hundreds of millions, and even the spectre of mass starvation before this crisis is passed. Rather than such details, time requires that I give you a global picture, in the hope that it will convey to you the gravity of the situation, and the need for our utmost further effort.

I have said before that calories are . . . [our principal] yardstick of hunger, of starvation, of famine, and finally death. And I may remind you that an average of 2,200 calories per person per day is the minimum in a nation for healthy human beings. And do remember that we Americans, the British, the Canadians, the Australians, the Swedes, the Argentinians, and most of the Western Hemisphere are consuming over 2,900 calories per day right now. If these 800,000,000 people should receive no more relief, and if we assume that their own remaining resources could be evenly distributed, which they could not, the measure of their hunger with the caloric yardstick is about as follows:

About 100,000,000 people would be reduced to the 2,000 calory level.

About 100,000,000 more people would be reduced to an 1,800 calory level.

About 150,000,000 more would be reduced to an 1,500 calory level.

About 150,000,000 more would be reduced to an 1,200 calory level; and

About 300,000,000 more would be reduced to a 900 calory level, or below—and that is . . . [certain] death.

As we descend this scale, we move step by step from the stage of hunger to the stage of disease and epidemics, to the stage of public disorder, to the stage of starvation of all but the strongest, and finally, at less than . . . [1,500] calories we come to mass starvation. . . . But long before a population is reduced to these lower levels, government would break down.

All this sounds like an engineering formula. It is; but it is a formula which means life and hope to nations. At the best we can do, it means gnawing hunger to millions, but it is not mass starvation.

We must prevent the descent to these lower levels. Reconstruction and peace in the world would go up in the flames of chaos if we fail.

The transcendent question is the available overseas supplies with which to fulfill this formula. And I shall discuss breadstuffs only, for they are the symbols of life and hope. The problem of fats is no less urgent, but I will not burden your memories with more figures than necessary. And in breadstuffs I include all human food cereals that are available.

We have two sources of breadstuffs supply for this crisis—the residues of the 1945 harvest in the surplus countries, and the earlier part of the coming harvests of 1946. The harvest of some countries comes in June, others as late as October, and some supplies from the . . . [early] harvest can be available to the countries of late harvests. If the present harvest prospects continue favorable, relief will come to the world within a few months. By September new supplies should be available and the immediate crisis will ease.

In March last, the Combined Food Board in Washington made an estimate of the amount of food needed by all the deficit nations for the first six months of 1946, and of supplies available from the food-surplus nations. These estimates of need were based upon the requirements as stated by the nations who must have overseas supplies. Adding in estimates of the need between June and the fall harvest, the total requirements of cereals were listed at, roughly, 26,000,000 tons. For the same period supplies were estimated at 15,000,000 tons. Thus, there was [apparently] an unbridgeable gap of 11,000,000 tons, or . . . [over] 43 per cent. And that would be a calory level below human endurance. That gap of 11,000,000 tons spells death to millions.

During these past months shipments have been moving, and mass starvation has so far been prevented. Our Mission examined the stocks now in the hands of each country and the amounts of their own production that could be expected. We measured the needs of each nation on a drastic caloric basis such as would pull them through, would prevent mass starvation, would maintain order and economic life. We kept the 1,500–1,800 calory bedrock figure always in mind. Most of the nations we visited joined earnestly with us in working out the very minimum they could do with, as they all realize the desperation of other nations.

The net of these drastic revisions was to reduce the total world requirements of breadstuffs by about 4,000,000 tons. By developing some new sources, by substitution of other cereals, by shifting between early and late harvests, by our sacrifices in America and by spreading sacrifice into other surplus areas, we estimate supplies for the hungry will be increased by a minimum of about 3,000,000 tons. Thus, the gap has been decreased from [about] 11,000,000 to 3,600,000 tons. But the gap is still there—and it is a tragic gap.

. . . There are Americans who believe it right, and a duty, to feed women and children even of a surrendered enemy. No one is the enemy of children. There are others who believe that the only hope of a peaceful world is to save the enemy peoples from starvation and thus start building them into peaceful, cooperative peoples. There are others who, remembering the immeasurable crimes the enemy has committed against all mankind, believe in "an eye for an eye," "a tooth for a tooth." To these, let me say that to keep five hundred thousand American boys in garrison among starving women and children is unthinkable. It is impossible because, being Americans, they will share their own rations with hungry children; it is impossible because hunger brings the total destruction of all morals; it is impossible because of the danger to American boys of sweeping infectious diseases, which rise from famine. It is unthinkable because we do not want our boys machine-gunning famished rioters. It is unthinkable because we do not want the American flag flying over nation-wide Buchenwalds.

And what of the children in Europe?

This 1,500 calory bottom level is dreadfully hard on children. It is hard because a larger portion of the average ration must go to heavy workers if essential services be kept going. While this diet, which is as much as 85 per cent bread and the balance a little fat, sugar and vegetables, will pull adults through, it is not adapted to children. Several nations give them priority in what little dairy supplies there are; extra food is given in some schools; and the charitable agencies are doing the best they can. But in all, they are touching only the fringe of the problem. The proof is an annual infant mortality rate as high as 200 per 1,000 among children under one year in many cities. The further proof is that there are somewhere from 20 to 30 million physically subnormal children on the Continent. After the war in 1919 . . . [to 1923], we gave a good extra meal a day, of 500 or 600 calories of restorative food, to . . . [15,000,000] children. I deplore that this special aid for children has had no counterpart through a wide-spread organization set-up after this war. Civilization marches forward upon the feet of healthy children. It is not too late to stop this most costly retreat and its debacle of endless evil.

Much the same could be said of tens of millions of children in Asia. There many millions of these children have been falling far short of full life since long before this famine. And they are harder to reach and help because of age-old rooted customs.

Our Mission has stimulated some action for children, both in Europe and Asia. I have already proposed not alone a systematic handling of this problem of sub-normal children, but a drastic reorganization of the world's food administration for the next harvest year. It is a primary job for the United Nations Organization if peace and good will are to be re-established on earth.

UNRRA, with its earnest staff, attends to about 20 per cent of the world's food needs. Their supply is by charity, of which the vast majority comes from America. But great as this work is, 80 per cent of the problem is not charity—it is the furnishing of supplies which people can buy [or borrow money for], yet they are just as hungry as the destitute.

Before closing, I should pay tribute to my colleagues on this journey, and to the great army of men and women in every nation over the world who are working unceasingly to save these millions of lives. The volunteer organizations of the religious bodies, of the Red Cross of many nations, are in the field, unceasingly doing their best—but they can remedy only a fraction of the suffering.

There are some hopes of further decreasing this gap of 3,600,000 tons.

First: Still more intensive conservation of breadstuffs and fats in North America. Before I went on this journey, we asked the American people to reduce their consumption of wheat products to two pounds per week per person and to cut their purchases of fats by 20 per cent. Hundreds of thousands of families have responded by cutting out wheat products all together. Public eating places in many cities have cooperated. . . . I earnestly hope that every American will remember that an invisible guest sits with him at every meal.

Second: We have need that every farmer bring every grain of cereal to market.

We are seeking for still further cooperation in other nations. The Latin-American states have responded to our appeals and to those of Pope Pius XII for cooperation. At President Truman's request, I shall visit these governments to consult with them on measures of coordination of our efforts.

If we can succeed in persuading every man and woman, every nation to do their utmost, we shall master this famine. And we shall save the lives of hundreds of millions from the greatest jeopardy in all the history of mankind. We shall have saved infinite suffering.

I was asked by the President to undertake . . . the further journey to the Latin-American states, [and with that] my service ends. The responsibilities of administration of the programs I have outlined lie with our officials. I bespeak for them the full support of all Americans in their efforts to meet this terrible world crisis.

In conclusion, do I need to reinforce this report with more urging to do your utmost? I may repeat again what I said three weeks ago from Cairo: "If every source of supplies will do its utmost, we can pull the world through this most dangerous crisis. The saving of these human lives is far more than an economic necessity to the recovery of the world. It is more than the only path to order, to stability and to peace. Such action marks the return of the lamp of compassion to the earth. And that is a part of the moral and spiritual reconstruction of the world." [2]

[2] *Ibid.,* pp. 221–28.

CHAPTER 30

MEXICO, PANAMA, COLOMBIA, ECUADOR, PERU, AND CHILE

The famine-relief clock was now striking 11:00. There was still time to close the gap between mass starvation and survival if we could secure full co-operation from Latin America.

We started from Washington on May 25, 1946, with our faithful crew and their planes. Dr. Julius Klein, who had served many years as Commercial Attaché in a number of South American countries and had been Undersecretary of Commerce in my Administration, generously agreed to substitute for Hallam Tuck, whose personal commitments compelled him to remain at home.

I may recall the service His Holiness the Pope had assured us in Latin America. It helped to open every official door.

Our Latin-American objectives were threefold:

1. To persuade the food-importing nations to suspend or greatly reduce further imports for the crucial months until September, when most of the harvests of the Northern Hemisphere would be in.

2. To get increased exports from countries which had or could create a surplus by conservation of rice, beans, corn, fats, meats, and sugar.

3. To get idle stocks of food in the Argentine into motion toward Europe and thus free North American supplies for the rest of the world. The Argentine was our major goal.

We visited eleven countries: Mexico, Panama, Colombia, Ecuador, Peru, Chile, Argentina, Uruguay, Brazil, Venezuela, and Cuba. Our

203

procedure was the same as in other nations we had visited, and our journey proved to be even more exhausting—if such a thing were possible—than those to Europe and Asia. I was pressed to speak in every country in order to help the government obtain popular acceptance of the necessary regulatory actions. Prior to our departure, we secured Spanish and Portuguese translations of my Chicago speech and our report to President Truman, which we distributed to the press of each nation we visited.

During the two weeks in Washington and New York before leaving for Latin America, we had a variety of experiences. One of these "incidents" had begun to unravel while we were on our previous mission. The newspaper headlines were blazing daily, and the radio hourly, with famine news from all over the world. Mrs. Franklin D. Roosevelt, former Governor Lehman, and Secretary of Commerce Henry Wallace decided they should do something about the situation. They made vivid emotional appeals to householders to make contributions of canned goods for the starving and secured the aid of much of the press and radio to advance their idea. They were sincere and enthusiastic in advancing their cause, and they meant to be helpful, but inasmuch as the usual one-pound can of vegetables or fruit contains less than one hundred calories of food values, it would have been necessary for each of the recipients to eat eighteen such cans daily, as against a little over a pound of mixed cereals and fats. Such a program implied shipping 90 per cent water.

Since their committee was without funds to pay for transport of the foodstuffs to the famine areas, they asked Director Fiorello H. LaGuardia of UNRRA to assume this burden. LaGuardia cannily refused to do so unless the committee raised four million dollars to pay for the job, whereupon it appealed to the public for the cash required.

The project had created diversion from the prosaic and absolutely essential campaign of Chester Davis' Famine Emergency Committee, which was urging the American people to reduce their consumption and waste of breadstuffs and fats and thus release the real food essentials into channels where we could get at them. Although the members of the Committee resented this nonsense and its resultant damage to their efforts, they disliked the idea of fomenting a dispute over it in the press. They put it up to me, but I had no palate for such quarrels, either.

The cat had to be killed somehow, however, because it was slowing down our conservation campaign. Therefore, I called in some of the newspaper publishers and the heads of the press agencies and explained the situation "off the record." I suggested that they tell the public why canned fruit and vegetables (which comprised most of the gifts) were not adaptable to famine relief and inform people that what was needed was either canned baked beans, condensed milk, or canned meat. As householders had few of these latter items to spare, the whole matter died quietly overnight.

During this same two-week period, I appeared before the appropriations committees of the Congress to support Mr. Truman's recommendations concerning aid to Japan, Germany, and Austria. The Congress made the necessary appropriations.

MEXICO

Our first destination was Mexico City, where we were met at the airport on May 26 by the Minister of Foreign Affairs, Dr. Francisco Castillo Nájera; the Minister of Finance, Eduardo Suárez; the Minister of National Economy, Gustavo Serrano; and the American Chargé d'Affaires, Raymond Geist. We received full military honors.

On arriving at our hotel, we immediately went into conference with the American officials to check their Mexican data with our own. It was obvious that Mexico could provide no important surplus to export, but then our major problem was to persuade them to suspend their imports until after the North American harvest.

The Minister of Foreign Affairs accompanied Mr. Gibson and me to an interview with President Manuel Ávila Camacho. He received us with great cordiality. I briefly presented the world crisis in food and the work of our mission. I stated that our remaining hope of preventing starvation was the co-operation of Latin America. I said that aside from the practical support we hoped for from Mexico, I also hoped for his personal support in some difficult situations ahead, particularly in the Argentine, where United States diplomatic relations were indeed greatly strained. I was aware that President Camacho was a friend of President Perón, dating from the days of their foreign service together as Military Attachés. President Camacho said he would instruct the Mexican Ambassador in the Argentine to place himself at my service and would communicate to President Perón that I had had no part in the frictions with the United States and was solely on a humanitarian mission. Mexico immediately stopped imports of food for the duration of the crisis.

PANAMA

Brigadier General Frank T. Hines, the American Ambassador, provided our lodgings in Panama. He had served as my personal aide when I was in the White House. General Hines arranged a meeting with President Enrique A. Jiménez of the Republic of Panama, the Panamanian Cabinet, and with the American officers in command of the Panama Canal.

There were no consequential food problems in the Panamanian Republic.

COLOMBIA

We arrived in Bogotá on May 30. We were met by the American Ambassador, John C. Wiley, and representatives of President Alberto Lleras Camargo. There was a Latin-American convention of Boy Scouts in progress in the city and the Colombian authorities substituted for a military ceremony a salute to us by Boy Scouts bearing the banners of each Latin-American country. We were also greeted by a most eloquent and understanding editorial in *El Tiempo*, the leading journal in Colombia. It described accurately the great food crisis in the world and urged the people and the Colombian Government to co-operate in full. We subsequently made good use of this editorial in the other Spanish-speaking countries.

Indonesian children receiving nourishment that will help fight malnutrition.

A young refugee from North Vietnam being served by a nun near Saigon.

A sad-faced Hungarian refugee eating bread and cheese in Vienna.

*Brother and sister sharing a cup of the "milk of human kindness"
in India.*

We had the usual food conference with our Embassy officials. In the evening, Ambassador Wiley arranged a meeting with President Camargo, the Cabinet members, and the leading publishers in Bogotá. We had the opportunity to present the world crisis and the purpose of our mission.

The President and his ministers were most co-operative, but Colombia had little food surplus to export. However, the President agreed to cancel their request in Washington for 50,000 tons of wheat, and he agreed to put on a conservation program to try to squeeze out some supplies. He asked that I make a public statement supporting these measures. My statement to the press on May 31 was the story of need and the unfilled gap. The Colombian press made considerable use of my Chicago address.

ECUADOR

We arrived in Quito on May 31. A meeting had been arranged by American Ambassador Robert M. Scotten so that our staff could confer immediately with Embassy officials on the food situation. He had also arranged an evening meeting with President José María Velasco Ibarra, his Cabinet, and our mission at the Presidential Palace, where until a late hour the President delivered a lengthy appeal to us on economic, political, and international matters, pressing Ecuador's needs for economic aid from the United States.

The next morning, at a meeting with the Ministers of Agriculture and Economics, they stated they could export 32,000 tons of rice— but they asked just double the world price for the rice. Our mission was not buying food, and we suggested they offer the rice to foreign buyers.

We took time off to visit some of the splendid cathedrals in Quito, where the days of glory after the Spanish Conquistadors still remained in magnificent silver and gold images and gold embroideries on the walls. But the worshipers looked hungry and cold.

PERU

We arrived in Lima on June 1. At the airfield there were military honors, bands playing the national anthems with vigor, a large crowd of cheering people, and a salute of fifteen guns.

We were lodged in the American Embassy [1] by the Chargé d'Affaires, Walter J. Donnelly. The Chargé was the son of a policeman, and had brilliantly passed the examinations for a position in the Commerce Department when I was Secretary. Later I had appointed him Trade Commissioner to various South American nations. Because of his outstanding ability and character, he was taken over by the State Department, where he rose to important ambassadorial posts.

President José Luis Bustamante Rivero arranged a meeting for our mission with his Cabinet members. Peru was in an economic mess of inflation and other ills. Because of her economic necessities, she had already restricted imports and imposed an austerity program on food consumption. The President requested that we issue my Chicago address to the public and hold a press conference to support his "tightening of the belt." [2]

[1] It seems the place was bare. The American ladies in Lima were shocked at the idea that my colleagues and I should go to a hotel, so they went to work and fixed the place up, bringing in their own silver and linen and all the odds and ends that make a house a home. It took weeks to accomplish, but I think they would have felt repaid if they knew the great comfort they added to our trip.

[2] Just to introduce a little interest into a story of human woe, I give an extract from the diary (which is in my possession) of the ever cheerful Hugh Gibson about a visit he paid to the Cathedral at Lima:

"Before setting out on my calls I went with Colonel Carlos Stewart, the a.d.c. attached to the Chief for a look at the Cathedral. It was getting dark and the Cathedral was closed and the man who had the keys had gone off somewhere for a drink. However a smiling priest roused some children and sent them after the father who came along in time. By now it was as dark as the inside of a fish. He lighted a huge candle taken from the altar and showed us its glittering gold and silver, as well as the carved stalls. Not much of an impression to be had this way, but he then led us to the other end of the tomb of Pizarro. The old brigand is laid out in a glass coffin as naked as the day he was born. There is a hole in his neck where his armor pressed. In a glass bottle are his heart, liver and other giblets as well as the identifying parchment found in the coffin when it was discovered in the crypt. I could not but feel that it was all an invasion of his privacy and that the least they could do for the old gentleman was to give him a shroud."

CHILE

We arrived in Santiago on June 4. American Ambassador Claude G. Bowers gave us a good food summary, to which he added an exposition of the political and economic situations of the country. We also learned from him of the great propaganda efforts being made by the Russian Communist Legation in Chile.

The President of Chile, Juan Antonio Ríos, was very ill, and I called on Vice-President Alfredo Duhalde Vásquez, who was acting head of the Government. Admiral Vicente Merino Bielich, acting Foreign Minister, gave a reception for several hundred people to meet with us. After sundry speeches, I introduced Dr. Klein, who in fluent Spanish gave them a description of the world famine and the purposes of our mission.

Chile was a nearly self-sufficient country in food. All of her officials were most co-operative and appreciative of our mission. They immediately stopped all food imports during the critical months and squeezed out some exports.

Through one of Ambassador Gibson's old diplomatic colleagues in the American Embassy, we received a warning that persons in the State Department had issued some sort of deprecatory note about our mission. (We got the actual text later in Rio de Janeiro.) They were frightened by what we might do regarding their war with President Perón.

CHAPTER 31

THE ARGENTINE, URUGUAY, BRAZIL, VENEZUELA, AND CUBA

THE ARGENTINE

Our major objective now was the food basket of Latin America: the Argentine. We arrived in Buenos Aires on June 6.

Prior to our departure from Santiago, we had sent the usual advices to the American Ambassador in Buenos Aires, giving the time of our arrival, and asked that accommodations be arranged for us. We were met at the airport by a secretary of the Embassy, who told Mr. Gibson that the Embassy building could not accommodate us. The Argentine Under Minister of Foreign Affairs, Ignacio A. Bunge, representing President Perón, also met us at the airport. Señor Bunge, listening in on this conversation, stated after introducing himself that he was related to the Bunge family of Belgium, with whom I was associated in the Relief during the First World War. With some possible show of indignation, he asked if we would be guests of the Argentine Government, to which I responded cordially. He quickly arranged with the airfield officials to take us to the leading hotel and said that quarters would be ready by the time we arrived.

Upon our arrival at the hotel, Mr. Gibson asked recently appointed American Ambassador George Messersmith if he could arrange a meeting for us with President Perón the next day, as our mission was dealing with a great emergency. The Ambassador seemed hesitant.

We were soon able to solve some of the mystery of the American Ambassador's apparent reluctance to arrange our meeting with President Perón. The State Department had been most active in opposing Perón in the recent elections. Under its instructions, the American Ambassador, Spruille Braden, had used the American Embassy as headquarters for one of the factions opposing Perón's election, and Perón would have nothing to do with him or with our State Department. The sum of all this was that some of the State Department officials were conducting a total war against Perón, and for our mission to be doing business with him was a total cross-up of the Department's policies.

Meanwhile, the Mexican Ambassador called, repeating his instructions from President Camacho, and asked if he could be of service. Mr. Gibson had taken the call and at once asked his old friend what was going on between the American Ambassador and the Perón regime. After being informed, Mr. Gibson asked if the Ambassador could possibly arrange an appointment for me with President Perón. In fifteen minutes he called back, saying that the President was most desirous to see me and had fixed the time for our meeting at 10:30 the following morning.

On learning that the Mexican Ambassador had arranged our appointment, Mr. Gibson concluded that the proper attitude on our part was to invite the American Ambassador to accompany me when I called on President Perón. Ambassador Messersmith accepted our invitation.

President Perón was most cordial to me and mentioned the advices he had received from His Holiness the Pope, and from President Camacho with regard to our mission. I briefly outlined the world food situation, pointing out that the available American, Canadian, and Australian overseas supplies were now practically exhausted and that the one great hope to avoid a great catastrophe was the Argentine. I suggested that his possible service to the famine nations in Europe would bring great appreciation to him from them. The President stated that the Argentine desired to co-operate but that there were many obstacles and difficulties to be overcome. He seemed restless in Ambassador Messersmith's presence, and suggested that he would assign the members of his Cabinet who were concerned with food and its transport to discuss those problems with me. He added that when we had all the information in hand, he would arrange another meeting with me.

In our discussions with the Cabinet members, they confirmed that the total stocks of grain, in the hands of the farmers and in warehouses, beyond Argentina's domestic needs were between three and four million tons. They had received requests for supplies from various European countries which wanted to buy the food on credit. They explained that there were certain difficulties in this matter and President Perón would explain them to me. The President, through one of his officials, invited me to meet with him at his private residence. The official indicated that Perón did not want the American Ambassador present and asked me to bring one of my Spanish-speaking colleagues. Mr. Gibson urged that Dr. Klein, who was fluent in Spanish and knew more of the technology of our job, should accompany me on this occasion.

President Perón opened our conversation by saying that there were certain political problems with the Washington Administration which he must explain to me. He said that the size of his unparalleled majority in the recent elections was largely due to the opposition of the American State Department and the activities of the previous American Ambassador in opposing his re-election. This had given him a prime issue in his campaign. He said I had no doubt seen some of the posters still remaining on the billboards. These proclaimed that the issue of the election was the attempt at tyranny by the "Colossus of the North." He said he was grateful to the State Department but that as an Argentine, he resented it greatly. (We had already learned that the Ambassador had made the Embassy the headquarters of the opposition.)

Señor Perón, however, returned to the purpose of our mission and explained that he was faced with two major difficulties in accomplishing what he himself and my mission wanted. First, although the war had been over for ten months, the American Government still maintained wartime trade restrictions against the Argentine. This severely curtailed Argentine foreign trade and greatly increased unemployment. The second difficulty was that the Argentine had, before the war, carried its gold reserve in the Federal Reserve Bank in New York and the Argentine banks had large balances in American banks —all of which had been impounded during the war and was still withheld. The President told me that as a measure of reprisal he had confiscated American branch banks in the Argentine and that he also intended to confiscate the American meat-packing plants, the automobile assembly factories, and everything else that was owned by North Americans.

At this moment, I concluded that my mission was just about over, but President Perón picked up some papers and said that his complaint was not against the starving people in Europe and that these papers were the executive orders which would land food in the foreign ports as fast as we could send the ships. He added that the European nations could have it on credit and that he would need to print the money without any deposited reserve with which to pay the farmers for it and for internal transport of it.

I could hardly believe his story of gold and trade restraints. However, I expressed my appreciation for his making the food available and said that while, as a Republican, I had no influence in these matters, I would report the situation to President Truman when I returned to Washington. We adjourned for lunch, at which Mrs. Perón was hostess. My appraisal of her was that she was a cross between Mrs. Franklin D. Roosevelt and Miss Hedy Lamarr, with the brains of the former and the good looks of the latter.

Upon my departure from the Argentine I issued a statement which contained this sentence:

It is a great service that President Perón is undertaking for all the hungry people in the world.[1]

When I arrived in Washington, I related to President Truman the co-operation in food matters of President Perón and told him of Señor Perón's statement of our continued seizure of their gold reserve and our continued restraints on Argentine trade. Mr. Truman

[1] *Addresses Upon the American Road, 1945–1948*, p. 253.

said he could not believe any such thing was possible. He picked up the telephone and called the State Department, reciting these matters, and asked if this were true. I heard only one side of the conversation, but that was sufficient. The President directed that these restraints on gold and trade be dropped at once. I suggested that I would like to inform the Argentine President of President Truman's action, as it would relieve the strain between the United States and the Argentine. Mr. Truman agreed, and I sent a cordial telegram to President Perón.

After my return, I learned that the Argentine had, for many months, maintained an embargo on shipments of flaxseed to the United States. Our American paint manufacturers were sorely in need of this material. The Argentine President lifted the embargo on it at once.[2]

URUGUAY

We arrived in Montevideo on June 11. Ambassador William Dawson arranged a meeting for our mission with President Juan José Amézaga and the Uruguayan Cabinet. It developed that they had a small margin of food remaining for export.

Uruguay was enjoying great prosperity. Aside from other impressive public buildings, the people of Montevideo had just completed a 2,500-bed modern hospital. There are very few of this size in the world. Maurice Pate reported that the condition of their children equaled that of Switzerland, which was his maximum praise.

BRAZIL

We arrived in Rio de Janeiro on June 12. American Ambassador William D. Pawley was an old friend. We made the usual call on

[2] Some years later, at a private dinner at which former President Truman was present, I recounted his courageous action. He confirmed the facts regarding these transactions.

President Major General Eurico Gaspar Dutra. We held the usual conferences with the Embassy staff about the food situation, and later talked with the Brazilian Minister of Agriculture and other food authorities, who were most co-operative.

The Brazilians had a surplus of about 100,000 tons of rice and about 100,000 tons of corn. They were exporting it in co-operation with the Combined Food Board. The Brazilian Government was carrying on an effective conservation program. It had been importing wheat from the Argentine, but agreed to suspend imports until after the critical months, thus increasing the pool of supplies available for famine-stricken countries.

The Ministry asked my help in trying to prevent the Communists and the Communist press from pouring poison into the Government's conservation policies. The Communists were asserting that the food would never reach the needy, but was being used for the personal profit of the Ministers and the North Americans. I answered these attacks at our press conference by saying:

In Brazil, as well as the thirty-seven countries which we have visited, wherever there is a Communist press (and that is in most of them), that press has universally attacked this effort to provide food for the hungry working people of the world, mostly on the ground that the food is to be used for political purposes. In Latin America it takes also the form that we are trying to take food from the people.

This unity of opposition is interesting, because the Communist press is aware that the Christian world is today denying itself of food in order that the working people in France, Belgium, Italy, and twenty other countries, may be saved from starvation. And among these people, there are millions of Communists who have received their full share and whose lives have been alike saved. It is still more interesting because of the fact that, after the first World War [in 1921], at the request of the Soviet Government I organized the relief of the great famine among the working people in South Russia, and received most fulsome documents of thanks and appreciation, signed by the highest officials of the Russian Government.

As we are [now] feeding Communists in all countries, there obviously has been no use of food for political purposes or no intent to make such use [of it].

There can be only one explanation; that is, that the universal party line of the Communist Party in every country is to try to break down the provision of food for hungry people, and thus produce chaos where they can fish in troubled waters. If this is not the case, it would appear that this is the time for Moscow to establish a new party line in the Communist press of the world.[3]

VENEZUELA

We landed in Caracas on June 17. The American Ambassador, Frank P. Corrigan, had arranged for President Romulo Betancourt to hold a session of his Cabinet and meet with our mission. We discussed the plight of the world food situation. Venezuela was importing about four to five thousand tons of food a month from the United States. It was stopped from Washington.

The President gave an elaborate dinner to the mission, his Ministry, and the American Ambassador. There were many eloquent speeches. I got no comfort out of it because I had had a bad fall that morning. It subsequently developed that I had cracked a vertebra in my spine. This was my additional contribution to alleviating the great famine. Since I felt I must finish our mission, I was trussed up with a plaster bandage and proceeded.

CUBA

We arrived in Havana on June 18. We were met by the American Chargé d'Affaires, Robert F. Woodward, and the Minister of State, Alberto Inocénte Álvarez. We had no important matters concerning food, but Gibson and I called upon the President, Dr. Ramón Grau San Martín. Our staff had a meeting with the Ministers of Foreign Affairs, Agriculture, and Commerce. The Cubans were co-operating by exporting all their available surplus of sugar, but they were demanding large imports of flour from the United States.

[3] *Addresses Upon the American Road, 1945–1948*, pp. 254–55.

President San Martín gave us a dinner at which I urged the Cubans to speed up their sugar exports and to reduce their imports of flour for the final month until our American crops were in. I was in no condition to be very effective. However, in accord with American policies, the Combined Food Board suspended Cuban flour shipments, since their stocks were sufficient.

CHAPTER 32

TRIUMPH OVER THE GREATEST
FAMINE IN WORLD HISTORY

On my return to Washington on June 19, I reported to the White House and saw the President the following day. Mr. Truman at once took the courageous action which released the Argentine surplus. I also found that our American conservation program under Mr. Davis had added an estimated 2,762,000 tons to our American exportable grains. While there would be millions of people who would be hungry until the next harvest, there would be no mass starvation, except in that part of China which was inaccessible because of transportation problems.

Mr. Truman pronounced our mission a triumph over seemingly insurmountable obstacles. The same day, I held a press conference, at which I issued a short statement and answered a multitude of questions. I reviewed the work of the mission and the almost universal co-operation of the nations we visited. I expressed our gratitude for their many courtesies.[1]

---

[1] In reply to questions, I gave these bits of information about our race with famine: we had traveled 50,711 miles by air; we had co-ordinated the efforts of 38 countries; we had conferred with 7 Kings, a Viceroy, 36 Prime Ministers, 135 other Cabinet members, 38 American Ambassadors or Ministers, 26 American generals, and a multitude of colonels and private citizens of all nationalities; I had held 42 press conferences, delivered 31 press statements, and made 24 public addresses. Our entire mission had cost the Government less than $4,000, in addition to the expense of operating the airplane, which would have been kept in service anyway. We had collected a great store of political opinions, and of more importance, made an appraisal of the march of Communism in the world.

I received a cordial invitation from Prime Minister W. L. Mackenzie King of Canada to address members of the Canadian Parliament in Ottawa on June 28. The great part which Canada and its representative on the Combined Food Board had played in providing supplies in the midst of this gigantic danger made it appropriate that I should pay tribute to their service. I accepted the invitation. In my address I said:

MR. PRIME MINISTER:

I have been honored by your invitation to make from Canada the final report upon my food mission to 38 nations. I am glad for this privilege. It gives to me the opportunity to pay tribute to the magnificent service Canada has given to the world. To Canada flows the gratitude of hundreds of millions of human beings who have been saved from starvation through the efforts of this great Commonwealth of the North.

Upon four nations—Canada, the United States, the Argentine and Australia—has fallen 90 per cent of the [burden of] overseas . . . relief [in] . . . this, the greatest famine in all human history. . . . Without this gigantic flow of overseas food, hundreds of millions [of people] would have died and other hundreds of millions would have survived only as permanent physical wrecks. And when we use this impersonal word "people," let us not forget that most of them are women and children. Far beyond our humanitarian responsibilities lay the necessity to save the political and social structure of the world from sinking into a chaos in which recovery and the making of peace would be impossible.

We can see the future more clearly if for a moment we look back over our months of effort to drive the wolf from the door of the world.

This crisis, of course, had its roots in the degeneration of agriculture and manpower in the war-torn areas. But to this was added the plunder . . . of food [by Russia] of the last harvests in Germany, Eastern Europe and Manchuria. . . . But on top of all these disasters has been the unparalleled coincidence of five great droughts—in the western Mediterranean, India, China, South Africa and a partial failure in crops in the Argentine.

The full realization of the impending calamity [to the world] came early in March [of this year].

I then briefly described our journeys, the results, and the closing of the tragic gap in supplies:

When the potential dangers were realized . . . months ago, the Combined Food Board estimated that there was an 11,000,000 ton gap in the necessary . . . [supplies] to meet the minimum demands of hungry nations. . . . With this gap facing us it did not seem possible to prevent mass starvation. I felt compelled to say publicly at that time, "Our task is now to minimize the loss of life."

On my return from Europe and Asia a month ago, my colleagues and I felt assured that as of May 1st the gap in the bare subsistence supply of cereals had been reduced . . . to about 3,600,000 tons, with a corresponding reduction in the gaps of fats and other essentials. This reduction was due to the development of new sources of supplies; to substitutions; to the success of our appeal for self-denial in the surplus food countries. The reduction of the gap was due especially to the willing acceptance in the food deficit countries of drastic curtailment of their requested import programs. . . .

Our determination has been to hold the lowest of them up to a level of 1,500 to 1,700 calories per person per day. If we could hold these levels it would at least prevent mass starvation. But even this drastic program was endangered by that tragic gap of 3,600,000 tons. If it could not be overcome, we were defeated.

But something like the widow's cruse is happening. In this two months since those estimates the world has developed even further additions to world supplies. The Latin-American states have greatly reduced their import requirements during the crisis months. Especially the Argentine is greatly expanding its contribution of supplies. The other Latin-American states are giving aid. The British Government has reduced its pipe line supplies. Larger diversions have been made in India from the surplus provinces to the famine areas. The conservation measures in Canada and the United States are contributing even more largely to our potential exports. The United States harvest has arrived earlier than usual. . . .

The precariousness of the situation is not over. Scarcely any of the major food deficit . . . [countries] have stocks of as much as 30 days' overseas food. . . . If we fail in shipments, mass starvation will be instantly upon us.

. . . if we have continued cooperative action of the various nations, mass starvation will be prevented, with one exception. That exception is China, where transportation to the interior and inadequate organization has rendered relief only partially successful.

In other famine areas there will be suffering. We truly need more supplies than just enough to prevent mass starvation. Many of the old people and the weaker children will fall by the wayside, nevertheless the great majority of the endangered will be saved. Beyond this saving of human life, the political and social stability of nations, upon which alone peace can be builded, will be preserved. . . .

I may say at once that I do not take the extreme pessimistic view of the world supplies after the coming harvests that has been expressed in several quarters. We can at least hope there will be no plundering by armies during the next year. We have reason to believe that there will not be five coincident great droughts again in one year. In three of these drought areas the harvest prospects are very much improved. . . . With continued favorable weather, we in North America seem destined to have abundant harvests again.

. . . The food situation of the world in the next year will not be easy, but next year in my view will not be one of such dreadful crisis and drastic regimes as the one which we are now in. . . .

This 1,500 to 1,700 calory bottom level in many areas is dreadfully hard on children. While it will see adults through, the kind of food is not the most suitable for children. Disease and mortality among the little ones are ever the sensitive barometers of starvation and poverty. Several nations have done the best they could by giving the children priority in their meagre dairy products; some extra food is given in some schools; and the scattered charitable agencies are doing the best they can in limited areas. But in all, they are only touching the fringe of the problem. Millions of mothers are today watching their children wilt before their eyes. The proof of this is an annual mortality rate in many cities as high as 200 per 1,000 among children under one year of age. The further proof is that there are somewhere from 20 to 30 million physically subnormal children on the continent of Europe. There are other millions in Asia.

After the first world war, we gave a good extra meal a day of restorative food, to . . . [15,000,000] undernourished children. I deplore that this special aid for children has had no counterpart through a widespread organization set-up after this war. And I repeat that civilization marches forward upon the feet of healthy children. We cannot have recovery of civilization in nations with a legacy of stunted bodies or distorted and embittered minds.

I . . . suggest that the redemption of these children be organized at once. . . . The job could be done with three or four hundred million dollars—a charge beyond any organized private charity but not a great sum from the world as a whole.

Mr. Prime Minister, I have held this statement to sober words. I have not tried to describe the grim visage of famine in action. I have not attempted to express the emotion which every decent human being feels in the presence of the scenes of hunger and of sickly children I have witnessed. Nor have I tried to express the sympathy and pride which swells in one's heart for those hundreds of thousands of heroic men and women in the world who are struggling to save these millions of human lives. They labor for their countrymen in villages, in cities and in the halls of government. They know that hunger is a destroyer far worse than war. Great as its toll of life may be yet its destruction of morals, of social and political institutions are infinite.

May I repeat here a statement I have made to men of government in each of these 38 nations?

"The world has ended a bloody and horrible era of killing of even women and children. The jeopardy to mankind by famine gives to us an opportunity to change the energies of the world from killing to saving life. These months can bring the glow of a new faith and a new hope for the dawn of a new era to mankind.

"To succeed is far more than a necessity to economic reconstruction of the world. It is far more than the path to order and peace.

"It marks the return of the lamp of compassion to the earth. And that is part of the moral and spiritual reconstruction of the world." [2]

[2] *Addresses Upon the American Road, 1945–1948*, pp. 259–66.

FAMINE CONTINUES IN GERMANY, AUSTRIA, AND JAPAN

INTRODUCTION

On January 5, 1947, Secretary of War Robert P. Patterson telephoned me, asking if I would again go to Germany and Austria, as a very serious crisis in food supplies had arisen there. I replied that the necessary data could be obtained by teletype from the military staffs or by cable from the American civilian staffs in Germany and Austria, I suggested that with this information, along with the previous experience of my colleagues and myself, we could settle on a new food program in Washington, without going overseas.

However, as I had grave doubts regarding the wisdom of the economic and political policies of our Government in Germany and Austria, I told him I would not refuse if the purpose of the mission were widened to include a report on American, British, and French administration in the respective zones and if the mission were undertaken on this enlarged basis and at President Truman's request. Further, I told the Secretary that I would require instructions to be issued which would open every door and every document. I was aware from my visit to Germany nine months previously (April, 1946) that the policies of the former Allies and ourselves there had created such wholesale destitution and unemployment that it was costing the American people hundreds of millions of tax dollars annually to keep the Germans alive.

I heard nothing more for some days, but on January 18, I received a letter from President Truman requesting me to undertake the mission for food purposes only, without reference to the wider aspects of the problem. It was reported to me by a friend in the War Department that certain Government officials had intervened and deleted

225

mention of the broad mission from the draft letter which had been prepared for Mr. Truman to send to me.

In the meantime, I learned that Mr. Tracy Voorhees, an Assistant Secretary of War, was pushing my appointment. I also learned something of the capacity for intrigue of some officials in the State Department. The Department's policies were influenced by men bent on the destruction of German industry and the punishment of the German people, regardless of the future impact on the economy and security of the United States and the rest of the world. These men concluded that my appointment encroached on their authority. On the day of Mr. Truman's first letter to me, and before I made any reply, stories of the mission appeared in the press. These hinted at the State Department's official disapproval and were openly critical of the proposed mission. Consequently, I was not in a particularly conciliatory mood when I responded to the call to Washington to talk with the President. However, Mr. Truman commented on these newspaper leaks and personal attacks with considerable indignation. I told him that from the data available, I could figure out closely enough a program of increased monthly food shipments without going to Germany. If, however, he were interested in a report and recommendations on the whole economic and political policies now being pursued and if I could be assured of a competent personal staff and specific instructions to the Military Government to open all doors, I would go.

The President's letter of request, dated January 18, 1947, mentioned the food problems and concluded with this paragraph:

I should, therefore, like to ask you to undertake this economic mission as to food and its collateral problems, and report to me upon it. It is hoped that methods can be devised which will release some of the burdens on the American tax payer.

CHAPTER 33

THE FOOD SITUATION IN GERMANY

I was able to secure eight able assistants, all familiar with Germany and most of them fluent in German. They were: former Ambassador Hugh Gibson; Dr. Dennis A. FitzGerald from the Department of Agriculture; Frank E. Mason, a former American Military Attaché in Berlin; Hugo Meier, as secretary, all from our 1946 journey; Dr. Louis P. Lochner, former Associated Press Chief in Berlin; Tracy S. Voorhees, Assistant Secretary of War; Dr. William H. Sebrell, Jr., Medical Director of the United States Public Health Service; and Dr. Gustav Stolper, a German-refugee economist and former member of the Reichstag.

The War Department furnished us with a DC-4 and an excellent crew, some of whom had been with us on our 1946 mission. We took off on February 2, 1947. On February 4, we arrived in Frankfort, where we visited American Army Headquarters, under command of General Joseph T. McNarney. On February 6, we arrived in Berlin and were met by General Lucius D. Clay, General William L. Draper, General Frank H. Keating, and others.

I had anticipated the usual method of the military to put on guided tours for visiting firemen, in which the perspective of the seen and the unseen is badly distorted, but this was not the attitude of either the American or British military and civilian staffs. General Clay was especially helpful—in fact the whole atmosphere was one of full co-operation. Some of these men were old friends, such as

227

General Withers A. Burress, Chief of the Army Intelligence Staff in Europe, and Ambassador Robert D. Murphy, United States Political Adviser for Germany. They gave every possible assistance.

I assigned each of my staff to a particular, critical subject. As for myself, I arranged to conduct forenoon conferences with the American or British officials in the district, including the second and third levels of authority. We held two such conferences in Berlin, one in Hamburg, and one in Stuttgart. In the afternoons we had meetings with German officials of the district. Many of these men were bursting with indignation at what was going on. It was easy, by asking questions, to stimulate a full discussion and get frank statements of their problems, which quickly disclosed that the spirit of the Morgenthau Plan was still being practiced, under directives from Washington, all along the economic, political, and administrative lines. Except in Berlin these conferences were held in public buildings, with the temperature hovering around freezing. No domestic heating coal had been available for months, and we might as well have met in the parks or in cold-storage plants. To sit all day in the cold proved very trying—even though I wore the heaviest of overcoats and at times a blanket besides, as did most of the conferees. One result for me was a sequence of severe colds. These were often coincident with take-off and landing hops in the unpressurized planes of those days. An injury to my hearing was the consequence.

In any event, we learned what was causing Germany's $600,000,-000 annual cost to the American and British taxpayers.

CHAPTER 34

GERMANY

The American and British commands requested my major recommendations on food, without waiting for my report to the President. They were: (1) an increase in the "average" ration to 1,550 calories from levels as low as 1,000 calories; (2) a supplementary ration for hard laborers, necessary to assure coal and other production; (3) a system of canteens serving a 500- to 600-calorie meal at midday, seven days a week, with special food for children, expectant mothers and the aged, to be conducted by devoted German women, mainly in schools (the Germans called it the *Hoover Speisung*); (4) an allotment of food to German and Austrian relief organizations for other distress cases; and (5) a food-import program to support these provisions.

Before leaving, I submitted a rough draft of my report to President Truman to General Clay and Ambassador Murphy, and I gladly accepted their suggestions regarding it. In my report to the President, dated February 26, 1947, I expressed my appreciation of the co-operation given me by the American and British officers in Germany:

Dear Mr. President:

I have now completed the Economic Mission to Germany and Austria, which I undertook at your request.

I enclose herewith a memorandum on the economic conditions affecting food supplies for the newly combined American and British Zones, together with estimates of supplies and costs involved in deficiency appropriations for the last half of the fiscal year 1946–1947 and appropriations for the fiscal year 1947–1948. . . .

I shall report separately on Austria, and at a later date I shall have some further report on other economic and health problems in these areas.

In this examination of food questions in the combined zones, I have had the invaluable service of Dr. Dennis A. FitzGerald in food questions and that of Dr. Wm. H. Sebrell, Jr., in nutritional and health questions, together with the able assistance in other economic questions of Mr. Hugh Gibson, Mr. Louis Lochner, Mr. Frank Mason, and Dr. Gustav Stolper. I have received the full cooperation of Generals McNarney, Clay, Draper, and Hester and their able staff, as well as General Robertson, Sir Cecil Weir and Mr. T. F. Griffin, and their able staff on the British side.

My thanks are also due to the devoted service of Mr. Tracy S. Voorhees, Special Assistant to the Secretary of War, and to the Air Transport Command for their cooperation and skill.

HERBERT HOOVER

The report has historic importance because it demonstrates the depth of misery to which the German people had been plunged by Hitler's warmaking, plus the vengeance of the Morgenthau Plan, which had been carried out in spirit, if not in letter.

REPORT ON AGRICULTURAL AND FOOD REQUIREMENTS

INTRODUCTION

At the time of her surrender, Germany had exhausted all of her reserves and most of her stocks of consumer goods and raw materials. We now know that, driven back into her own borders, she would have blown up in chaos within a short time without further military action.

Promptly after the surrender, her liquid resources from which she could have been provided with supplies were seized and divided as reparations. The population thus became largely dependent for its life upon the armies of occupation.

It is hardly necessary to repeat that parts of Germany were annexed to Poland and Russia and that the shrunken territory was divided into four military occupation zones between the Russians, French, British and

Americans. The American and British Zones have now been administratively combined, each nation bearing one-half the expense, and this report relates to that area only.

CHANGES IN POPULATION AND MANPOWER

The changes which have taken place in population profoundly affect all economic problems. The population of the combined zones in 1939 was about 34,200,000. The Germans expelled from the Russian and Polish annexations together with those from Czechoslovakia, Hungary, and Austria, have raised the population in the American and British Zones to about 41,700,000. It is estimated that an additional 1,000,000 will come into this area by December 1947. There are also about 400,000 British and American military and civil personnel. Thus, the two zones will have to accommodate about 43,000,000 people, bringing the population approximately 9,000,000 above that in 1939.

The skilled manpower and the ratio of working males in the population have been greatly affected by the war. For the whole of Germany, it is estimated that 5,700,000 [men] were killed or permanently injured. It is also estimated that over 3,000,000 prisoners of war are [still] held in work camps in Russia; 750,000 in France; 400,000 in Britain, and 40,000 in Belgium. The detention of large numbers of skilled Sudeten German workmen in Czechoslovakia bears on this problem.

As applied to the American and British Zones, this represents a present subtraction of over 6,000,000 of the most vital and most skilled workers in the population. Likewise, the 90,000 Nazis held in concentration camps and the 1,900,000 others under sanctions by which they can only engage in manual labor naturally comprise a considerable part of the former technical and administrative skill of the country, and the restrictions upon them, however necessary, add to administrative and industrial problems.

One consequence of these distortions is that in the age groups between 20 and 40 there are 6 men to 10 women, and in the age group between 40 and 60, about 7 men to 10 women. Thus, there are in these groups between 6 and 7 million more women than men. The results upon productive power are bad enough, but the consequences to morals are appalling.

HOUSING

The housing situation in the two zones is the worst that modern civilization has ever seen. About 25 per cent of the urban housing was destroyed by the war. Therefore, 25 per cent of the urban population must find roofs from among the remaining 75 per cent, in addition to all the destitute "expellees" and other groups brought in. There has been little repair of damaged houses, due to lack of materials and transportation. The result of all this is that multitudes are living in rubble and basements. The average space among tens of millions is equivalent to between three and four people to a 12'x12' room. Nor is the overcrowding confined to urban areas, for the "expellees" have been settled into every farm house. One consequence is the rapid spread of tuberculosis and other potentially communicable diseases.

COAL

The shortage of coal is, next to food, the most serious immediate bottleneck to both living and the revival of exports to pay for food. The Ruhr, which is now almost the sole coal supply of the Anglo-American Zones, is, due to lack of skilled men and [lowered] physical vitality in labor, producing only 230,000 tons per day, as against a former 450,000 tons per day. Of the present production, a considerable amount must be exported to surrounding nations which are also suffering. The shortage leaves the two zones without sufficient coal for transport, household and other dominant services, with little upon which to start exports in the industry.

The coal famine all over Western Europe and the unprecedented severity of the winter have produced everywhere the most acute suffering. As an example in Germany, no household coal has been issued in Hamburg since October. Other German cities have been but little better off.

AGRICULTURAL PRODUCTION

It must be borne in mind that about 25 per cent of the German pre-war food production came from the areas taken over by Russia and Poland. Moreover, the Russian Military Zone in Germany was a large part of the bread basket of Germany. Some millions of tons formerly flowed into the American and British Zones from these areas. These sources now contribute nothing.

The British and American armies and civilians are entirely fed from home. The large Russian army is fed upon their zone.

Due to a lack of fertilizers, good seed, farm implements and skilled labor, the 1946 agricultural production in the American and British Zones was [only] about 65 per cent of pre-war. A generalized appraisal indicates that in the American Zone the harvest of 1946 yielded a supply, beyond the needs of the farmers (self-suppliers) equal to about 1,100 calories per day for the "non-self suppliers." The similar supply in the British Zone was about 900 calories per day average to the "non-self suppliers." These amounts contrast with 3,000 calories of the pre-war normal German consumption.

With the efforts being made to improve agricultural production, there is an expected small increase from the harvest of 1947, especially in potatoes (if better seed is provided in time). The steps which I recommend, however, should show greater production from the 1948 harvest.

FOOD DISTRIBUTION

This terrible winter, with frozen canals and impeded railway traffic, has rendered it impossible to maintain even the present low basis of rationing in many localities. The coal shortage and the consequent lack of heat, even for cooking, has added a multitude of hardships. The conclusions in this report as to the food situation are, however, not based upon the effect of this temporary dislocation, but upon the basic conditions to which the winter has added many difficulties.

From the food point of view, the population of the combined zones has been divided as below, based upon the German census undertaken last autumn. The table must not be regarded as precise for the different groups, as the Berlin Sector was not distributed on the same basis as others. It is, however, accurate enough for food computation purposes.

"Self-suppliers," i.e. farmers and their families		7,640,000
"Non-self suppliers," i.e. urban population:		
Prospective and nursing mothers	660,000	
Children 0–6 years of age	3,070,000	
Children 6–15 years of age	4,495,000	
Adolescents, 15–20 years of age	2,100,000	
"Normal Consumers," 20 years up	17,910,000	
Moderate hard workers	2,500,000	
Heavy workers	1,910,000	
Extra heavy workers	720,000	
Displaced persons	680,000	34,045,000
Total population, two zones		41,685,000

The base ration is 1,550 calories per person per day to the "normal consumer" group, with priorities and supplements, as the situation requires or permits, for other groups. For instance, milk and fats are given in priority to nursing mothers and children up to six years of age; more food, including more meat, is given in supplement to hard workers, etc.

This basic ration for the "normal consumer" compares with the minimum temporary maintenance food intake recommended for "normal consumers" by eminent nutritionists, as follows:

	Present German	Recommended Minimum	Per Cent Deficiency
Carbohydrates	283 grams	335 grams	16%
Fats	24 grams	45 grams	47%
Protein	52 grams	65 grams	20%
Calories	1,550	2,000	24%

Thus with the deficiency in quantity and in fats, protein and other nutrients, the 1,550 [calorie] ration is wholly incapable of supporting the health of the groups which do not have supplements.

NUTRITIONAL CONDITION OF THE POPULATION

The nutritional conditions of the above different groups . . . are:

(A) The 7,640,000 self-suppliers are, naturally, in good condition.

(B) The supplements and priorities in special foods given to 3,730,000 prospective and nursing mothers, and children under six years of age, appear to be enough to keep them in good condition.

(C) Over half of the 6,595,000 children and adolescents, especially in the lower-income groups, are in a deplorable condition. Their situation is better in limited localities where school feeding has been undertaken but outside these limits stunted growth and delayed development is widespread. In some areas famine edema (actual starvation) is appearing in the children. A study of groups of boys between the ages 9 and 16 years showed 5.5 lbs. under minimum standard weights, with girls 5.1 lbs. below such standard. Other groups studied showed even worse conditions.

(D) A considerable part of the "normal consumer" group of 17,910,000 is likewise in deplorable condition.

This group comprises the light physical workers and is in large majority women and many are aged. . . . Some part of this group are too poor to purchase even the 1,550 calorie ration.

In any event, a large part of the group shows a steady loss of weight, vitality and ability to work. A study in the British Zone shows urban adult males over 19 pounds and females nearly 5 pounds under proper weight. A study in the American Zone showed from 5 to 20 pounds under proper weight. Famine edema is showing in thousands of cases, stated to be 10,000 in Hamburg alone. The increased death roll among the aged is appalling. In persons over 70, in three months last autumn the increase [in the number of deaths] was 40 per cent.

(E) While the workers' rations, due to supplements, are perhaps high enough in themselves, yet the universal tendency is for the worker to share his supplement with his wife and children, and therefore it does not have its full effect in supplying energy for the worker himself.

(F) The 680,000 Displaced Persons are about one-third in the British Zone and two-thirds in the United States Zone. In the British Zone they receive the German ration only. In the United States Zone they receive supplements which amount to 700 calories per day, so there can be no doubt as to their adequate supply in that area. In fact, the American ration is above the "normal ration" of the other nations on the Continent, except the former neutrals.

These nutritional conclusions are based upon surveys made by Dr. Wm. H. Sebrell, Jr., of the United States Public Health Service, who was a member of my Mission. At my request, he also visited Italy, France, Belgium, Holland and Britain, to study the comparative nutritional situations of these countries with that of Germany. He reports that the nutritional condition in those countries is nearly pre-war normal, while the special German groups that I have mentioned are not only far below the other nations but disastrously so.

A NEW PROGRAM

The Anglo-American bi-zonal agreement of last autumn calls for an increase of rations by 250 calories per day at some undetermined date. Such an increase is highly desirable. However, the world shortage in cereals, evidenced by the early reduction of bread rations in several other nations, renders such an increase impossible until after the harvest of 1947. Such a program also implies increased import supplies which, in terms of grain, would add 1,260,000 tons and $136,000,000 annually to costs, above the already huge burden upon the taxpayers of our two nations.

As the present base of 1,550 calories for "normal consumers" is not enough to maintain health in many children or health and working energy in many adults, I propose a different program. This new approach is to repair the weakest spots in the nutritional situation. I believe that this method will accomplish the major purpose of the proposed general increase in ration as nearly as can be accomplished within the limits of available supplies and finances for the remainder of the fiscal year 1946–1947.

In many ways, I believe it is a better program, and if this method proves a successful remedy during the next few months, it may modify the necessity of so large an increase in imports in the fiscal year 1947–1948 as has been proposed under the bi-zonal agreement.

There are two groups to which this repair of weakness should be given quickly:

First are the children over six years of age and the adolescents. The number of this group who are undernourished is estimated to be about 3,500,000 or more than 50 per cent. To cover this group and assure that the food reaches the child, the British in their zone, aided by the Swedish and other charities, are giving a small ration in certain schools. There is no systematic school feeding in the American Zone. A system of soup kitchens [canteens] to provide a hot meal of appropriate body-building foods (meat, fats, milk, etc.) of at least 350 calories daily is imperative for the children in the worst areas of the combined zones, if a future Germany of wholesome character is to be created.

In order to start this system at once, I recommend using the Army surplus 10-in-1 rations now en route and certain excess stocks not adapted to Army feeding and now in control of the American Occupation Forces. These resources can form the major base of this system for a considerable period. This is the more possible as it is proposed to slaughter during 1947 over 5,000,000 head of [emaciated] cattle, hogs and sheep in order to lessen the animal consumption of ground crops, and a portion of these meats and fats can be applied to this program. These various supplies, together with some minor cereal allotments, should carry the program for six months.

The second group demanding immediate relief is the "normal consumer" group of about 17,910,000 persons, now receiving 1,550 calories per day. I strongly recommend several lines of action. (a) A certain portion of them should be advanced to the group of moderate heavy workers and receive the supplement applicable to that category. (b) An emergency supply of cereals should be allotted to the German welfare organizations with which to provide a supplement to families in need and the soup kitchens. (c) I recommend that the aged in the "normal consumers" group, and others where medically certified, be issued tickets upon the soup kitchens for the meal of 350 calories per day during the school week, to be consumed either at these kitchens or taken home. These supplemental measures will substantially improve, and will at least carry over, the most needy part of this group.

By aid to the children and adolescents, some pressure will be removed from the "normal consumer" group, who naturally tend to cut their own food to help their children.

In support of the above program for children and "normal rations," I have included in the recommended deficiency appropriation an emergency supply of 65,000 tons of cereals. These measures, as I have said, are in substitution for the great increase otherwise necessary to import for the proposed program of a lift in the whole ration system by 250 calories.

In addition to these measures, I have included in the sums given below which I recommend to be appropriated for the balance of this fiscal year 1946–1947 an amount necessary for the shipment of 400,000 tons of surplus potatoes from the United States. The object is two-fold.

Due to spoilage during this unprecedented winter, and other causes, there are not enough potatoes by 250,000 tons to cover that portion of the minimum 1,550 calorie ration until the next harvest. Certainly we cannot allow the ration to fall below its already dangerous levels.

Of even more importance, most of the potato seed of our zones normally comes from the Polish-annexed area and the Russian Zone and is not available. If we can forward 200,000 to 250,000 tons of good potato seed, with some already in hand, we should be able to assure a yield from the 1947 harvest of 5,000,000 tons, and thereby effect some savings in overseas foods imports for the fiscal year 1947–1948.

NECESSARY IMPORTS AND FINANCE

The supply and finance of food and collateral relief imports and the development of exports with which ultimately to pay for these imports, has been organized upon the basis of dividing foreign trade into two categories:

Category "A" covers imports of food, fertilizers, and petroleum products for the civil population. This Category is to be paid for by appropriations, and thus one-half by the taxpayers each of the United States and the United Kingdom. It has not been determined whether seeds fall in this group. In my opinion they should be, and I have included them in my estimates of supply and cost which appear below.

Category "B" is under the "Joint Export-Import Agency," which regulates the importation of raw materials and the export of coal, some other raw materials and manufactured products. The organization started with a certain working capital and all exports of coal and other commodities are credited to this fund until the exports exceed the raw material imports, when the surplus will be applied to the cost of Category "A." It is hoped that the export surplus will begin to contribute to Category "A" in the last half of 1948 and cover virtually all the cost in the calendar year 1950.

Therefore, the cost of Category "A" for the balance of the 1947 fiscal year, in which a deficiency appropriation is involved, and the whole of the 1948 fiscal year, will fall upon the taxpayers of America and Britain.

COST AND SUPPLIES OF CATEGORY "A" IMPORTS
FOR THE LAST HALF OF FISCAL YEAR 1946–47

The program of supplies and costs to cover Category "A" for the six months from January 1st to July 1st, 1947 will appear large compared to the program given later for the whole fiscal year . . . [July 1, 1947, to July 1, 1948]. The reasons are that imports were unduly low during the last six months of 1946 and the drain on indigenous food unduly large. Also, it is necessary to include the cost of purchases and shipments prior to July 1st so as to provide in June for arrivals in Germany during the period July 1st to August 15th, for which appropriations for the 1947–48 fiscal year cannot be available until after July 1st. This works to lessen the burden on the fiscal year following that date. I have, as said, included the allotment of 65,000 tons of cereals to support the "normal ration" group, and the potato imports.

The following is the estimated cost for both zones; for the six months January 1st to July 1st, 1947, in which are included the supplies already shipped for this period:

Cereals (wheat equivalent) 2,505,000 tons	$288,000,000
Other foods, 720,000 tons	54,000,000
Fertilizers	17,500,000
Seeds	12,500,000
Petroleum products (civil population)	12,000,000
Total	$384,000,000

The United States contribution of one-half of this is $192,000,000.

What portion of these expenditures are already covered by appropria-

Not peek-a-boo, but a prayer of thanks offered by children in Kenya.

Distributing CARE packages to Hungarian refugees in Wolfgang See, Austria.

Herbert Hoover and Pope Pius XII during their conference in the Vatican.

Herbert Hoover and Mahatma Gandhi after food talks in New Delhi.

tions, and what portion must need be covered by deficiency appropriations, is not known to me.

SUPPLIES AND COSTS FOR FISCAL YEAR . . .
[JULY 1, 1947, TO JULY 1, 1948]

In considering the supplies and cost of Category "A" for the fiscal year 1947–1948, the supplemental supports I have proposed to strengthen the children, adolescents and "normal ration" group, should undoubtedly carry through these groups until October, especially with the Spring and Summer produce. Therefore, it will not, in any event, be necessary to increase the general ration by the 250 calories provided in the bi-zonal agreement until that date. It is my hope that the revised methods by which the weak places in the system are strengthened may partially or wholly avoid this necessity after that date. I have, however, provided in the estimates an item of $62,300,000 for such an increase after October. I have also included in these estimates an enlarged fertilizer and seed program. It is my belief that these latter measures will greatly lighten the burden on our taxpayers in the fiscal year . . . [July 1, 1948, to July 1, 1949].

The following is my estimate of the supplies and costs needed for the fiscal year . . . [July 1, 1947, to July 1, 1948], covering Category "A":

Cereals (in terms of wheat) for 1,550 calorie level, 2,785,000 tons	$278,500,000
Cereals for "normal consumers" emergency supplemental feeding, 192,000 tons	19,200,000
Child feeding program (includes special foods), 130,000 tons	35,000,000
Other foods, 450,000 tons	75,000,000
Fertilizers (available)	45,000,000
Seeds	27,000,000
Petroleum products for civil population	25,000,000
	$504,700,000
Cost of ration increase to 1,800 calories on or about October, 1947	62,300,000
Total	$567,000,000

of which the United States share of 50 per cent amounts to $283,500,000. Due to these changes in method, the above program is different from that submitted by the War Department for the fiscal year 1947–48, but the total cost is no greater.

It is my conviction that these appropriations for Category "A" for both the . . . [July 1, 1946, to July 1, 1947] and the . . . [July 1, 1947, to July 1, 1948] fiscal years should have first consideration, even in priority to appropriations for military purposes. The occupational forces cannot be reduced without these assurances of minimum food supply. From the point of view only of maintaining order, the need for these forces is not great, if we can meet the food needs. . . .

FURTHER SAVINGS TO THE TAXPAYERS THAT CAN BE MADE

There are ways by which these costs could be reduced, although they are not certain enough to be deducted in advance against appropriations which must now be determined.

1. If these changes in rationing program render the general calorie lift unnecessary, there would be a saving of $62,000,000.

2. If through the 1947 deficiency appropriation the seeds are provided in time, there should be substantial additions to the German potato harvest, in relief of . . . [July 1, 1947, to July 1, 1948] expenditures. If the fertilizer and seed recommendations for the fiscal year 1947–1948 are accepted, there should be savings by increased indigenous production in the year . . . [July 1, 1948, to July 1, 1949].

3. There would be savings if prices proved lower and if climatic conditions for the indigenous crops turned out exceptionally favorable.

4. The Potsdam Declaration results in Germany having no consequential overseas shipping. If we could effect some temporary operation by German crews of, say, seventy-five Liberty ships, now laid up, to transport food and raw materials, all of the expense could be paid by the Germans in marks, except for fuel, and thus save a very large amount of dollars otherwise coming from the American and British taxpayers. This would probably amount to $40,000,000 per annum.

5. A further saving of possibly several million dollars could be made for the taxpayers if the large American Army return equipment, now being transported at high ocean rates, were sent home on the return voyages on these Liberty ships.

6. There are food surpluses in the control of other nations than ourselves and the British. They comprise possible increased catches of fish in Norway, Sweden and Denmark, which otherwise are little likely to find a market, and some surpluses possible from the South American States. It

would seem to me that some supplies could well be furnished by these nations, being repaid as indicated below, pari passu with the British and ourselves.

7. The Germans lost a considerable part of their deep sea fishing fleet. If more such boats could be found and leased from American surplus small shipping, the fish supply could be greatly increased. The fishing grounds in the Baltic and North Seas are being limited against German fishing. As there are ample supplies of fish in these seas, it seems a pity that with this food available, British and American taxpayers are called upon to furnish food in substitution for fish the Germans could catch for themselves.

Fish is particularly needed, as the present diet is sadly lacking in protein content.

8. A still further saving to British and American taxpayers is possible if maximum expedition could be made of exports of German manufacture. The Joint Export-Import Agency is doing its best, but such exports are hampered by the lack of coal for manufacture; by Trading-with-the-Enemy Acts, and restrictions on free communication together with limitations on dealings between buyers and sellers. The restoration of trade is inevitable, and every day's delay in removing these barriers is simply adding to the burden of our taxpayers for relief that could otherwise be paid for in goods. No one can say that in her utterly shattered state, Germany is a present economic menace to the world.

Should there be such good fortune as to realize all these possibilities, we could not only increase the food supply to health levels but also lessen the joint costs by $150,000,000 during the fiscal year 1947–1948. . . .

GERMAN REPAYMENT FOR THESE OUTLAYS

The great sums hitherto spent on relief of the German civilian population from outside Germany's borders, together with those in the future, should not be an irrecoverable expenditure to our two Governments.

I have, therefore, urged upon the American and British authorities that it be announced as a policy, and stipulated in all peace arrangements, that these expenditures for the relief of the civil population (Category "A"), past and future, should be made a first charge upon the economy of Germany and repaid from any future net exports from Germany before any payments to other nations of any kind.

At my instance, all Allied nations in the first World War agreed that German civilian relief expenditures at that time should be repaid from any liquid assets and ranked ahead of any reparation claims. They were so repaid. The grounds which I advanced at that time are no less valid today. By these relief expenditures, we are rebuilding the economy of the German people so that other payments can be made by them. These costs should be a sort of "Receiver's Certificate." If this policy be pursued, these appropriations for relief asked from the Congress, and the Parliament, can become a recoverable expenditure and not a charity loaded onto our taxpayers. It would seem that a tax upon exports, of some per cent, to be paid in dollars after July 1, 1949 might be an effective implementation of such a provision.

ORGANIZATION

I have made certain recommendations to the joint Military Governments of the two zones as to organization matters, which I believe will improve administration, now that bi-zonal operation, under larger German responsibility, has been undertaken.

CONCLUSION

It may come as a great shock to American taxpayers that, having won the war over Germany, we are now faced for some years with large expenditures for relief for these people. Indeed, it is something new in human history for the conqueror to undertake.

Whatever the policies might have been that would have avoided this expense, we now are faced with it. And we are faced with it until the export industries of Germany can be sufficiently revived to pay for their food. The first necessity for such a revival is sufficient food upon which to maintain vitality to work.

Entirely aside from any humanitarian feelings for this mass of people, if we want peace; if we want to preserve the safety and health of our Army of Occupation; if we want to save the expense of even larger military forces to preserve order; if we want to reduce the size and expense of our Army of Occupation—I can see no other course but to meet the burdens I have here outlined.

Our determination is to establish such a regime in Germany as will prevent forever again the rise of militarism and aggression within these people. But those who believe in vengeance and the punishment of a great mass of Germans not concerned in the Nazi conspiracy can now have no misgivings, for all of them—in food, warmth and shelter—have been sunk to the lowest level known in a hundred years of Western history.

If Western Civilization is to survive in Europe, it must also survive in Germany. And it must be built into a cooperative member of that civilization. That indeed is the hope of any lasting peace.

After all, our flag flies over these people. That flag means something besides military power.[1]

When published, this report received an astonishing public response. It seemed to me the whole press editorialized favorably, and I received thousands of letters of approval. It was evident that the American heart was free of vindictiveness and ready to respond to human appeals.

Soon after this report appeared, the British decided they could not undertake their share of food costs, and the whole burden fell upon the United States. The food programs I initiated were put into action as far as appropriations from Congress permitted.

[1] *Addresses Upon the American Road, 1945–1948*, pp. 269–85.

CHAPTER 35

THE RESULT OF ALLIED ECONOMIC POLICIES

Much of the burden on the American taxpayer was due to the strangulation of German production and, consequently, exports which could have paid for Germany's imports of food and other supplies. The background of this policy was the Morgenthau Plan to limit industry in Germany.[1] This was a program of vengeance, bringing great suffering to the German people, stifling the European recovery, and creating additional expense to the American taxpayer. In a letter to President Truman, I said:

March 18, 1947

DEAR MR. PRESIDENT:

I am sending you herewith my conclusions upon the problems of reviving German industry and thus exports with which to relieve American and British taxpayers from their burden in preventing starvation in Germany. These problems also involve economic stability and peace in Europe.

Whatever may have been our policies in the past, I am convinced that the time has come to face the realities that have developed. The mission you assigned to me would be less than performed if I did not state the stark situation and make such recommendations as seem to me necessary.

I wish again to express my appreciation to you for your consideration, to my colleagues Mr. Hugh Gibson, Dr. Gustav Stolper, Dr. Dennis A.

---

[1] This plan was in action, at least in spirit, through an executive order dated April, 1945, and known as "Directive J.C.S., 1067." The text of these drastic orders is given in various publications, including *Bulletin of the Department of State*, v. 13, no. 330, Oct. 21, 1945, p. 596 ff.

FitzGerald, Dr. William Sebrell, Jr., and Messrs. Louis Lochner, Frank Mason and Tracy Voorhees, and to our military and civil officials in Germany.

HERBERT HOOVER

My report on the second part of our mission follows.

THE REPORT

Inquiry into the economic policies in Germany which would relieve financial support from the United States was one of the subjects assigned to my mission to that country. Aside from a mass of information and statistical material secured on this journey, I have been familiar with German economic problems over many years, including my experience before and after World War I. In view of the gravity of the crisis which confronts the world, it would be an ill service if I did not state my conclusions fully and frankly.

These conclusions are not the product of sentiment nor of feeling toward a nation which has brought such misery upon the whole earth. They are not given in condonement of the enormity of her crimes. They are the result of a desire to see the world look forward, get into production and establish a lasting peace. They are based upon the stern necessities of a world involved in the most dangerous economic crisis in all history.

At the present time the taxpayers of the United States and Britain are contributing nearly $600,000,000 a year to prevent starvation of the Germans in the American and British zones alone. The drain is likely to be even greater after peace unless the policies now in action are changed. Therefore, entirely aside from any humanitarian and political aspects, policies which will restore productivity in Germany and exports with which to buy their food and relieve this drain upon us are of primary importance.

But our economic interest is far wider than this. We desperately need recovery in all of Europe. We need it not only for economic reasons but as the first necessity to peace. The United States, through loans, lend-lease, surplus supplies, and relief, in the last two years, has spent, or pledged itself to spend, over fifteen billions of dollars in support of civilians in foreign countries. Even we do not have the resources for, nor can our taxpayers bear, a continuation of burdens at such a rate.

There is only one path to recovery in Europe. That is production. The whole economy of Europe is interlinked with German economy through the exchange of raw materials and manufactured goods. The productivity of Europe cannot be restored without the restoration of Germany as a contributor to that productivity.

SOME ASSUMPTIONS

In order to offer constructive conclusions as to economic policies which will relieve the American taxpayer and will promote economic recovery in Europe, I make six assumptions, which I believe will be accepted by sensible people. They necessarily include certain political aspects which underlie all these economic problems.

First. I assume that we wish to establish a unified federal state in Germany, embracing mainly the present American, British, Russian and French military occupation zones, with economic unity and free trade between the states. I shall refer to this area as the "New Germany."

Second. I assume that our objective must be to clear German life of the Nazi conspirators and to punish those who have contributed to this conspiracy, which murdered millions of people in cold blood and brought this appalling disaster upon the world.

Third. I assume that we will not make the major mistake of Versailles, but will complete absolute disarmament of the Germans so that they shall not be able again to engage in aggressions; that this disarmament will embrace destruction of all military arms, fortifications and direct arms factories, with certain control of industry; that the Germans will have *no* army, *no* navy, and *no* air forces, retaining only a constabulary in which no Nazi or previous army officer may be employed; that this disarmament must be continued for a generation or two, until Germany has lost the "know-how" of war and the descent of militarism through birth.

Fourth. I assume that these requirements must be safeguarded by international guarantees and effective police service by the nations.

Fifth. I assume, in our own interest and that of Europe, that we wish to restore the productivity of the continent, that we wish to revive personal freedom, honest elections and generally to reconstruct the German people into a peace-loving nation cooperating in the recovery of Western civilization.

Sixth. I assume that the United States will not join in such guarantees and policing unless the treaty with Germany is so concluded that it contributes to the restoration of productivity and lasting peace in Europe and promptly relieves us of drains upon our taxpayers.

THE GERMAN ECONOMIC PROBLEMS

The German economic problems have two aspects:

First, the long-view, broad economic policies toward the New Germany which alone can produce the reconstruction of Europe and peace.

Second, our immediate problems in the joint Anglo-American military zones during the interregnum pending peace.

I therefore divide this discussion into these two parts.

PART I: THE LONG VIEW ECONOMIC PROBLEM

The long-view economic problems involved in the peace with the New Germany and its aftermaths are greatly affected by war destruction, the boundary settlements for the New Germany, the plant removals for reparations, and the policies with respect to "war potential" of industry.

These effects may be summarized:

1. There was considerable destruction of non-war industry from the air and otherwise during the war. The loss to peaceful productivity has not been determined, but it is considerable.

2. The proposed annexations to Poland and Russia, and the possible annexation of the Saar Basin by France, will take from Germany, as compared to 1936,* about 25% of her food supply, about 30% of her bituminous coal and about 20% of her manufacturing capacity.

3. The population of Germany in 1936 was about 68,000,000. The population of the New Germany by 1949 will be about 71,000,000, due to the expulsion of Germans from the Polish and Russian annexations, from Czechoslovakia, Hungary, Austria, Yugoslavia, Roumania and the return of prisoners into this area.

4. The Allied economic policies toward Germany are of two categories: the first involves world safety, and the second, reparations for wrong done:

a. There has necessarily been, or will be, a demolition of all arms plants as part of disarmament. This destruction, however, has included some plants which might have been converted to peaceable production.

b. Reparations have been provided by assignment for removal to the

---

* I have adopted 1936 as a basis for economic comparisons because it was a full year before German industry was distorted by her annexations and her most intensive armament activity.

different Allies of certain percentages of "usable and complete industrial equipment." What proportion of Germany's peaceable productive plant has been, or is, in the course of removal in the French and Russian zones is not known. Certainly they have been very large from the Russian zone. The total for all Germany amounts to an important segment of its peaceful productivity. These removals include a large amount of "light industry" (producing mostly consumers' goods) as well as "heavy industry" (producing mostly capital goods). The removal of plants from the American and British zones has been halted because of the refusal of Russia and France to cooperate in inter-zonal economic unity as provided for at Potsdam.

5. In addition to the above courses of action, there have been general policies of destruction or limitation of possible peaceful productivity under the headings of "pastoral state" and "war potential." The original of these policies apparently expressed on September 15, 1944, at Quebec, aimed at:

"converting Germany into a country principally agricultural and pastoral,"

and included,

"The industries of the Ruhr and the Saar would therefore be put out of action, closed down. . . ."

This idea of a "pastoral state" partially survived in JCS Order 1067 of April, 1945 for the American zone. It was not accepted by the British. The "pastoral state" concept was not entirely absent in the Potsdam Declaration. It was partially ameliorated or its name changed for another concept, the "level of industry," developed by the agreement of March 26, 1946, and signed by Russia, Britain, France and the United States. This agreement was a compromise between the drastic terms proposed by Russia and France and the more liberal terms proposed by the other two nations.

One major theme of this "level of industry" concept is to destroy Germany's "war potential." Under this concept certain industries are to be blown up or prohibited, others are to be limited as to production. The emphasis was placed upon the limitation of "heavy industry" with the view that Germany could export enough goods from "light industry" to buy her food and necessary raw materials.

The absolute destruction or prohibition includes ocean-going ships, shipbuilding, aircraft, ball bearings, aluminum, magnesium, beryllium, vanadium and radio-transmitting equipment, together with synthetic oil, ammonia and rubber. Some of these provisions may be essential to disarmament. Such exceptions are not included in the discussion which follows.

Beyond these prohibitions, however, the "level of industry" concept provides elaborate restrictions, mostly on heavy industry. The following items are illustrative:

Iron and steel production to be reduced from 19 million tons (as in 1936) to a capacity of 7.5 million tons, with a maximum production of 5.8 million tons and only the "older plants" to be used.

Heavy machinery production to be	31% of 1938
Light machinery production to be	50% of 1938
Machine tools to be	38% of 1938
Electrical machinery to be	from 30% to 50% of 1938
Agricultural implements to be	70% of 1936
Automobiles to be	10% of 1936
Trucks to be	67% of 1936
Basic chemicals, including nitrogen, calcium carbide, sulphuric acid, chlorine and alkali to be	40% of 1936
Cement to be	65% of 1936
Electric power produced to be	60% of 1936
No new locomotives until 1949.	
Some "light industries" were also to be limited:	
Textiles to be	77% of 1936
Paper to be	65% of 1936
Boots and shoes to be	70% of 1936
Precision instruments and optics to be	70% of 1936
Miscellaneous chemicals to be	70% of 1936
Pharmaceuticals to be	80% of 1936
Dyestuffs (export) to be	58% of 1936

THE CONSEQUENCES TO FOOD SUPPLY

We may first examine what has happened, and what will happen, to the German food supply under all the circumstances of annexation and industrial controls.

Germany in 1936 was, by most intensive cultivation, able to produce about 85% of her food supply. This 85% has now been reduced by 25% through the Russian and Polish annexations, or is down to about 64% because even a larger population is to be concentrated in the New Germany.

Her production, however, was greatly dependent upon intensive use of fertilizers. The New Germany will require at least 500,000 metric tons of nitrogen and 650,000 tons of phosphoric anhydride, she having sufficient potash.

Under the level of industry agreement, the domestic production of nitrogen eventually would be reduced to under 200,000 tons; the production of phosphoric anhydride would be reduced to about 200,000 tons. A larger production of nitrogen is allowed pending an opportunity to import. Part of this reduction is due to the "level of industry" steel reduction from which some nitrogen and a large percentage of phosphoric anhydride requirements were obtained as by-products.

From these figures it is obvious that a great discrepancy exists between minimum agricultural needs and the possible fertilizer production under the "level of industry" plan. If we persist in these policies, unless there are large imports of fertilizer, Germany's food production is likely to drop under 60% of her requirements even with an austere diet.

New Germany, if there is to be a will to work, to maintain order and to aspire to peace, must have an average food supply of at least 2600 calories per person per day, with adequate fats and protein content. (The . . . [German prewar] average being . . . about 3,000 calories.)

Taking the above limitations into consideration and based upon actual experience in the American and British zones, and extending that experience with adaptations to the Russian and French zones, the indications are that New Germany would need, at present prices, to import over $1,250,000,000 annually in food and animal feed alone.

At the end of the war Germany had a very large nitrogen capacity. Despite losses from war destruction, its potential production was still about 700,000 tons per annum. This capacity, if it had been preserved, would have supplied not only her own needs but large exports to neighboring countries as well. Fertilizers are now sorely needed all over Europe for crop restoration. Therefore, through the fertilizer reduction Germany not only loses in her own food production but her export potential to pay for food, and the crops elsewhere in Europe are reduced.

CONSEQUENCES OF "LEVEL OF INDUSTRY" UPON "HEAVY INDUSTRY"

The effect of the agreed "level of industry" is stated in American official reports that "The 'heavy industry' products for which Germany was noted will virtually disappear from her exports."

I have exhaustively examined the production and exports of Germany over some years in the light of this "level of industry" and they amply confirm this statement. What the result may be is indicated by the fact that her exports during peace from now-restricted "heavy industries" comprised between 60% and 70% of the total German exports. In 1936, for instance, a generally prosperous year, they amounted to about $1,900,000,000 out of a total of about $2,700,000,000, both figures converted into present prices. Under the "level of industry" most of this 60–70% is to be abolished, and Germany must pay for most of her imports from exports of "light industry."

Germany must not alone import food and animal feed, but also reduced amounts of copper, lead, zinc, iron ore, leather, cotton, wool, and other raw materials. Due to the prohibitions, she must import all of her oil and rubber, and considerable nitrogen for fertilizers.

It is indeed a cynical fact that today we are supplying Germany with oil and nitrogen at the expense of the American and British taxpayer, at a rate of $70,000,000 per annum, which, except for the "level of industry" and the Russian refusal of zonal cooperation, Germany could have produced herself.

CONSEQUENCES UPON LIGHT INDUSTRY

As I have said, the assumption is that exports from the German "light industry," from coal and native raw materials, such as potash, can pay for her imports of food and other necessities. There are two reasons for believing this assumption to be completely invalid.

Had there been no loss of "light industry" plants by annexation, had there been no destruction of them by war, had there been no removals for reparations, they could not have produced enough exports to pay the food bill alone. And the situation is made doubly impossible by the restrictions now imposed on what "light industry" is left, as, for instance, on textiles.

If Germany is to buy food and the necessary imports of raw material for the "light industry," she would require not only complete restoration to pre-war level in "light industry" but a much larger equipment than she had even before the war.

Then Germany, with the expansion of these industries, would be in a competitive field of consumers' goods with all the rest of the world whose "light industries" have been little damaged by war.

SOME ECONOMIC ILLUSIONS

There are several illusions in all this "war potential" attitude.

a. There is the illusion that the New Germany left after the annexations can be reduced to a "pastoral state." It cannot be done unless we exterminate or move 25,000,000 people out of it. This would approximately reduce Germany to the density of the population of France.

b. There is an illusion in "war potential." Almost every industry on earth is a "war potential" in modern war. No industry (except direct arms manufacture) is a war potential if the energies of a people are confined to the paths of peace. If Germany be disarmed in the way I have assumed above, there must be a control commission to see that they do not have any army or any navy. And two score of intelligent men, as part of that commission, could see that there is no arms production and that no industry is manufacturing or storing materials for evil purposes. Moreover, industry is not likely to waste its substance, either by storing or manufacturing for war, when there is no army or navy to use it.

The question here is not "level of industry." The real question is whether the Allied nations will stick to their abolition of militarism itself in Germany. If they do that, there is little danger from "war potential" in industry.

c. Another illusion is that the "light industry" in Germany can be expanded to a point where she will be able to pay for her imports. In my view, it cannot be done for years, and even then it is doubtful in the face of competition with the "light industries" of other parts of the world.

d. The over-all illusion is that Germany can ever become self-supporting under the "levels of industry" plan within the borders envisioned at present for New Germany.

e. A still further illusion is that Europe as a whole can recover without the economic recovery of Germany.

CONSEQUENCES TO EUROPE GENERALLY

Thus there is a still wider aspect of this "level of industry"—the needs of the rest of Europe. Germany had been for a century one of the great European centers of production of capital goods—"heavy industry," which I may repeat are construction materials, factory equipment, railway equipment, electrical and heavy machinery. The other nations of Europe are in desperate need of such goods for reconstruction from war damage. Moreover, a considerable part of the European equipment on these lines is

German-made, and today, they cannot even get replacements and spare parts, in consequence of which their productivity lags.

From the standpoint of other nations, the expansion of "light industry" to a point of self-support for Germany will, by competition, injure these industries in the rest of Europe. On the other hand, the products of "heavy industry" is Europe's first necessity for recovery.

It must not be overlooked that Germany was the market for every nation in Europe and such a reduction of her economy will tend to demoralize the industries and employment in those countries. For instance, Germany was the market for over half the exports of Turkey and over one-third those of Greece. In consequence, their loss of this market contributes to increase the relief they seek from us now.

Another illustration is the proposed limits on steel. Large and efficient steel and iron plants, undamaged or only partly damaged, are standing idle in Germany. Formerly the Germans imported millions of tons of iron ore from France and Sweden. These mines, under the "level of industry," must remain idle until a new steel industry is built elsewhere. That will require years and an amount of capital that is not in sight. In the meantime, Europe needs steel for reconstruction as she never did before.

To indicate the anxiety of surrounding states a memorandum of the Netherlands Government of January 1947, in presenting the absolute necessity to the surrounding nations that a productive economic state be created in Germany, said: "The provisions of the plan for reparations and the level of German economy of March 1946 require to be revised . . . it is inadvisable to lay down maximum quota for production of German industries including the iron and steel industries."

The sum of all of this is: Germany, under the "level of industry" concept, unless she is to be allowed to starve, will be a drain on the taxpayers of other nations for years and years to come. In the meantime, if her light industries were built to become self-supporting, she would become an economic menace to Europe; if her heavy industries are allowed to function, she has an ability to export and would become an asset in Europe's recovery. To persist in the present policies will create, sooner or later, a cesspool of unemployment or pauper labor in the center of Europe which is bound to infect her neighbors.

We can keep Germany in these economic chains but it will also keep Europe in rags.

A NEW ECONOMIC POLICY

Therefore, I suggest that we adopt at once a new economic concept in peace with New Germany.

(1) We should free German industry, subject to a control commission, which will see that she does no evil in industry, just as we see that she does not move into militarism through armies and navies.

The difference between this concept and the "level of industry" concept is the saving of several hundred millions of dollars a year to the American and British taxpayers. It is the difference between the regeneration and a further degeneration of Europe.

(2) The removal and destruction of plants (except direct arms plants) should stop.

(3) A further obstacle to building Germany as an essential unit of European economy arises from the Russian Government's acquiring a large part of the key operating industries in their zone. Germany in peace must be free from ownership of industry by a foreign government. Such ownership can thwart every action of control or of up-building by joint action of other nations. German industry must be operated by Germans if any international control is to work, if she is to recover production and is to serve all nations equally.

(4) There can be no separation or different regime of the Ruhr or Rhineland from the New Germany. That is the heart of her industrial economy. Any control commission can dictate the destination of coal or other exports from that area and even such control would not be needed after the era of scarcity passes from Europe.

PART II: THE INTERREGNUM BEFORE PEACE

How long it may be before there is such a constructive peace with Germany, no one can tell. It may be long delayed. In the meantime, we are faced with the feeding of the people in the Anglo-American zones on a level just above starvation until we can develop enough export goods from these zones so that the Germans may pay for their food. I have said, American and British taxpayers are called upon for about $600,000,000 a year for relief.

We have an admirable staff in Military Government of Germany under Generals [McNarney,] Clay and Draper but their administration is constantly frustrated in building up the needed exports to pay for food and minimum raw material imports. A large part of these delays is due to the following:

a. The Russians and the French have failed to carry out the provisions of the Potsdam agreement for economic unity in the four zones. The Russian zone ordinarily produces a surplus of food but that surplus is used elsewhere, thus increasing the burden of imports on the Anglo-American zones. Both the Russian and French zones are producing industrial commodities which would relieve necessities in the Anglo-American zones and could contribute to exports with which to pay for food. The net effect is that the United States and Britain through relief are paying Russian and French reparations.

b. The inability to determine what specific plants are to be the victims of "level of industry," or destruction or the removal for reparations, produces stagnation because the Germans do not know where to begin work.

c. There is lack of working capital with which to import raw materials for such industries as are allowed to function.

d. An inflated currency and no adequate banking system hampers all forward movement in such industry as is left.

e. While de-Nazification and de-cartelization are necessary and important certain phases of them limit recovery. They are so involved as not to warrant description here.

CONCLUSION AS TO THE BI-ZONAL ADMINISTRATION

If, however, we cannot get a quick and sound peace on the lines I have recounted, the Anglo-American zones should abandon the destruction of plants, the transfer of plants for reparations and the "level of industry" concept, and start every plant, "heavy" as well as "light," which can produce non-arms goods. This will relieve far more rapidly great costs to our taxpayers; it will do infinitely more for Europe than American loans and charity.

Indeed the Congressional Committee on Postwar Economic Policy urged, on December 30, 1946, that the "levels of industry" be ignored wherever they conflict with exports so that there may be earlier recovery and payment for food.

The violation by Russia and France of the agreement for economic unification of the four zones of military occupation and the additional burdens this imposed upon us in consequence certainly warrant our ignoring all agreements for "level of industry," transfer and destruction of non-arms plants. . . .[2]

President Truman proceeded to release the economic shackles on Germany. She then began her economic recovery.

A BY-PRODUCT OF OUR RECOMMENDATIONS IN GERMANY

The food programs which I initiated were at once put into action, as is indicated by the following extracts from letters from General Lucius D. Clay and Secretary of War Robert P. Patterson:

7 March 1947

My dear Mr. Hoover:

. . . Authority has been received from the Secretary of War to implement the program recommended by you in your report to President Truman. We shall put this program into effect at the earliest practicable date.

I am deeply grateful to you for your sympathetic understanding of our problems here in Germany. If adequate funds are appropriated to meet our minimum needs it will be largely through your understanding and help.

Lucius D. Clay

7 April 1947

Dear Mr. Hoover:

Thank you for your letter of 3 March and the printed copy of your report which the War Department had furnished us by radio.

We are ready to move into the child feeding program in the next few days. . . .

If it were not for your report, I know that we would face disaster in the months ahead. As it is, I believe we shall pull through with an appreciable economic revival and without substantial loss to communist penetration and influence.

Also, we can sense even now the improvement in American thinking and feeling toward the German problems which has come about from your report. In the long run, that may be even more valuable to us than

[2] *Addresses Upon the American Road, 1945–1948,* pp. 83–97.

the appropriation; although this latter need was so urgent from our viewpoint as to overshadow the former. . . .

No one else could have accomplished for us what you did. We are grateful, not only because we were honored by your visit, but also because your report has made possible the accomplishment of America's real objective in Germany.

LUCIUS D. CLAY

April 16, 1947

DEAR MR. HOOVER:

I have been advised by General Clay's headquarters that the child feeding program for the occupied German Zone will become effective about the middle of this month, and it appears that we may expect good cooperation in its implementation from all concerned.

General Keating, Deputy Military Governor of OMGUS, advised me that, at a recent conference sponsored by the German Executive Committee for Food and Agriculture to complete arrangements for the program in line with your recommendations, the following was requested:

"The conference members requested that Mr. Hoover and the US/UK Governments be informed of the appreciation and gratitude that it felt for their support of a special child-feeding program for German children. German participating agencies state program promises to be extremely popular and beneficial."

I should like to add again my gratitude to the above message.

ROBERT P. PATTERSON

A report from the Military Government on June 19, 1947, stated:

The School Feeding (Hoover) Program is now in operation successfully in all Laender in the Southern and Northern areas and in Bremen. . . .

. . . By the beginning of the 103rd ration period (23 June) the entire permitted quota of 3,550,000 children will receive the supplemental meal at school of 350 calories daily. . . .

The importance of this program cannot be over-estimated both from its nutritional value to the children and its public relations value between Military Government and the German people.

The numbers of children who were fed were rapidly increased.

I received thousands of touching letters from the children and from their parents in all parts of Germany, for the service was put on under my name. Among them was this one from thirteen-year-old Friedrich Wilhelm Langguth of Coburg, Bavaria:

I want to thank you very much for your fine child feeding program. Our daily meals taste wonderful, especially because we became always hungry during school. We are three brothers and one sister, and all of us, except my eldest brother, who is already 18 years old, get the school-feeding. It is a great support for our dear mother, when we come from school after taking such a fine meal, because my mother apprehended very much, about our dear father, who is still a Prisoner of war in Moscow and whom the Soviets do not let home. . . . If every people will help the other, like you does, we should have a lasting peace soon.

Another typical letter came from twelve-year-old Liselotte Massholder of Heidelberg. Translated, it read:

Honored Mr. Hoover! . . . you have brought great joy to us with the school feeding program. We were very happy when our teacher told us to bring dishes along. We went home with beaming faces. The next day we returned with dishes in our hands. We were so excited that we were very restless. . . . At 2:30 p.m. the janitor rapped at the door and said, "Children, today you're going to get something good!"
. . . Two nice Red Cross sisters handed out the food. . . .
The food was still very hot, wherefore we placed it on the window sills and continued to study intensely. During the big recess we ate the sweets with great relish. I have already gained four pounds in eight days. Dear Mr. Hoover, you are now feeding us hungry mouths every week with good food. You have helped German youth out of a great hunger disaster. That's why I thank you most sincerely! [3]

In the middle of May, 1947, there was a sudden and unexpected minor crisis in German food. The hard winter had prevented early planting of vegetables, and there was some miscalculation of stocks. But the whole amounted to about two weeks' food and was remedied by quick imports. As it attracted considerable press comment, I issued, on May 15, a statement explaining the situation to take

[3] These letters were also published in Louis P. Lochner's book *Herbert Hoover and Germany* (New York, The Macmillan Company, 1960), pp. 197 and 199.

some of the pressure off General Clay and our Military Administration. I reviewed the temporary causes and freed the Military Government from blame. Secretary Patterson referred to this in a letter dated June 13:

DEAR MR. HOOVER:

I wish to express, both officially as Secretary of War and for myself personally, my deep sense of gratitude to you for the most recent great service which you have rendered to us in your courageous and vigorous support of our requested appropriation for Fiscal Year 1947 for Government and Relief in Occupied Areas. If we obtain this appropriation in full or without a very large cut, it will be due in principal part to your action. . . .

Now in your recent testimony and press statement, supporting so effectively our request for the funds necessary to carry this work on through the next fiscal year, you have done everything that one man can do, and more than any other man living would be able to do, in giving aid to the War Department toward the successful discharge of this responsibility.

With deep appreciation,

ROBERT P. PATTERSON

A CAMPAIGN FOR CLOTHING

Upon my return from Europe on February 23, 1947, I took up in several directions the problem of clothing the destitute in Germany and Austria. I first secured the aid of the American Friends Service Committee in the job of collecting unused piece goods from manufacturers. I then arranged for the War Department and the War Assets Administration to assign a very large quantity of used Army and Navy clothing for these purposes. I also secured the withdrawal of much of this kind of material which had been classified for surplus sale by the War Assets Administration. This action was also justified by the fact that the sales were not covering the costs of selling.

I also interested the Girl Scouts in a program of sending layettes for babies to all countries in need. They did a magnificent job. A typical statement of mine which they used as a quotation in their campaign was:

Tens of millions of children in Europe are underclad. There is nothing that should so appeal to the children of America as for each of them to prepare and send them a garment. There are no enemies among children.

As a final word on Germany, I include here a letter dated September 30, 1959, twelve and one-half years after our mission, from Louis Lochner, who accompanied me on the mission to Germany:

September 30, 1959

DEAR CHIEF:

My wife and I have just returned from a series of visits to friends and relatives which took us as far eastward as Hannover. Already upon our arrival two weeks ago in Essen, the heart of German industrial production, we had been struck by something, the confirmation of which came so frequently during our trip, that I feel justified to present it to you as a conclusion:

There is so marked a difference in the stature of the young German women and men in their late teens or early twenties as compared with that of their parents that the fact is inescapable that there must be some connection between the towering figures of the youngsters and the food on which they were raised. In other words, the post-war Hoover Child Feeding Program of 1947 and the years following has paid off in a manner that perhaps even you—certainly we, who were members of your team on The President's Economic Mission—could not envisage.

At first, I confess, I was merely bewildered and could not figure things out. I merely *saw* what seemed like a miracle. I had sat at the feet of Dr. David Starr Jordan and heard him as a biologist state before audience after audience how the French population of his day was on an average two inches smaller than that of the days of Napoleon—all because the best and the bravest had become soldiers and were killed, leaving the procreation of the next generation to the weak, infirm and unstable, with a resulting deterioration of the race.

Suddenly it dawned on me that there must be some cardinal difference between what happened to the youth of the post-Napoleonic period of France and the post-Nazi period of Germany. How come, I wondered, that a totally defeated nation, compelled by Hitler to produce "cannons instead of butter," could raise such strapping youngsters as we now see constantly? It dawned on me:

Mr. Hoover came to prostrate Germany—and for that matter, to all

Europe—just in time to reverse the process and make "butter instead of cannons" a reality.

To reassure myself that I, who am by no means an expert on nutritional and biological questions, am not totally wrong, I have asked husky, healthy teenagers and young people in their early twenties wherever I had an opportunity, whether they had been recipients in their early years of the "Hoover-Speisung," and all replied enthusiastically in the affirmative. I have asked their elders as to whether in their opinion the juvenile feeding program and the astounding height and apparent well-being of their offspring might be due to the "Hoover-Speisung." Again the reply was "most definitely so."

This is only the unscientific opinion of one of your humble disciples, but I thought it might interest you to know that one of our happiest and most impressive experiences in Germany thus far has been this realization of the undreamed-of-efficacy of the measures for the rehabilitation of Germany which you brought about.[4]

LOUIS P. LOCHNER

[4] Dr. Lochner gives his own account of our mission in his book *Herbert Hoover and Germany*, pp. 170–201.

CHAPTER 36

AUSTRIA

President Truman's directive to our 1947 mission included Austria. General Mark W. Clark, as American High Commissioner for Austria, was in charge. An hour after my arrival in Germany, I received a telephone call from General Clark in London, where he had gone to meet General Marshall to join a mission to Moscow. General Clark expressed regrets that he would not be in Vienna to receive me, but assured me he had given instructions to his staff to give our mission the fullest possible co-operation.

My report to President Truman on March 11, 1947, covered food matters and the necessary steps for relieving the American taxpayers of their financial burden.

ON AUSTRIAN AGRICULTURE AND FOOD
REQUIREMENTS—ECONOMIC REORGANIZATION

INTRODUCTION

It is impossible to make clear the economic and relief problems of Austria without a paragraph on her history.

By the Treaty of Versailles in 1919 Austria was reduced from an empire to a small state of between six and seven million population, over-weighted by the large city of Vienna with its 1,500,000 people.

Being left with too little agriculture to feed herself and too little industry to buy food through export of goods, the deficits between her imports and exports from 1919 to 1931 were met largely by foreign charity and "loans" from institutions and governments, including the United States. She finally crashed into bankruptcy in 1931 setting the fire of financial panic which swept Europe and finally the whole world.

After 1932 the country, rid of accumulated debt, made slow but substantial progress and by 1938 seemed to have reached stability and self-support. At that time she was forcibly annexed by Hitler. After annexation, the Germans stripped the country of the bank reserves, confiscated many industrial establishments, and large farm estates.

The Allied Armies invaded the country in April and May 1945 dividing it into four separate zones for military government under the French, American, British, and Russian Armies.

An election held in November 1945 resulted in the establishment of a constitution and parliamentary government, which government is, however, subject ultimately to the direction of a control commission representing the four Allied Powers.

The people being exhausted of food supplies, relief measures were carried initially by the American and British military authorities. This lasted about twelve months until April 1, 1946, when UNRRA undertook the work. UNRRA (whose funds were 98% American and British Commonwealth) is now winding up its service. The remainder of the fiscal year . . . [July 1, 1946, to July 1, 1947] will fall upon some new organization of relief. Such aid will certainly need to be carried on for the fiscal year . . . [July 1, 1947, to July 1, 1948] and probably considerably longer before recovery of Austrian industry enables her to exchange goods for her necessary food imports.

WAR DESTRUCTION

Aside from the vitality of the state drained by the Germans, there was considerable damage from the war. Fortunately, there was less destruction to manufacturing industry than in most combat areas. The railways suffered considerably but have been generally restored. The largest damage was to housing and to public and important cultural buildings.

In the city of Vienna, which suffered most, some 15,000 buildings were completely destroyed out of 65,000 damaged. Expressed in apartment units, over 110,000 or 21% of the city's shelter was made uninhabitable with consequent dreadful over-crowding, and thousands living in the rubble.

AGRICULTURAL PRODUCTION

Austrian agriculture never did supply more than 70% of her needs, the balance being imported. Due to the lack of fertilizers and agricultural machinery the harvest of 1946 was [only] about 60% of normal. Thus, between the normal deficiency in production and the low yields, the present volume of needed imports is very large.

FOOD DISTRIBUTION

The 7,000,000 population, from a food-rationing point of view, can be classified as follows:

"Self-suppliers"	1,200,000
Partial "self-suppliers"	700,000
Expectant and nursing mothers	90,000
Children 1–3	330,000
Children 3–6	370,000
Children 6–12	620,000
"Normal consumers"	2,100,000
"Employees"	600,000
Moderately heavy workers	800,000
Heavy workers	400,000

There is some duplication in these numbers due to "Partial self-suppliers." There are some 550,000 displaced persons in Austria, 450,000 of whom are included above and 100,000 of whom are provided for from non-Austrian sources.

The ration is at present 1550 calories for "normal consumers" with priorities in dairy products and special foods for the mothers group, and children up to twelve years. There are varied supplements in meats, fats and breadstuffs for the different "workers'" groups.

Examination of the nutritional situation of these groups showed that their condition was fairly good. There was no consequential famine edema. The weak spots were the lack of universal school feeding of children and more effective aid for indigent "normal consumers." Therefore, more systematic school feeding is necessary and further provision should be made for the indigent.

The nutritional condition is better than when I examined the situation a year ago. Although the official ration generally parallels that of Germany, insofar as calories are concerned, the condition of the people is distinctly better in Austria.

Compared to Germany the ration is better balanced, especially in the children's group, and there is a larger amount of supplemental food outside the ration. This arises from the larger amounts of unrationed food (such as vegetables except potatoes), larger black market supplies, a certain amount of child-feeding by foreign voluntary agencies and the very large number of food packages sent to friends and relatives from abroad. Altogether it is estimated that these supplements to the rationing system would represent an addition of at least 350 calories *per diem* if evenly distributed, bringing the "normal consumer's" ration up to 1900 calories.

The present food levels appear adequate to prevent any disaster but must be regarded as "emergency maintenance" which cannot be continued over years.

PROPOSED ORGANIZATION OF CONTINUED RELIEF

The United Nations has proposed a fund of $610,000,000 for relief to certain countries of which Austria is one. The United States contribution, recommended by our State Department, is $350,000,000, or 57%. The fund is presumed to cover only the period from the imminent end of UNRRA to the end of 1947—about nine months. The United Nations estimates contemplated a higher food level than that which I have felt possible or necessary during the emergency, and they include certain industrial reconstruction aids in addition to food, medicine and such agricultural supplies as seed, fertilizers and insecticides. While the program recommended by the United Nations is admirable and desirable, I have felt it necessary, in view of world supplies and the drains upon the American taxpayer, to make estimates only for food, medicines and agricultural supplies, and upon more limited levels of caloric intake.

The relief program can be divided into two periods: (a) from the end of UNRRA to the end of the fiscal year [July 1,] 1947, and (b) for the fiscal year . . . [July 1, 1947, to July 1, 1948].

REQUIREMENTS FOR THE REMAINDER OF THE
FISCAL YEAR 1946–1947

The program necessary for the period after UNRRA winds up—until July 1, 1947—is difficult to estimate until final amounts of UNRRA supplies are known. However, the requirements of food and medicine beyond the UNRRA program are roughly estimated at about $30,000,000 to July 1st [1947]. I have made no estimates for fertilizers or seed for the 1947 crop beyond the UNRRA supplies, as no more could arrive in time.

This sum will need to be provided either from Army deficit appropriations or from the newly proposed $350,000,000 fund. Whatever the source, the control of the distribution of American supplies should be placed in the hands of the American Army Command in Europe. The reason is that these supplies should be coordinated with the supplies for Germany, as both should be procured in common and shipped through the port of Bremen and over German railways. Moreover, Army agents can not only supervise distribution, but can also adjust our activities in relief to that of other nations contributing to Austria.

FISCAL YEAR 1947–1948

As relief must continue at least until the end of the fiscal year . . . [July 1, 1947, to July 1, 1948], I have felt it better to face the fact now rather than renewed appropriations later.

The program for the fiscal year 1947–48 will depend somewhat upon the crop of 1947, which cannot as yet be determined. All estimates should be revised at that time. My preliminary estimate of requirements is:

Cereals	430,000 tons
Meats	5,600 "
Fats	35,000 "
Pulses	114,000 "
Sugar	9,000 "
Seeds	60,000 "
Fertilizers	150,000 "
Medicines	$5,000,000

The total cost of such a program is estimated at about $125,000,000.

FINANCE

Thus the estimated cost of this program from the end of UNRRA until July 1, 1948, or about 15 months, is about $155,000,000. . . .

What amounts the other nations may contribute to Austrian relief have not yet been determined. The British have made a grant of 10,000,000 pounds sterling to Austria but I understand only a minor part can be used for dollar purchases. If the whole $610,000,000 fund be subscribed as recommended by the United Nations, then the 57% of the cost to the American taxpayer would be about $86,000,000. If other nations fail to respond, it may be necessary to lower the level of relief.

The estimates for Austria under the $610,000,000 United Nations program are about $148,000,000 for nine months only, but relief will need to go on at least until July 1, 1948. If it were continued six months more at this same rate, it would entail a further sum of about $100,000,000, or a total of about $248,000,000, as contrasted with $155,000,000 I have estimated.

As said, the lower costs that I propose are due to short world supplies and a food level that while austere is I believe sufficient to maintain health and vigor. Further, the $610,000,000 program includes support for industrial rehabilitation which I discuss later.

NECESSARY STEPS TO END THE LOAD
ON THE AMERICAN TAXPAYER

The problem of how soon Austria can become self-supporting by exports with which to buy her own food is of first interest to the American taxpayer. No report on Austria that does not face this situation is worth preparation. So long as such a balanced economy cannot be created (unless we wish to see terrible starvation) a large part of the deficit will fall upon the taxpayers in the United States and other nations. And this at a time when the whole world is struggling with huge problems of recovery.

There can be no real solution until there is a peace treaty which entirely frees Austrian economy to produce and export.

However, two alternative situations must be considered:

First, the interregnum between now and a peace treaty.

Second, the economic basis of a treaty under which Austria may regain self-support.

THE INTERREGNUM

Austrian economy, even in the interregnum before peace, requires the import of machinery, coal, certain raw materials, such as textiles, leather and metals, in order to manufacture both for consumption goods and for export. She already has developed some exports. The Austrian government has set up a sort of pool into which foreign exchange from these exports and otherwise is deposited and from which payments are made for industrial imports. The United Nations estimated her exports and other foreign exchange sources for the year 1947 at about $125,000,000. It is my belief that, at this rate, if the agricultural and food necessities can be provided without present drain on these exchange resources, Austria can manage her own industrial import program, as well as can be expected with the limitations of the times, without calling for aid from taxpayers of other nations in this field.

There is no way to estimate how long it will be before a constructive treaty shall be concluded. However, there are certain cooperative steps between the occupying powers that could be taken during the interregnum which would decrease needed food imports and increase exports so as to contribute to payment for food.

As I have said, pending peace, the Austrian government is subject to a quadrupartite commission of American, British, Russian and French representatives, and the country is separated into four military zones. The original intention was that there should be economic unity of the zones. That has not been fully carried out and full use of Austrian resources is not being brought into play, the result of which increases the burden upon our taxpayers.

The greatest difficulty in cooperation is with the Russian zone. Under the Potsdam Declaration, each of the four nations was to have as *German* reparations any *German* assets in its Austrian zone. Under these provisions each military government requisitioned such property. A very large segment of Austrian economy is under such requisition. Our American requisitions amounted to some two hundred enterprises but these have been assigned to the Austrian Government to operate in trust pending some settlement of the whole question. The other governments have been urged similarly to assign such ownership so as to increase Austrian productivity, self-support and recovery.

Under the Russian interpretation of the Potsdam Declaration, they have not only requisitioned a large amount of fertile land, but a great number of industrial plants. The Austrians claim that a large part of them were not in reality German assets. Disregarding questions of legality upon which I am not passing judgment, if the produce from these lands were released to Austria, together with relaxation of other requisitions, it would decrease the food imports by at least 70,000 tons per annum. Many of the requisitioned industrial plants are used otherwise than to support Austrian economy or exports. Another way to moderate this load on Austrian food supply would be the reduction of Russian armies to the minor levels of the other powers. In any event, the load upon the taxpayers of other nations during the interregnum is greatly increased, both for food imports and the diminished exports with which to pay for it.

AUSTRIAN ECONOMY IN PEACE

The Allies, in the Moscow Declaration of November 1, 1943, declared the annexation of Austria "null and void," "shall be liberated from German domination," "reestablished as free and independent." Thus classed as a "liberated state," it has been presumed that Austria will be free of reparations.

It can be said at once, however, that if the requisitioned assets are to be removed or operated for other than Austrian economy or by other than the Austrians themselves, there can be little hope that Austria can recover self-support for many, many years.

On the other hand, if Austria's land and industrial equipment were entirely freed by a peace treaty and the burden of foreign armies removed, we might reasonably expect her to begin to contribute to the cost of food imports by the latter part of 1948 and to become self-supporting in two or three years thereafter. Otherwise she is likely again to be the poorhouse of Europe for years to come and her people constantly be dependent for life upon foreign aid.

The Austrian people are making a brave fight to reestablish the principles of Western Civilization. Their officials are able and effective. They should enlist our sympathy, our support and all the influence we can summon in her reconstruction.[1]

I returned home from Germany and Austria via Rome and London. I went to Rome at the invitation and request of the Italian Prime Minister, who asked me to advise his government on methods of food administration, and I visited London in order to present my recommendations affecting the British Zone. Both countries enthusiastically applauded my proposals to abolish the continued strangling of German productivity, which was having adverse chain reactions in both Britain and Italy.

[1] *Addresses Upon the American Road, 1945–1948*, pp. 294–302.

CHAPTER 37

JAPAN

In January, 1947, Secretary of War Patterson asked that I recommend to him members of a mission who would visit Japan, for the situation there was similar to that in Germany. As related in Chapter 28 of this memoir, I had studied the Japanese food and economic situation in May, 1946, at the request of President Truman.

In Japan, as in Germany, the American people were spending hundreds of millions of dollars annually to keep starving people alive, yet at the same time forbidding the reconstruction of that nation's industries, a program which, if permitted, would enable the Japanese to help themselves.

I recommended a mission which included, among others, Colonel R. L. Harrison of the Department of Agriculture as Chairman, Captain Tracy B. Kittredge, and W. Hallam Tuck. The inclusion of Hallam Tuck gave the mission a veteran of many investigations in countries all over the world.

Prior to the creation of the mission, Secretary Patterson had set up a committee under Mr. Clifford Strike to examine and report generally upon the economic and political situation in Japan. The Secretary sent me a copy of the Strike report and asked for my conclusions on the Japanese situation. On May 7, 1947, I sent the following letter to Secretary Patterson, expressing my opinions on the Japanese situation:

DEAR MR. SECRETARY:

You and Mr. Clifford Strike did the honor to consult with me on measures proposed to end the industrial paralysis in Japan. You presented me with a proposed new level of industry (which I refer to as the "new level").

Since our discussion, I have re-examined my notes upon this subject made during my visit to Japan in May 1946. I have re-read the various agreements and reports on reparations, war potential, the "original" level of industry and other regulations. I have now had time to digest more fully the very able Strike report and to include in my thinking the constructive report of the Recent Food Commission under Colonel R. L. Harrison.

At the outset I wish to say that when I think of the white crosses over tens of thousands of American boys in the Pacific and the millions of butchered Chinese, I sympathize emotionally with Draconic measures of punishment. But when we look to the real interest of the United States and the future peace of the world, we must confine punishment to the war leaders and realize that we must live with this 80,000,000 people.

I had prepared an elaborate analysis of the economic and reparations situation in Japan. However, the only matters of interest are my conclusions.

I am convinced that there must be a revolutionary change in the whole concept of "levels of industry," "plant removals" for reparations and destruction of peace industry plants, if the Japanese people are to produce enough exports with which to pay for their food and other necessary imports, or become a stable and peaceable state. That drastic change is necessary must be evident by now from the fact that the American taxpayer is called upon to furnish upwards of $400,000,000 in the next fiscal year to keep the people barely alive; and unless there are revolutionary changes, it will continue indefinitely.

The "original" concepts in economic and military policy which contributed to this situation arise partly from the inadequate data at the time upon which the policies were based and upon several illusions.

As to the data, I may point out just two instances as illustrative. The food deficiency in Japan was under-estimated. The estimate of Japan's foreign trade deficit under these regulations showed a deficit for 1947 of under $20,000,000, whereas experience proves the deficit to be over $400,000,000.

Without giving more instances, it is safe to say that there was an under-estimate of the thin margins of the Japanese economy and the destruction to it from war and her territorial separations.

Of the illusions, the first is that to demilitarize Japan it is necessary to do little more than to destroy or remove all arms fortifications and direct arms factories and to prevent *any* army, *any* navy, *any* air force, *any* munitions or aircraft manufacture, and to enforce such a regime over a generation or two until Japan loses the know-how of war.

The second illusion is the whole concept of control of "war potential" in industry of the type which can contribute to peace economy. All industry is "war potential" in total war. Very little industry is war potential (except arms manufacture) if a country has a forced demilitarization such as I assume above. Another part of this illusion is that these major "levels of industry" can be enforced and a nation function without a complete "planned economy" directed by foreign agents. On the other hand, to watch a major free economy, to see it is directed to no evil, is a simple problem of inspection. People are not going to manufacture for war where there is compulsory elimination of militarism.

The third illusion is that Japan can ever be self-supporting in food. That is impossible with only 15% of arable land in a state the size of California with 80,000,000 people; all her modern history she has imported 15 to 20% of her food and now the population has been increased by six or seven million expellees. One-third of the population of Japan must live by export industry.

The fourth illusion is that there are any consequential reparations to be had from the removal of industrial plants overseas. The buildings, foundations, water, electrical and other connections in such plants have no value for removal. All that is removable of any use is motive power and machine tools, all second hand. The cost of tearing them out, crating them, shipping them to some area where there is neither skilled labor nor skilled management and to build new foundations, buildings and connections, leaves even these values comparatively trivial.

These ideas in action or threat of action have created the present economic paralysis.

I may say from my knowledge that General MacArthur has long sought the remedy to these matters. The engineering Committee under Mr. Strike, which you appointed, in its able report of February 22nd, recommends radical changes in "level of industry" and plant removal plans. General MacArthur strongly supported their recommendations. But the "new level" of industry submitted to me does not even fulfill the urgent Strike recommendations. In my opinion the Strike recommendations did not go nearly far enough.

My suggestions are:

First. Allow the removal to claimants of machine tools and equipment from such munitions factories as cannot be converted into peace-time production. Assess by independent engineers the actual value to any proposed recipient of peace-time plants, deducting the cost of removal and shipment, and then call upon Japan to pay such a sum over the years and to retain the plants.

Second. Do away with the whole concept of "level of industry," both "original" and "new." Establish a few absolute prohibitions such as monopolies, arms manufacture, aircraft construction, speed (but not size) of ships, and install a general watch to see that industry is devoted to peace-time production.

The sum of my reasons are:

(a) No further industrial repressions are necessary to preserve peace in a perpetually demilitarized country.

(b) The continued uncertainty of plant removals and the present proposed levels of industry are bound to continue the paralysis of export industry.

(c) We cannot find competent American men over the years to competently direct the kind of planned economy for Japan which either the "original" or "new" limit of industry plus the export-import controls amount to. We could find the minor inspection staff to see that Japanese industry does no evil.

(d) The development of de-monopolized private enterprise is the only hope of increasing the standards of living in Japan. Thereby is the only possibility of holding her people as a bulwark against the Communist invasion of Asia.

(e) Japan's full productivity (except arms) aids in the recovery of her neighbors.

(f) It is the only way Japan can be gotten off the back of the American taxpayer.

Finally, may I say that what the world needs today above all things is recovered peace-purpose productivity. The United States does not possess the strength to bear the deficient productivity which now dominates industry all over the world. Chains on any productive area are chains on the whole world. We need a larger vision of the primary basis of world peace which is productivity. Otherwise there would be a disintegration of Western Civilization everywhere.[1]

[1] *Addresses Upon the American Road, 1945–1948,* pp. 98–102.

MORE AMERICAN RELIEF ACTIVITIES

REHABILITATION OF FAMINE CHILDREN—THE UNITED NATIONS INTERNATIONAL CHILDREN'S EMERGENCY FUND (UNICEF)

My lifelong identification with relief enterprises, which started in China with the Boxer Rebellion, resulted in many other appeals after our 1947 relief mission to Germany and Austria. One of these was the United Nations International Children's Emergency Fund (UNICEF).

During and after the First World War, my colleagues and I had set up the methods and conducted the organization for the rehabilitation of some fifteen million child victims of famine.[1] As I have related, we made some progress toward establishing such relief in Poland in the early months of the Second World War but were stopped by the British blockade. We had made a great effort to establish relief for children in the small German-occupied democracies during the war, but had been able to make very little progress, again because of the British blockade.

After Mr. Truman became President in April, 1945, my old colleagues and I determined to try again. We organized a public meeting at Carnegie Hall on May 8, and at this time were able to demonstrate factually the consequences of neglect as they were dis-

[1] Herbert Hoover, *An American Epic* (Chicago, Henry Regnery Company, 1959–64), Vol. III.

closed by the liberation of Western Europe. When, on May 28, President Truman called me to the White House and requested my advice on a number of subjects, I naturally brought up for discussion this great world problem of impending famine.

Then in February of 1946 I was called by the President to undertake a mission to co-ordinate world food supplies to meet the great famine. I again raised the problem of caring for the starving children. On February 8, I included in a public statement the following:

> . . . There should be organization of special food to undernourished children and mothers over the whole of Europe, including Germany. The infant mortality is very high everywhere on the Continent and unless special supplies are available it will be still higher. In some areas it is now over 50%. Peace and progress will not be restored if those who survive are to be infected by a generation of men and women stunted in body and distorted in mind. . . .[2]

As previously stated, I recruited the invaluable Maurice Pate for the specific duty of investigating the condition of the children in each of the thirty-eight countries we visited. He had directed our child-feeding operations, first in a part of Belgium during the First World War, then for Poland during and after the Armistice, and again in 1939.

I have given Mr. Pate's appraisal of the condition of children in each of the nations we visited in 1946. There were between twenty and thirty million needy children in Europe and untold numbers in Russia, the Middle East, and Asia. We determined to make the civilized world aware of this problem. Accordingly, I made public statements on the subject from New York on March 14 and 16; from Prague on March 28; from Warsaw on March 30; from Helsinki on April 1; from London on April 5; from Brussels on April 8; from Vienna on April 15; from Cairo on April 19; from Bangalore on April 26; from Washington on May 13; and from Chicago on May 17, 1946.

On May 13, 1946, I again informed President Truman that the rehabilitation of children was urgent. On May 20, a meeting was

[2] *Addresses Upon the American Road, 1945–1948,* p. 163.

called in Washington by the United Nations to consider food questions. There were delegations from thirty nations present, and I was asked to speak. My statement on the child problem was:

Special feeding and medical care of physically subnormal children should be organized systematically and should be the sole charitable contribution of governments. That is the most needed reconstruction effort in the world. It does not call for large figures.[3]

The Conference agreed with me, and passed a resolution recommending that the matter be taken up officially by the United Nations. A small group of my former associates, including Arthur Ringland of the State Department, Congressman Christian Herter, and others, undertook to push it along.

I have previously mentioned my address to the Canadian Parliament on June 28, 1946, in which I urged action in behalf of the debilitated children. Prime Minister Mackenzie King assured me that he would instruct the Canadian officials at the United Nations to support my proposals. Meanwhile, I urged action on my friends in the British, Polish, Belgian, French, and other delegations to the United Nations. A United Nations Assembly on December 11, 1946, passed the resolution we proposed, establishing the "United Nations International Children's Emergency Fund" (UNICEF). Dr. Ludwik Rajchman was made Chairman of the organization.

I felt that the success of the new effort could be assured only by having someone of long experience in this work as Director. Maurice Pate fitted the qualifications perfectly. Fortunately, Dr. Rajchman had been associated with Mr. Pate in Poland during the First World War and supported him. Pate was appointed on January 8, 1947. The following day I received this note from him:

DEAR CHIEF:
Yesterday afternoon I spent half an hour with Trygve Lie who afterwards announced my appointment as Director of the U.N. Children's Fund.

[3] *Ibid.*, p. 231.

Lie approves 100% all the principles on which the A.R.A. [American Relief Administration's] European Children's Fund operated after World War I.

The U.N. Children's Fund Committee of 26 national delegates will gather occasionally to discuss policies and programs. But Lie says . . . that I report directly to him (Lie); that I am completely responsible for the choice of my own personnel and the direction of the operation in every respect.

We already have a little money in the Treasury but allocated expressly for food, so Lie is advancing initial expenses for the C.F. from his general funds. Actually the Children's Fund of U.N., however, is to stand on its own feet and we are to receive and disburse our own funds.

The plan on which I am now working jointly with Arthur Ringland and Chris Herter calls for a program of $450,000,000 . . . of which $100,000,000 is to come from the U.S. government.

With a small selected staff I shall be devoting 90% of my time here in Washington on this first objective: support from the U.S. government. This is our keystone and when its achievement appears possible, all the other angles will then be brought into the picture.

I shall need much help and advice as time goes on—and will bring the full story up to you in New York as soon as you return.

MAURICE

THE REHABILITATION OF CHILDREN
IN GERMANY

As noted in my account of my visit to Germany and Austria at President Truman's request in the winter of 1947, I arranged with the military authorities that a child-feeding organization should be set up at once for those countries along the lines of our successful efforts in 1919–23. I also secured the inclusion of the costs in the Congressional appropriations. As has been mentioned, the German organization was known as the *Hoover Speisung*. The organizations were entirely independent of the United Nations. We thus provided for regular extra meals for more than six million children in addition to those covered by Pate's organization as it spread over other countries.

To finance UNICEF, I appeared before the House Appropriations Committee in support of a fifteen-million-dollar appropriation for the first year. Mr. Pate's organization was able to begin active relief in June, 1947. By August, it was well under way.

Maurice Pate is an unusual soul. He is a great administrator as well as a persuasive evangel for children. During the ensuing years, his organization effected the rehabilitation of literally many tens of millions of children. He established it so firmly in the everyday life of scores of nations that it is now a permanent measure of basic human welfare.

Up to the end of 1963, Mr. Pate had raised over $420,000,000 in contributions from governments and individuals. In addition, countries given assistance by UNICEF had committed the equivalent of $885,000,000 to the organization as internal matching funds. Altogether, $1,305,000,000 had thus been programed for the benefit of needy children since UNICEF began its operations in 1947. In addition, the United States, Canada, Switzerland, Austria, and the Netherlands furnished to UNICEF more than 1,200,000,000 pounds of dry skim and whole milk, either free or at low cost, representing an additional contribution of well over $180,000,000 dollars. Therefore, the total program as of December, 1963, amounted to the equivalent of nearly $1,500,000,000.

During its first years, UNICEF's resources were devoted largely to meeting the emergency needs of children in the form of food and clothing. In December, 1950, the General Assembly of the United Nations directed UNICEF to shift its emphasis from stop-gap emergency aid to developing programs of long-range benefit for children, mostly in economically underdeveloped countries. UNICEF is now at work in 115 such countries or territories.

Mr. Pate made the following statement on June 5, 1962:

No one man in the world has ever understood better the problems and the needs of children, and no one man has ever done more in their behalf than Herbert Hoover. . . .

It was Mr. Hoover who originally had the idea of setting up in the framework of the United Nations, the United Nations Children's Fund. Over these past fifteen years Mr. Hoover has given this work his constant support and encouragement. UNICEF, now operating in 107 countries and territories, has given benefits to many tens of millions of children and mothers. Mr. Hoover's foresight in this action has resulted in programmes for the benefit of children of a value of over one billion dollars, of which the beneficiary countries themselves have put up more than two-thirds of the funds.

CHAPTER 39

CARE, INC.

Another post–World War II organization should be added to the roster of relief efforts of my colleagues and me in that period. After World War I, we had organized an extensive system of remittances of packages from persons in the United States to needy persons in Europe. As a result, over 129,000 tons of food were sent to the needy during that period.[1] This service was so effective that I determined it should be set up again after World War II.

I sent for General William N. Haskell, who had directed relief and reconstruction on my staff in Rumania and Armenia in 1919–20 and in Russia in 1922–23. I suggested to him that the world needed a re-establishment of the food-package system. The world situation now being different, I suggested the shipment of single packages on orders received with cash payment. I also suggested, as a start, using the Army's surplus of "10-in-1" rations already packed. Each contained about thirty pounds of food with a nutritional value of about forty thousand calories. The Army was glad to make a low price to get rid of the surplus.

The organization required working capital, and I suggested that we enlist the support of the various religious and voluntary organizations engaged in European relief, each to subscribe a few thousand dollars to start the work. I helped the General to secure twenty-seven such organizational members, each to be represented on the

[1] *An American Epic,* Vol. III, Chap. 32.

board of directors. We then arranged bank loans to further finance the "pipeline."

In November, 1945, the organization was launched under the title "Co-operative for American Remittances to Europe, Inc." (CARE). It was to be a nonprofit operation, but the packages were to be sold with a small margin to cover overhead and contingencies and to repay and strengthen its capital. Any ultimate surplus profit was to go to the member societies.

I persuaded some of my old staff to aid the General. The plan succeeded beyond all expectations. Soon the Army "10-in-1" rations were exhausted, and the organization prepared its own packages, ultimately expanding to cover clothing and other articles.

On my trip to Germany in 1946, I secured permission, which had been previously refused, for CARE to operate in the Allied Military Zones in Germany and Austria, and arranged for the transport and distribution of the packages.

General Haskell resigned to undertake other duties in March, 1947, and was succeeded by his able assistant, Paul C. French. Aside from the packages CARE sold for specific individuals, it also accepted gifts in money for the free delivery of packages to needy persons at the discretion of CARE managers in various countries.

I declined any official connection with the organization because of other responsibilities elsewhere as the head of many educational, charitable, and scientific institutions. I did, however, have certain moral responsibilities for CARE, and its officers repeatedly sought my support and advice. In 1948, Murray Lincoln, the Chairman, and Mr. French, fell into difficulties with their unwieldy board of directors. Some of the minor organizations wished to restrict operations and distribute more dividends. They also found that direct contributions to their particular charities had fallen off in favor of CARE packages. Messrs. Lincoln and French appealed to me in their difficulties. I thereupon arranged that the War Department insist upon their continuance under the War Department agreement of 1946 with regard to Germany, and I induced the State Department to discourage any reduction of activities. I reinforced this by stating that I would set up a new organization if the member societies insisted on restrictive operations or upon liquidation. All of which settled this immediate trouble.

I made numerous public statements in CARE's support. In May, 1948, Mr. French asked my assistance to secure free transport to Europe for the packages as a part of the Marshall Plan operations. I sent the following telegram to my Congressional friends:

I understand there will be before your Committee the question of appropriations of transportation of CARE packages under the E.C.A. As I was largely instrumental in founding this institution which has resulted in great savings to the American taxpayer, I hope you can accept the recommendations of this organization for free transport.

The free transport was obtained.

Up to June 30, 1963, CARE had delivered packages of food, clothing, and other articles valued at more than $578,000,000. It brought relief to an immense number of families, since the packages furnished an invaluable addition to the sparse rations in many countries. CARE, as does UNICEF, continues to broaden the scope of its relief assistance. MEDICO recently became a service of CARE. In addition, CARE administers Peace Corps units in Colombia, Sierra Leone, Guatemala, and Pakistan. And still another new field is education. CARE's "Self-Help Program" provides educational tools and trained professional assistance.

HUNGARIAN REFUGEES

I was again called into urgent service at the time of the Hungarian uprisings in the last months of 1956. I accepted the honorary chairmanship of an organization called "First Aid for Hungary, Inc.," which had been formed as the result of a meeting of several prominent Americans of Hungarian descent called by Dr. Tibor Eckhardt on October 29, 1956; it was organized to render vital services in a sudden emergency. Our immediate objective was to bring aid to the hundreds of Hungarian Freedom Fighters who had been forced to seek refuge in neighboring Austria and had thus cast an enormous burden upon that country.

We were one of only two foreign charities actually operating at the Hungarian border during those first frenzied weeks. Immediate aid was rendered through seventeen first-aid stations, four field kitchens, and three mobile pharmacies set up in the border zone to distribute clothing and medical supplies. We were also able to send food and medical supplies into Hungary itself—at first by direct shipment, then through the International Red Cross, and finally by direct shipment again. During the latter part of this organization's life, as Russian tanks halted the flow of Hungarians across the border, we turned our attention to aiding the refugees in camps in Austria and for several months provided a number of them with supplies, especially for children, and also with care for the sick, wounded, and maternity cases.

In February, 1957, we determined upon a specific program to deal with the emergency created by the interruptions of studies, particularly of high-school age children. We supported programs in Austria, Belgium, Germany, and the United States by providing funds and textbooks.

Later, our efforts were extended to the problem of higher education for refugee students. Aid to the education of these young people took some of our work out of the realm of the temporary and gave it an added significance of future and permanent value. My personal feelings on the matter were conveyed in a message of mine which was read at the Protest Meeting for the Hungarians in Madison Square Garden on November 8, 1956:

Every people striving for freedom has over our whole national life appealed to the American heart. But seldom in these hundred and sixty years has any people shown such magnificent courage and sacrifice as we have seen in these past few weeks in Hungary.

Whatever we can do to alleviate their suffering and to protest this wickedness must lie on the American conscience.[1]

Among the officers of the organization, in addition to myself as Honorary Chairman, were Dr. Tibor Eckhardt, President, and Mr. Tibor Jahoda, Treasurer. Through October 31, 1957, the total funds raised amounted to $1,143,055.43.

[1] *Addresses Upon the American Road, 1955–1960,* p. 29.

SOME LAST REMARKS

CHAPTER 41

THE FINAL CHAPTER

On its journey to thirty-eight countries, our mission necessarily met with the heads of state, Prime Ministers, Ministers of Foreign Affairs, Ministers of Agriculture and Commerce, parliamentary leaders, and military officials. While our major interest was relief of the famine, all on our staff were concerned about the forces moving in the world and their impact upon our country—and especially with the spread of Communism. Invariably, except in the Communist countries, the officials in every country insisted upon a discussion of the Communist danger, which had greatly increased since the war. They talked frankly about Communist infiltration and conspiracies in their own as well as in neighboring states. At no time were we in conflict with our State Department, for at all of our important meetings we were accompanied by our American Ministers or Ambassadors, many of whom started such discussions.

All of us made many notes and collected many documents. Upon our return, I concluded that the best way I could summarize this disheartening information would be with statistical tables, which I include here. They are arranged in different categories of the advancement of Communism by showing populations and square miles of the countries involved.

The first category was the areas annexed by the Soviet Union as a result of the Tehran Agreements:

	Square Miles	Inhabitants
Finnish Provinces	17,600	450,000
Polish Provinces	69,900	11,800,000
Bessarabia	17,100	3,200,000
Bukovina	2,300	500,000
Estonia	18,300	1,122,000
Latvia	25,400	1,951,000
Lithuania	21,500	2,957,000
Königsberg area	5,400	1,187,000
Areas annexed from Czechoslovakia	4,900	731,000
Total	182,400	23,898,000

Under the Tehran Agreements, the following countries or peoples in Europe had been provided by Stalin with Communist presidents, Communist ministries of about eight members, and, at most, two representatives of the "other liberal elements":

	Square Miles	Inhabitants
East Germany	42,900	18,807,000
Albania	11,100	1,186,000
Bulgaria	42,800	7,160,000
Czechoslovakia	49,300	12,463,000
Hungary	35,900	9,224,000
West Poland	120,400	24,500,000
Rumania	91,600	16,007,000
Yugoslavia	95,600	16,339,000
To enumerate the full extent of the Communist spread, we should add Russia itself, with	8,600,000	193,000,000
Total	9,089,600	298,686,000

Under the Secret Far Eastern Agreement, made public on February 11, 1946, and other commitments, the following areas in Asia were now controlled by the Kremlin:

	Square Miles	Inhabitants
North China Communist		
Government of Mao Tse-tung	1,200,000	60,000,000
Manchuria	503,000	43,234,000
Mongolia	625,900	2,000,000
North Korea	48,500	9,100,000
South Sakhalin	13,900	415,000
Kurile Islands	3,900	18,000
Tannu Tuva	64,000	65,000
Total	2,459,200	114,832,000

The grand total of peoples and areas under Communist rule was therefore about 437,416,000 persons and about 11,731,200 square miles. In 1939, before the war, there was one Communist country; by 1946 there were twenty-three nations or parts of nations dominated by Communism. Moreover, the progress of Communism in the world after the Second World War was not limited to the areas which had actually been made Communistic. There were eleven countries [1] which emerged from the war with Communists in their ministries and with organized Communist political parties:

	Square Miles	Inhabitants
France (Europe only)	212,700	42,519,000
Belgium (Europe only)	11,800	8,388,500
Italy (Europe only)	116,200	45,646,000
Austria	32,400	6,653,000
Chile	286,300	5,191,000
Mexico	764,000	22,776,000
Venezuela	352,200	4,189,000
Peru	482,300	6,208,000
Guatemala	45,450	3,706,250
Bolivia	537,800	3,787,800
Iran	628,000	3,000,000
Total	3,469,150	152,064,550

[1] The countries in this group gradually eliminated the Communists from their ministries. To this extent, the march of Communism was pushed back, but active Communist parties and Communist conspiracies still continued without ceasing.

The spread of Communism did not end in 1946. To the political entities under Communist domination at that time we must add at this writing:

	Square Miles	Inhabitants
Cuba	44,000	6,743,000
New Guinea	151,000	730,000
China	3,746,453	669,000,000
Indonesia	735,865	92,600,000
Total	4,677,318	769,073,000

The point is perhaps debatable, but it appears that South America's British Guiana and some of Africa's new nations, Ghana and Guinea, for example, show the effects of Communist influence in their governments.

My friends will forgive me if I recall a nationally broadcast address (June 29, 1941) I made when Mr. Roosevelt had set up a tacit alliance to join Russia in the war:

Six weeks ago I made a statement to the American people upon the relations of the United States to this war.

That address has received large approval. It has naturally been disliked by the extremists. That is the psychosis of war. That disease has two outstanding symptoms. Those who catch it lose their reason in the fever of emotion. And in that fever intolerance rises to a pitch where it seeks to frighten men from free speech by defamation.

I shall speak again without betraying the emotion that arises within me when the whole destiny of my country is imperiled. I can hope to appeal only to reasoning people. And it is cold reason, not eloquence, that America needs today.

Momentous events have happened which greatly change the shape of things. They must be incorporated in American thinking. There is the war between Hitler and Stalin. Propaganda of fear or hate to force us into war has been intensified. It comes from foreign sources, from Cabinet officers and American organizations. They urge step after step of executive actions which would drag us into war.

There are those who argue that we are already in this war. The Constitution of the United States provides that Congress has the sole authority to declare war. It is equally their responsibility to see that this country does not go to war until they have authorized it.

The only reason for not submitting the matter to the Congress would be that Congress could not be trusted to do their bidding. Or that the people, through them, should not be allowed a voice. No president in a democracy should take that responsibility. If Congress decides to go to war, then we willingly give all and we willingly surrender all our freedoms necessary to win that war. And until Congress shall by Constitutional action declare war, no man in America may demand the end of debate on this issue of Peace or War.

No man can tell what the kaleidoscopic changes in this appalling situation may be. We must constantly reappraise its dangers. The constant question is what we should do now. But there are certain courses of practical statesmanship; there are certain eternal principles to which we must adhere. There are certain consequences to America and civilization which we must ever keep before our eyes.

In the last seven days that call to sacrifice American boys for an ideal has been made as a sounding brass and a tinkling cymbal. For now we find ourselves promising aid to Stalin and his militant Communist conspiracy against the whole democratic ideals of the world.

Collaboration between Britain and Russia will bring them military values, but it makes the whole argument of our joining the war to bring the four freedoms to mankind a gargantuan jest.

We should refresh our memories a little.

Four American Presidents and four Secretaries of State, beginning with Woodrow Wilson, refused to have anything to do with Soviet Russia on the ground of morals and democratic ideals. They even refused diplomatic recognition. They did so because here is one of the bloodiest tyrannies and terrors ever erected in history. It destroyed every semblance of human rights and human liberty; it is a militant destroyer of the worship of God. It brutally executes millions of innocent people without the semblance of justice. It has enslaved the rest. Moreover, it has violated every international covenant; it has carried on a world conspiracy against all democracies, including the United States.

When Russia was recognized by the United States in 1933, the Soviets entered into a solemn agreement that they would refrain from any propaganda, any organization, or from injuring in any way whatsoever the tranquility, prosperity, order or security in any part of the United States.

Seven years later, the Dies Committee reported unanimously and specifically that the Communist Party in the United States is a Moscow conspiracy, masked as a political party; that its activities constitute a violation of the Treaty of Recognition; that under instructions from Moscow the Communists had violated the laws of the United States; that throughout the entire time they had been supplied with funds from Moscow for activities against the American people and the American Government. The Dies Committee only confirmed what most Americans already know. Is the word of Stalin any better than the word of Hitler?

In these last weeks it is declared not only by public officials but by labor leaders themselves that the strikes which hamstring the defense of the United States have been Communist conspiracies. Thus Russia has continued her mission of destroying our democracy down to last week.

Less than two years ago, Stalin entered into an agreement with Hitler through which there should be joint onslaught on the democracies of the world. Nine days later Stalin attacked the Poles jointly with Hitler and destroyed the freedom of a great and democratic people. Fourteen days later Stalin destroyed the independence of democratic Latvia, Lithuania and Estonia. Ninety days later on came the unprovoked attack by Russia on democratic Finland. Is that not aggression and is not every case a hideous violation of treaties and international law?

Stalin has taken advantage of the very freedoms of democracy to destroy them with the most potent fifth column in all history. He contributed to the destruction of France. He has daily implanted class hate in America and a stealthy war against our institutions.

We know also Hitler's hideous record of brutality, of aggression and as a destroyer of democracies. Truly, Poland, Norway, Holland, Belgium, Denmark, France and the others are dreadful monuments. But I am talking of Stalin at this moment.

One of the real compensations America received for our enormous sacrifices in the last war was from the large part we played in establishing the democracies of Finland, Poland, Estonia, Latvia and Lithuania. We nursed them in their infancy. We spent hundreds of millions to help them grow to manhood. Does America feel quite right about aiding Stalin to hold his enslavement of them? That is where power politics will carry us. No doubt we will promise to aid Russia. But the war to bring the four freedoms to the world will die spiritually when we make that promise.

If we go further and join the war and we win, then we have won for Stalin the grip of communism on Russia, the enslavement of nations, and more opportunity for it to extend in the world. We should at least cease to tell our sons that they would be giving their lives to restore democracy and freedom to the world.

Practical statesmanship leads in the same path as moral statesmanship. These two dictators—Stalin and Hitler—are in deadly combat. One of these two hideous ideologists will disappear in this fratricidal war. In any event both will be weakened.

Statesmanship demands that the United States stand aside in watchful waiting, armed to the teeth, while these men exhaust themselves.

Then the most powerful and potent nation in the world can talk to mankind with a voice that will be heard. If we get involved in this struggle we, too, will be exhausted and feeble.

To align American ideals alongside Stalin will be as great a violation of everything American as to align ourselves with Hitler.

Can the American people debauch their sense of moral values and the very essence of their freedom by even a tacit alliance with Soviet Russia? Such an alliance will bring sad retributions to our people.

If we go into this war we will aid Stalin to hold his aggression against the four little democracies. We will help him to survive and continue his terror and his conspiracies against all democracies. We should stop the chant about leading the world to liberalism and freedom.

Again I say, if we join the war and Stalin wins, we have aided him to impose more communism on Europe and the world. At least we could not with such a bedfellow say to our sons that by making the supreme sacrifice, they are restoring freedom to the world. War alongside Stalin to impose freedom is more than a travesty. It is a tragedy. . . .

We cannot slay an idea or an ideology with machine guns. Ideas live in men's minds in spite of military defeat. They live until they have proved themselves right or wrong. These ideas are evil. And evil ideas contain the germs of their own defeat. . . .

No man can see what the future may bring. Whatever that future may be, only one defeat can come to America. We have no need to fear military defeat if we are prepared. Our only defeat would be if we lost our own freedoms and our potency for good in the world. . . .

There is no course we can pursue amid these stupendous dangers that is perfect, or without risks, or that may not require change. But let me propose for reasoning people a course for us at this time which avoids the most destructive forces and holds fast to the most constructive forces. And that program is neither defeatist, nor isolationist, nor interventionist.

We should give every aid we can to Britain and China within the law, but do not put the American flag or American boys in the zone of war. Arm to the teeth for defense of the Western Hemisphere, and cease to talk and to provoke war. Uphold Congress steadily in assuming the responsibility to determine peace or war. Stop this notion of ideological war to impose the four freedoms on other nations by military force and against their will. Devote ourselves to improving the four freedoms within our borders that the light of their success may stir the peoples of the world to their adoption.

The day will come when these nations are sufficiently exhausted to listen to the military, economic and moral powers of the United States. And with these reserves unexhausted, at that moment, and that moment only, can the United States promote a just and permanent peace. . . .

Here in America today is the only remaining sanctuary of freedom, the last oasis of civilization and the last reserve of moral and economic strength. If we are wise, these values can be made to serve all mankind.

My countrymen, we have marched into the twilight of a world war. Should we not stop here and build our defense while we can still see? Shall we stumble on into the night of chaos? [2]

We not only stumbled, we fell.

[2] Herbert Hoover, *40 Key Questions About Our Foreign Policy* (Scarsdale, New York, The Updegraff Press, Ltd., 1952), pp. 1–7. An earlier and somewhat longer version of the address was released to the press on June 27, 1941, two days prior to the broadcast. During the interim, however, events occurred so rapidly and the world situation changed so much as a result that I decided to revise my remarks and make them more forceful before going on the air. For lack of time, the press release was not changed accordingly, and it was inadvertently reprinted in *Addresses Upon the American Road, 1940–41*, pp. 87–102. The text included here is, of course, the one I actually delivered.

EPILOGUE

EPILOGUE

A brief résumé of Volumes I, II, and III of *An American Epic* might interest the reader.

Volume I, published in 1959, gave an account of the relief of ten million people in Belgium and Northern France during four and one-half years of German occupation and its aftermath.

Volume II followed in 1960. It told of American relief to 170,000,-000 people in the Allied and neutral nations from the United States' entry into the war in April, 1917, until the Armistice in November, 1918. This volume also described the "organization behind the front" in forty-five nations to meet the food shortages, acute famine, and reconstruction problems created by the First World War.

In Volume III, which appeared in 1961, I described the "front line" of relief—nation by nation—to more than 1,281,150,000 people from the American entry into the war in April, 1917, to the final victory over famine and pestilence in September, 1923. Also included is a rather detailed description of relief to Communist Russia from 1921 through 1923.

        ✿   ✿   ✿

I give a review of some of the pertinent paragraphs from the Introduction of Volume I, with some rephrasing, because they also apply to Volume IV.

For thousands of years, the question "Am I my brother's keeper?" has echoed in the conscience of mankind. The American people were the first in history to accept that obligation as a nation. Never before has a nation

301

undertaken such burdens, consciously and collectively, that human life, and even civilization, might be preserved.

Our people accomplished this task of compassion by self-denial, by longer hours of labor and greater tax burdens—and with no return other than to their own consciences.

❖   ❖   ❖

I participated in many of these efforts in both wars and I have had access to a mass of documentation hitherto not available to others. And I have had the assistance of my many colleagues in its preparation. Thus perhaps I alone am in a position to tell the whole magnificent story.

❖   ❖   ❖

Reduced production of food, medicine, and clothing is the inevitable consequence of total war. Men are drafted from farms into armies; manufacture of agricultural implements is turned to munitions-making; fertilizers are turned into explosives; farms, homes, and processing and industrial plants are destroyed. Blockade and counter-blockade are imposed to reduce enemy nations by starvation; thousands of ships carrying supplies are sunk at sea.

❖   ❖   ❖

The result of these wars was not peace.

When the fighting ended, hundreds of millions of people were faced with famine in some degree and often with its evil handmaiden, pestilence. Both wars left an inheritance of debilitated and diseased children who, without succor, would have burdened the world with dwarfed bodies and warped minds.

❖   ❖   ❖

Except for the sufferings of the early Pilgrim fathers, the American people have never known real famine. Even in the Confederate States during the Civil War there was enough food to maintain public health.

No one who has not seen famine with his own eyes can have understanding of its hideous reality. Mothers at every meal watch the wilting away of their children. Gaunt mothers search for food, carrying emaciated children too feeble to walk. Long streams of refugees flee from the famine areas, carrying their children and a few possessions; many dead lie at the roadsides. Few people die directly from starvation, for disease intervenes.

❖   ❖   ❖

Relief and reconstruction require billions of dollars, the purchase of scores of millions of tons of supplies from overseas, the management of enormous fleets of cargo ships, and, at times, the taking over and managing of railways, waterways, and coal mines in areas of economic chaos. The distribution of seed to restore crops in desolated areas and great supplies of tools and machinery are a prime necessity. All of this requires a great organization of equipment and medicines to stop the spread of pestilence and to stamp it out.

* * *

Throughout these long years, American men and women have been called upon to abandon their responsible positions and their home life to administer these huge lifesaving enterprises. They never failed to respond, with little or no remuneration. The services of these Americans have been as vital to mankind as the money or the provision of supplies.

* * *

It is difficult to portray the immensity of the tasks to relieve great famines. Statistics throw but a dim light on the overwhelming problems of organization. But perhaps the reader will have a better understanding of these tasks if I relate that during the First World War and reconstruction period, my colleagues and I had organized famine relief and reconstruction in forty-five nations. During this time, some 1,281,150,000 people were provided with the necessary margins of food, medicine, and clothing.

And after the Second World War, to meet the world-wide famine, we had need to organize thirty-eight nations of over 1,400,000,000 people, of whom 800,000,000, without overseas supplies, would have had less food than the prisoners in Buchenwald. Most of these 800,000,000 would have died of mass starvation or disease.

* * *

The giving of these supplies and services from America was, in a considerable part, direct charity. From many nations the United States received obligations to repay the cost. But these obligations, in billions of dollars, were far greater than the debtors could ever possibly repay. We received but a small repayment, and in the end, we forgave the debts. It is impossible accurately to enumerate these sums. A rough estimate could mount as high as fifty billion dollars. From this gigantic effort we were left with a substantial part of our national debt and thus to an unending tax burden on the American people.

* * *

Over the years, many different American organizations took part in these operations. Other nations contributed within their means in these emergencies, but 95 per cent of the financial burden of these enterprises in saving human lives during both of these wars and their aftermaths was borne by the American people.

*   *   *

These four volumes dealing with American undertakings in human service contain the record of many actions unique in the written history of the world.

Our operations were conducted in the midst of war, of revolution, and of reconstruction. Through the pages of these volumes march every outstanding civilian leader and the high military commanders. The necessary exposition of economic and political backgrounds throws a bright light on many phases of history.

*   *   *

This history of American enterprises of compassion does not suffer from a lack of documentation.

The largest collection of documents, articles, books, diaries, and records relating to these subjects is located in the Hoover Institution on War, Revolution, and Peace at Stanford University. Other sources are the Library of Congress and the libraries of the great universities. Still other essential materials are in our own government departments and the official records of the other nations engaged in total wars.

More than 3,500,000 documents had to be examined during the preparation of these volumes. Obviously, it was impossible for me to examine personally all of this mass of information. But I have had the aid of long-time associates and my staff, who have reduced the number which I had need to inspect to about 400,000 items, as my homework over the years.

*   *   *

There were many exciting episodes which might appear to be incredible were they not completely documented. I have reduced the documentation to those of major importance. Since such documents are at times verbose and repetitious and contain many diplomatic superfluities, I have limited quotations to their essential paragraphs, but have indicated deletions. The full text of the documents may be found in the Hoover Institution on War, Revolution, and Peace or in the places indicated in the footnotes. Part of these documents have been published. Many more of importance have not hitherto been made available to the public.

*   *   *

Previous experience of mankind with famines lends emphasis to this narrative. The first war-created famine of which we have some detailed record was that which followed the Thirty Years' War in Europe three hundred years ago. It is said that one-third of the population of Europe perished as a result of famine and pestilence. But because of American efforts, there was no mass starvation or mass loss of life by pestilence following the great wars of this century.

❖   ❖   ❖

These American sacrifices and labors not only saved human lives, they saved civilization for the Western world. They erected dams against the spread of Communism.

❖   ❖   ❖

But no amount of documents, statistics, accounts, reports of negotiations, or incidents can adequately reflect the ideals, the courage, and the sacrifice of the tens of millions of Americans who participated both directly and indirectly in these great enterprises. They are the true authors of *An American Epic*.

And what of this little group of a few hundred Americans whose names occur and recur in this narrative of *An American Epic* stretching over forty-nine years?

Most of them served without monetary compensation. Perhaps a few of them who had families to support received a small salary, but it was far below possible earnings at home. Some of them received out-of-pocket expenses. A few of them paid their own expenses. But their reward was indeed great, for hourly they witnessed the saving of human life, aid to ailing women and children, and the growing stability of governments.

The friendships that were made during the performance of common tasks, under stress, anxiety, and hardship, lasted all their lives. And these simple ties grew into affection for one another. Many of these devoted Americans rose to the highest positions in their professions and positions in government.

They will receive no monuments of stone. Perhaps a line from Pericles' great oration of more than two thousand years ago serves as their epilogue:

Their story . . . lives on far away, without visible symbol, woven into the stuff of other men's lives.

INDEX

INDEX

X
main

DATE DUE

A 3/-2 17Apr'67			
NOV 3 0 1984			
APR 1 7 1991			
MAY 0 1 1996			
GAYLORD			PRINTED IN U.S.A.